SEMPLICE

DINO JOANNIDES

SEMPLICE

REAL ITALIAN FOOD
INGREDIENTS & RECIPES

DINO JOANNIDES

Contents

This book is dedicated to
Sarah, Alexander and Edward,
my dear wife and sons, along
with Alexandre (Aleco)
and Anna, my parents. My
gastronomic genes were clearly
passed on by my late father.

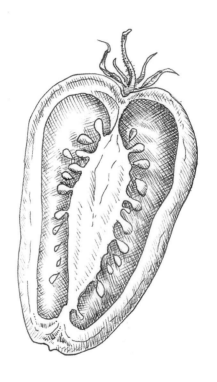

Always choose the finest ingredients, this will help you make a good impression. This is the first commandment of those who are passionate about food, it's the conditio sine qua non *for the success of any dish.*

Pelligreni Artusi, *Science in the Kitchen and the Art of Eating Well, 1891*

It is not only one [thing] that inspires me. Of course, the various markets where fresh products are being offered [are inspiring], but it is not only the various markets. Even a little conversation with a fisherman or the old ladies who find the wild herbs are an inspiration to me.

Fulvio Pierangelini

Introduction

Some years ago I had the good fortune of visiting a *sfogline* (maker of fresh pasta) in Bologna. Considered by many to be among the finest makers in the world, her pasta was simply superb, the best I had ever tasted. The secret, she whispered, was quite simple: use the very best eggs and the very best flour and, of course, years of know-how. I spent a blissful couple of hours with her, discussing the finer points of making fresh pasta. When our time was up, I lamented I was flying back to London later that day, but asked if I could purchase a couple of kilos of her tagliatelle with a view to cooking them that evening with butter, prosciutto di Parma and Parmigiano Reggiano. Her expression changed immediately; her body stiffened with indignity. 'This pasta needs to be eaten within three hours of preparation; you are flying back to London so you are unlikely to be home for at least six hours. I'm sorry, sir, it's impossible. I cannot let you have any of our pasta.'

That wonderful *sfogline*'s attitude to her art captures for me the essence of Italian food and how seriously good producers take their role in the process. Italian food is characterized by its extreme simplicity, with many well-known dishes having very few ingredients. However, it is its very simplicity that sometimes obscures the most important element in Italian cooking – the understanding and sourcing of ingredients. It is quality that lies at the heart and soul of Italian cooking.

Over the 30 years or so that I have been working in and cooking Italian food, I have watched as industrially produced, over-pasteurized pasta using poor-quality eggs and flour has become the norm. Today, as John Mariani observes in his book *How Italian Food Conquered the World* (see page 467), Italian food is the most popular in the world, but with popularity comes commerce, and with commerce comes ubiquity, and with ubiquity, very often, comes mediocrity. Brilliant marketing and mass production has led to almost all Italian ingredients, including such staples as olive oil, balsamic vinegar, cheese, cured meats, canned tomatoes and, indeed, pasta, being available on the shelves of retailers large and small the world over, to such an extent that otherwise discerning consumers no longer know what is good and bad because they have never tasted the good.

This book aims to set things straight by providing a definitive guide to sourcing the ingredients necessary to produce perfect contemporary Italian dishes. It also hopes to provide the reader with an understanding of Italian cooking in the early part of the 21st century, together with recipes that can be prepared by a home cook. It's a big aim, but by making the ingredients come first, allowing them to become the spark that inspires the dish or meal, I hope I can deliver.

Each chapter will deal with a particular category of ingredient – pasta, fish, fruit and so forth – and within that, each item will be defined in some detail (origin, history, locality). Then there are insights and tips that will show how to source and select 'the best'. Where relevant, the recommendations will cover price points to suit all pockets. Only sometimes will I require you to splash out!

The book offers over 70 'authentic' recipes, but (inevitably) authenticity and ownership of recipes and their ingredients are fought over – perhaps more in Italy than any other country. The result is ferocious regionalism and even quasi 'vendettas' among those who lay claim to having the 'true' recipe. The fact is that the truth does not exist. Recipes can vary from town to town, village to village, or even from street to street, so the pursuit of authenticity is in many ways a fool's errand. However, that is not to say that each dish has no discernible boundaries. Like evolution in nature, variation in cooking occurs across the landscape until the variation is far enough from the original that a new dish is patently different from, but as good as, the original. Take, for example, the classic three-ingredient dessert zabaglione, made with egg yolks, sugar and a sweet (often fortified) wine. In southern Italy it is prepared mostly with Marsala, whereas in Piedmont, the northern region from which the dish is said to originate, 'zabaione', as it is known, is prepared with Moscato d'Asti. Recently I had the latter version with a fourth ingredient, namely, shavings of white Alba truffle. It was both an unexpected discovery and a superlative variant of a fairly common dessert.

To go even further into the minefield, some argue that Italy no longer has a national cuisine because Italian food is now made and eaten globally. They argue that there is only a collection of regional or local recipes, which often have origins outside Italy. I shall step lightly and leave that debate for politicians rather than food lovers.

For myself, I certainly believe in the existence of an Italian cooking style where there is more of a pattern within boundaries than a rigid set of rules. These boundaries are difficult to explain. For Italians and those of us immersed in Italian cooking, they are largely intuitive.

I hope this book will, in some small way, act as a companion to readers, taking them by the hand and leading them through the maze so that in due course they will be able to look back and discern and enjoy more fully some of the landscape.

The recipes in this book have come from many sources, mostly in Italy and therefore genuinely Italian, but a few from elsewhere. Some have been passed down through my family; others have come from home cooks, farmers or producers, as well as amateur and professional chefs I have had the privilege of encountering on my travels over many years.

Many writers have helped to create a wider understanding about the essence of Italian food. Among the greats from Italy were Pellegrini Artusi writing in the late 19th century, Ada Boni in the 20th, and Luigi Veronelli, who was a huge influence until his death in 2004. Outside Italy, Elizabeth David and Marcella Hazan did more than most to educate those in the English-speaking world. My hope is that I can encourage you to go back to the basics that these seminal writers championed in their lifetimes.

The Italian word that best captures this approach, and is the essence of this book, is *semplice* – simple and straightforward.

Buon appetito!

Dino Joannides

My Approach

Ingredients & Cooking

Food and wine are very important to me, my family and friends, and meals are cherished for both gastronomic and social reasons.

My approach to food, in terms of sourcing ingredients and cooking them, always starts with the objective of producing a meal that forms part of a balanced and varied diet. As a family, we try to cook and eat together at least once a day. I recognize that this is a luxury for many people who, for various reasons, do not have the time or inclination to source, cook and eat together on a daily basis, but it's something well worth trying to achieve, and I hope this book will help you to do so.

I do not tend to think about what I am going to cook until I have started the process of seeing what is available. My choices are therefore market-driven. More often than not, I choose food that is seasonal and from trusted sources. This is at the core of what is often called the Mediterranean diet, which evidence suggests has many health-giving benefits.

If you are able to grow some of your own food, especially fruit and vegetables, you will find that following a seasonal approach to ingredients and cooking becomes second nature. But there's nothing to stop you buying seasonally too. I buy food from people I trust and have usually built up a relationship with. My father once told me when I was a child that after family, partners and close friends, the most important people you should get close to are the best fishmongers, butchers, bakers and greengrocers you can find.

When possible, I try to buy food from local independent sources. Not only is this handier, but it also has the advantages of boosting the local economy and being more environmentally friendly. However, I sometimes have to travel great distances to obtain something, and I do occasionally use an online shopping source.

In my experience, you should aim to buy the best possible ingredients you can find at a given time. If you cannot find them, or the price is prohibitive, do not settle for something mediocre or second best. Start again and consider a completely different ingredient, and possibly even a different dish.

Avoiding waste makes good economic sense, but it is also socially responsible; it makes you think and plan ahead. For example, by boiling a good chicken on Sunday night, you have the essentials for several meals during the week, plus leftovers for sandwiches.

There is no getting away from it — to find the best ingredients, you have to do your homework and try to find out as much as you can about their origins and the producer or farmer. The food industry is huge, and the marketing spend is obviously commensurate with its size. Many mass-produced products or produce are promoted as being of superior quality, almost artisanal, when nothing could be further from the truth. This global marketing phenomenon is certainly present in Italy, and remains part of the Italian food supply chain.

Unfortunately, alongside misleading marketing there are many examples of outright fraud. Consequently, I recommend taking a sceptical approach to the majority of marketing related to food.

Italians are no different from Anglo-Saxons when it comes to marketing food and are, in fact, masters of what writer Michael Pollan describes as 'supermarket pastoral'. The best illustration of this, as noted by John Dickie, professor of Italian studies at University College London, is probably the mass-produced biscuit brand Il Mulino Bianco 'baked' in the industrialized Po valley. For millions of consumers in Italy and beyond the brand will be forever associated with a remote white mill near Chiusdino in Tuscany. The TV advertising campaign, involving the renowned film-maker Giuseppe Tornatore and composer Ennio Morricone, was such a success that the mocked-up mill used in the advertisement became first a quasi pilgrimage destination, before being converted to an *agriturismo* (farmhouse holiday destination).

The scepticism I encourage should also be applied to some ingredients or products that qualify for legal protected status – PDO (Protected Designation of Origin), DOP (Denominazione di Origine Protetta), PGI (Protected Geographical Indication) or IGP (Indicazione Geografica Protetta). Whilst useful for indicating provenance and, in effect, protecting intellectual property, these designations provide no guarantee that the specific product is particularly good or will be to your taste. However, it is common for participants right along the food supply chain to suggest otherwise.

I, like many others, have had very poor PDO Mozzarella di Bufala Campana and Parmigiano Reggiano. In my opinion, this is simply down to the individual producer not making a good enough product, or one to my taste.

The Slow Food Foundation's Italian Presidia (organizations that list protected products) currently include over 224 foods from 1600 small-scale producers – fishermen, butchers, bakers, cheese-makers and pastry chefs – all identified by the Presidia Slow Food brand. This project has a number of objectives, including the

sustaining of quality products at risk of extinction, the protection of unique regions and ecosystems, the recovery of traditional processing methods and the safeguarding of native breeds and local plant varieties.

The Slow Food movement and the foundation are discussed more fully in the history section (see page 44), but it is fair to say that, from the point of view of the consumer, the Presidia endorsement is generally a good indicator of excellence and quality. This is backed up by fairly robust standards, regulation and ongoing monitoring. Of course, the Presidia are not foolproof, and a listed product may sometimes cease to deserve its listing, perhaps through over-production, or a decline in quality, or having edged towards the slippery slope of commodification (the opposite of artisan or traditional).

It should be noted that there are thousands of excellent products and producers in Italy that have no protection or endorsement, and it remains a joy to discover them.

Travels & Evolution of Italian Cooking

Some writers claim that Italian food is now the most popular in the world, attributing its popularity to Italian migration to virtually every corner of the planet. Paradoxically, though – due to major food businesses mass-marketing variants of Italian cuisine with its associated products, and the influence of high-profile chefs and food writers – what constitutes an Italian dish or recipe can range from something you might actually eat in Italy to abominations such as pineapple-topped pizza. That is not to say that Italian food in foreign lands has not evolved to produce delicious dishes, some of which have even found their way back to Italy. In fact, I find it particularly interesting that the popularity of Italian food has often led to the 'Italianization' of other countries' cuisines or emerging food cultures.

Aside from the influence of migration, tourism and mass media, the spread of Italian cooking owes a great deal to the mass production and brilliant marketing of Italian ingredients, which can now be found on the shelves of retailers all over the world. It should also be noted that the Italian state has played an important role in promoting Italian food and pursuing policies that boost exports.

The Italian Diaspora

On the whole, the main waves of emigration from Italy post-unification (1848–70) were driven by poverty. The first wave, between 1861 and 1900, saw in the region of seven million people emigrate, of which an estimated 66 per cent came from the northern parts of the country. Roughly half that total headed to other European countries, whilst the rest went mainly to North and South America, as well as to Australia and New Zealand.

In the second period of mass migration, between 1900 and 1914 (at the start of the First World War), about nine million people, the majority mainly from the rural south, emigrated mainly to North and South America. During the war itself, the flow of emigration reduced to a trickle; but as soon as the war ended, it restarted, particularly during the first five years of the Fascist period (1919–24).

Following the Second World War, there was a third wave of emigration, this one attributed as much to war damage and organized crime, especially in the south and Sicily, as to poverty.

Most estimates at the time of writing suggest that there are at least 60 million people of Italian origin around the world – roughly the same number as the current population of Italy. The largest concentration is in Brazil, with the majority living in and around São Paulo.

Italians constitute a large proportion of the population in Argentina and Uruguay, and significant numbers of Italian migrants made their way to Venezuela and Canada in the post-war period.

From the late 19th century onwards, the USA has been the main destination for Italian migrants, and those who originally settled in the cities of New York and Boston formed the basis of what is now called the Italian-American community.

I have had the opportunity of tasting Italian cooking in many countries around the world, and it is clear to me that the Italian settlers adapted to their new environment — often an ethnic and cultural melting pot — by integrating elements of other cuisines into their own regional food. Take provoleta, for example, a locally produced provolone or provola cheese that is melted on the *asado* (grill) used to cook the meat that is served after it. I first tasted this non-Italian invention in Buenos Aires, but it can be found in Uruguay and other cities in Argentina. The melted cheese is normally seasoned with herbs such as oregano, but is sometimes flavoured with the chimichurri sauce used for

the grilled meat. I have discussed provoleta with my good friend Diego Jacquet, the acclaimed Argentinian chef-patron of two London restaurants. His second one, Zoilo, aims to showcase the melting pot of cultures that make up Argentinian cuisine, which of course has many Italian influences. Today at Zoilo, Diego makes his provoleta in a small copper frying pan and tops it with honey, almonds and oregano. It is an absolute delight.

In New York City, Marco Canora, one of the very best Italian-American chefs, produces outstanding 'Italian-inflected' food at his restaurant Hearth and in his Terroir wine bars. Using ingredients sourced from farms in or around New York State, he makes superb seasonal dishes — the same methodology as would be used in Lucca, where his family originates. His gnocchi are the best I have eaten anywhere, and the recipe for them appears on page 116.

Tourism

In her paper *From Migrant Food to Lifestyle Cooking* (see page 469), Ulrike Thoms has noted that movements of migration and travel are important factors in the transfer of foodstuffs and the establishment of relationships of exchange between countries and continents. Food and wine, along with culture, sun, sea and mountains, are certainly amongst the reasons that people choose to holiday in Italy.

Holiday-makers, of course, sometimes need guidance, and the British publisher John Murray was quick to recognize this. In 1829 he produced the seminal *Handbook for Travellers on the Continent*, which also featured food and restaurant recommendations. Other guides, such as *Bradshaw's* and *Baedeker*, soon followed suit. Since then, some guidebooks have had an even stronger focus on food. In 1914 the French Touring Club produced a book that inspired the Italian publication *Guida Gastronomica d'Italia* (1916). The next major event was in 1956, when the *Michelin Guide* for Italy was first published, by which time driving holidays were well established. In 1990 Gambero Rosso, publishers of the influential *Italian Wine Guide* and *Food and Wine* magazine, produced their first restaurant guide for Italy. Travellers have therefore always been well catered for, and that pattern continues.

Low-cost airlines have now edged out driving holidays for most people, and have brought many wonderful Italian cities within easy reach. For less than the cost of a taxi to the airport, you can immerse yourself in the local gastronomy and bring back superb ingredients. Just remember to take a good guidebook.

The *Michelin Guide* is not necessarily everyone's idea of a gastronomic barometer for a given country, but the 2014 edition for Italy lists 281 one-star restaurants, 40 two-star and eight with three stars. Italy is third in the European rankings for three-star restaurants, France being first with 27, and Germany second with 11. This is a commendable record, and Italy deserves to be considered a leading gastronomic nation.

While visiting the Far East, I have come across exceptional Italian cuisine in Japan, and I have been lucky enough to eat two superb meals in Hong Kong — at Umberto Bombona's Otto e Mezzo, the first Italian restaurant to gain three Michelin stars outside Italy. The quality of sourcing in Far East restaurants is often outstanding. Indeed, I know many producers of the finest Italian foods, and it is the norm for them to export as much as 40 per cent of their premium products to Japan rather than to other European countries or the USA.

Mass Media

The publication of Italian cookbooks started as a trickle in the 20th century, became a torrent by the 1980s, and now, in the early 21st century, has become a flood.

While published recipes are less important in Italy because versions of dishes are passed on within families, and approaches to quantities and cooking are best described as intuitive, they are a growth area elsewhere.

In the English-speaking world the most important works on Italian food remain those by Elizabeth David, Marcella Hazan and Anna del Conte. A number of top chefs and restaurateurs in the UK have also published very good Italian cookbooks, including Franco and Ann Taruschio, Giorgio Locatelli, Rose Gray and Ruth Rogers, Alastair Little, Jacob Kenedy and Theo Randall. In the USA, Mario Batali has been prolific both in opening restaurants and writing books dedicated to Italian cuisine.

In terms of reach, though, it is TV chefs who tend to influence the mass market. Jamie Oliver, Antonio Carluccio and more recently (in her *Nigelissima* phase) Nigella Lawson are most likely to influence the average UK household, whilst in the US, Batali is high profile, as are Nick Stellino and Giada De Laurentiis.

While diligent marketing has done a great deal to raise the gastronomic profile of other countries, such as Spain and parts of Scandinavia, in my view, Italy remains out in front. You still have more chance of eating well there in any randomly chosen restaurant than in any other country in Europe.

Cookbooks remain a growth segment in print publishing, just as food-related programmes do in broadcasting. And don't forget the Internet. Vast quantities of data are available at the click of a mouse, be it from professional chefs, food writers, producers, bloggers or simply dedicated amateurs. To research a dish online and compare different recipes or cooking methods can all be done in a matter of minutes. Similarly, and just as easily, Italian ingredients can be purchased online and delivered pretty much anywhere.

The Role of the State

The Italian state has consistently promoted the export and distribution of Italian food, and generally the cooking and food culture of Italy's regions. This has been done mainly through the Italian Institute for Foreign Trade (ICE).

Another government initiative offered aid to consortia of food producers on the understanding that they would work together to export around the world. Unfortunately, some of these consortia became scams for obtaining grants that never resulted in any export activity. By the turn of the 21st century, the country's economic situation was looking bleak, so export funding was reduced. However, many of the diligent consortia, who work on a non-profit basis and are partly funded by producers or from export sales, have continued to thrive.

A good example of such a company is Export 3P, known as Gourm.it, based in Mantova. Focused mainly on promoting world-class cheese and the finest cured meats, the business is run by a group of passionate Italians and provides export promotion and distribution services to over 20 top-notch producers. Apart from small ad hoc contributions from the PDO consortia, they are completely self-funded. Gourm.it has successfully exported artisan food products to Japan, Britain, France, Germany, Hong Kong, Russia and North America, where it ends up in shops and restaurants.

In her book *Italian Food*, written in the early 1950s, the writer Elizabeth David noted that 'the difficulties of reproducing Italian cooking abroad are much the same as the difficulties attendant upon any good cooking outside its country of origin, and usually they can be overcome'. In fact, Italian emigrants, and the subsequent generations that were born in the countries where they settled, managed to do so.

If it was possible in the 1950s, there is no excuse for not doing so today. Information about Italian cooking and ingredients is now fairly ubiquitous, and consumers in most parts of the world can access food products that are 'Made in Italy', and source good local ingredients to accompany them. Outstanding Italian food has never been more accessible.

History, Tradition & Preservation

While the main purpose of this book is to provide the reader with an understanding of Italian cooking in the early part of the 21st century, that understanding is not possible without some reference to the past. Only by looking back can we see the origins of ingredients and dishes, as well as their diffusion.

The territory that now defines Italy was fairly late in appearing in the annals of food history. It is thought that the Italic people (part of the Indo-European migration westward into Europe) introduced rudimentary agricultural techniques in the 12th century BC.

Thereafter, it is possible to trace the introduction of certain foods and techniques that have become indelibly linked with Italy. Olive trees and vines, for example, are thought to have been brought over by the Etruscans in the 11th century BC, but were certainly present in the early Greek colonies of southern Italy around 770 BC. Later, the influx of Celts into northern Italy in the 5th century saw the introduction of salt-based meat-curing techniques and a greater propensity for the consumption of pork.

All these developments owed something to the Phoenician bases founded in Sardinia and Sicily in the 8th century BC. They became key points in the food and produce trade routes connecting the shores of the Mediterranean.

Rome

During the period that covers the Roman Empire (753 BC–AD 476) there were a number of key events that are important from a food perspective. Also, there are many texts that provide insights into what certain parts of the population were eating.

Rome developed from a mid-sized city-state, gaining supremacy of the Italian peninsula and forming one of the largest empires in history. Its territory encircled the Mediterranean, taking in not just Europe but parts of Africa and Asia too.

The Romans called the Mediterranean *Mare Nostrum* (Our Sea), and international trade flourished under their aegis. This was stimulated by the commercial export of crops such as olives, grapes and wheat, which were produced on the *latifundia* – large private estates worked by peasants or slaves. Many farming and herding methods then used were the products of war, being taken from the Carthaginians, whom the Romans defeated in 146 BC. Imports included cherries, peaches, apricots, guinea hens and peacocks.

At this time spices also started to arrive from the East, creating connections with kingdoms as distant as China.

As noted in Capatti and Montanari's cultural history of Italian cuisine (see page 465), 'During the years of the Roman Empire the Mediterranean was a formidable melting pot of different cultures and their diverse culinary traditions. It embraced all the diversity within reach and dispatched it onto a circuit of exchange that ultimately wound up in the capital, a gigantic commercial emporium and center of consumption.' They also note that a careful reading of ancient writers, such as Horace, reveals established links between places and produce. Tuscany, for example, was already associated with wild boar, while Ravenna was noted for asparagus and Campania for semolina wheat.

De Re Coquinaria (On the Subject of Cooking), often referred to as the oldest cookbook in the world, appeared around the 5th century AD. The author is unknown, but is often referred to as 'Apicius', after the Roman gastronome Marcus Gavius Apicius, who lived in the 1st century AD and whose name became synonymous with fine living. The text is a collection of recipes and recommendations by multiple authors and it circulated in manuscript form throughout Europe. The first printed edition appeared in 1498. Whilst providing some insight into what a certain social strata may have been eating — pulses for the poor, and exotic items such as flamingo for the rich — it is less useful in illustrating links between cooking in that period and the development of regional or national dishes. However, it certainly had some influence in spreading the notion of Italy having a distinctive cuisine.

Interestingly, the manuscripts of some Roman writers did in fact find their way back to Italy around the middle of the 15th century, but their impact on cooking or gastronomy was minimal.

Between AD 500 and 1000, successive waves of conquerors, including Ostrogoths, Byzantines, Lombards, Franks and Arabs, captured and recaptured strategic cities in the Italian peninsula and the island of Sicily. Part of their legacy was to introduce new foods and food cultures. To take just one example, the Arabs in Sicily (and to a lesser extent in Apulia and Campania) spread the idea of smallholdings, brought in new irrigation systems and introduced oranges, lemons and pistachios. So successful were these introductions that one cannot imagine Sicily today without its citrus groves and pistachio trees.

Whilst the Romans followed the Greeks in regarding wheat, grapes and olive trees as markers of agricultural development and urban civilization, the Germanic peoples of Europe still relied on hunting and gathering, alongside raising livestock. Their diet was therefore rather different, having a stronger reliance on meat, milk, butter and beer. When these Barbarians, as the Romans called them, took over the western part of the empire, there was a fusion of these two diets. This, according to Capatti and Montanari, was a major factor in creating a new European food culture during the Middle Ages. The other significant influence was the Catholic Church, which imposed certain rules about what could be eaten and when.

Influential Writings

Various works on gastronomy were produced during that time. Those by Bartolomeo Sacchi (known as Platina) were particularly important and influential. His *De Honesta Voluptate et Valetudine* (On Honest Pleasure and Good Health), produced about 1470, was based firmly on sources and practices of that time — it owed nothing to classical Roman texts. As the historian John Dickie points out, it was probably the first cookbook to be published using the revolutionary technology of print, so it gained a wider audience and influence throughout Renaissance Europe than had previously been possible.

What is of particular interest in Platina's work is that the recipes are largely 'borrowed' from a well-respected artisan chef called Martino de Rossi. Rossi had served masters from Lombardy to Campania, and his recipes clearly show a synthesis of the cooking from various major cities. These were written up in his own work, *Libro de Arte Coquinaria* (The Art of Cooking), produced around 1465. Now considered a seminal text in Italian gastronomic literature, it is also a historical record of the development of cooking on the Italian peninsula during the Renaissance.

John Dickie also makes the point that although many of the foods and recipes covered by Martino de Rossi were increasingly familiar, maybe even seminal, both Rossi and Platina clearly suggest that contemporary cooking in the cities was much more important than that of ancient Rome. This change is underscored by the great historian Fernand Brauduel in his classic study of Italy between 1450 and 1650; he too highlights the importance of cities in both socio-economic and cultural terms.

In the 16th century, Bartolomeo Scappi, a renowned chef for several cardinals and eventually Pope Pius IV, attempted to create a kind of synthesized Italian culture in texts that listed products and provided about 1000 recipes. His book *Opera l'arte et prudenza d'un maestro Cuoco dell'Arte del Cucinare* (The Art and Craft of a Master Cook), published in 1570, is a very detailed 900-page volume that goes far beyond recipes by providing numerous tips and information on sourcing and provenance. However, these efforts eventually gave way slowly but surely in the 17th and 18th centuries to an increasing emphasis on regional diversity. And this continued to happen, despite the very strong French influence then being felt on all matters related to cooking and serving food.

The transalpine influence of French gastronomy is most noticeable in Piedmont, particularly in Turin. This can be seen in *Il Cuoco Piemontese Perfezionato a Parigi* (A Piedmontese Cook Schooled in Paris), written anonymously in 1766 and lifted largely from *La Cuisinière Bourgeoise* (The Middle Class Cook) by Menon (a pseudonym). Despite the French influence and title, the book does include a few local dishes and ingredients. The influence of French cuisine on Italian food and vice versa is much debated, a subject that arouses fierce passion. Without wishing to yield too much, I tend to agree with John Dickie, who has noted, 'Italian food would not be Italian food without the French'.

Other local cuisines also made their way into print. Some of the best examples are Vincenzo Corrado's *Il Cuoco Galante* (The Gallant Cook, 1773), *Il Credenziere di Buon Gusto* (The Confectioner of Good Taste, 1778) and *Del Cibo Pitagorico* (On Pythagoran Food, 1781), all of which represent Naples and Campania. These books were popular in their particular localities, but it is unknown if they had influence elsewhere.

Post–unification

The history of Italian food after unification in 1870 is in many ways the most interesting. Whilst the new state was developing politically and economically, regionalist and sub-regionalist food cultures remained strong. Furthermore, some regional dishes managed to cross over into general use, and to achieve a measure of national and international recognition. It is from this point that the term 'Italian food' can be said to have some meaning.

In post-unification Italy one of the most famous collections of recipes is Pellegrino Artusi's *La Scienza in Cucina e l'Arte di Mangiare Bene (The Science of Cooking and the Art of Fine Dining)*. Originally self-published in 1891, it sold more than 200,000 copies by the time Artusi died in 1911. The original first edition had 475 recipes, but that number grew to 790 by the 13th edition, the last one before Artusi's death. The book has never been out of print and has been translated into many languages.

The first publication of the book was almost perfect timing, coming shortly after the unification of Italy and being written in Italian rather than a regional dialect. Artusi was a Florentine merchant from Forlimpopoli in Emilia-Romagna, and his conversational and witty prose, coupled with anecdotes, was very well received by the educated and affluent middle classes. This was quite an achievement given that French cuisine was in vogue, and Vittorio Emanuele II, king of the newly unified Italy, was a devotee of it, favouring butter rather than virgin olive oil. Reflecting this, the majority of the cookbooks in print were written by chefs either trained in France or who wrote in French for other professional cooks.

Despite the scope of Artusi's book being focused on the food of Tuscany and Emilia-Romagna, it is considered the most important cookery text of post-unification Italy. Indeed, it is still used today and serves as an inspiration for both professional chefs and home cooks. However, perhaps Artusi's most important contribution to the young nation was to provide an insight into the diversity of food and recipes to be found in Italy, and to create a new vocabulary to build on.

One of the big problems in diffusing any kind of information was that the majority of the population was illiterate. Added to that, people still spoke in dialect and remained proud and protective of their local culture and traditions. At this juncture very few dishes can be said to have spread nationally. The most famous case of one that did so was pasta with tomato sauce, which, according to the historian Stefano Somogyi, was discovered by troops marching through the south (see page 469).

The central government used both the school system and the military as vehicles to try to standardize food habits all over the country. Many of the rations given to soldiers, such as coffee, pasta and hard cheeses, also became staples for large sections of the population when the men took them home on leave because they had developed a taste for them.

A very important development in homes and restaurants during the post-unification period was the adoption of Russian table service, which involved presenting dishes in a particular order rather than all at once. This led to the structure still used today:

> *Antipasti* — small bites or appetizers, often salumi and/ or vegetables, eaten at the beginning of the meal
> *Primo* — first course, often soup or pasta
> *Secondo* — main course, normally meat or fish
> *Contorni* — side dishes, very often vegetables, served with the main course, but rarely on the same plate; it is the only stand-alone course
> *Formaggi* — cheese, may be served as well as, or instead of, dessert
> *Dolce* — dessert, often just fruit

This structure was not accepted by everyone at the time, and there were certainly regional differences as to what constituted a particular course. Also, some questioned whether so many courses were necessary. As it turned out, the diets of the rural and urban lower classes remained very similar to that eaten in the 18th century, with change only really occurring after the Second World War.

Nowadays, the structure of six or seven courses is most often used for formal meals, feasts or special occasions, with maybe two or three individual elements served at everyday meals.

During the First World War, men from all over the country were brought together – perhaps for the first time outside their own region. It was an eye-opening experience in many ways, one of which was that they were exposed to each other's regional food. The poet and historian Olindo Guerrini, who published *L'Arte di Utilizzare gli Avanzi della Mensa* (The Art of Using Leftovers) in 1917, gives a good insight on the food culture of the period.

The Fascist period (1922–43) had a major impact on Italian food, both culturally and economically. In its attempts to build a national identity, the state promoted the ideologically driven idea that there were cultural and historical connections with imperial Rome. Consequently, local languages, food and traditions were repressed. On the other hand, a number of new products were introduced at that time, including concentrated meat stock, baking powder and instant chocolate. And in 1926 the National Agency for the Scientific Organization of Work was founded and this led to the modernization of kitchen utensils and a number of new appliances.

The application of modernity to cooking can first be seen in the work of the Futurists, a group of artists and thinkers led by the poet Filippo Tommaso Marinetti. In the early years of the 20th century they proposed a new diet and modern food culture, dismissing traditional food and recipes. Even pasta was off-limits, being compared to an oppressive religion that killed the individual's creative spark. It can be argued that Marinetti was the father of the low-carb diet. In reality, despite much press attention at the time, the food ideas proposed by the Futurists had little or no impact on the Italian population.

In the period leading up to the start of the Second World War, the Italian state, perhaps influenced by Germany, promoted the policy of autarky (self-sufficiency). As part of this drive, wheat production in the north increased hugely, rivalling the traditional sources in the south. The outcome was that Italy became self-sufficient in cereals by 1940.

During the Fascist period, the Italian National Tourist Board (ENIT) commissioned the artist Umberto Zimelli to

produce culinary maps of Italy as part of its promotional activities. In later years, food companies used the same technique to promote themselves within the context of culinary Italy.

For those interested in travelling around Italy and discovering its diverse gastronomic delights, the Touring Club of Italy published its first guidebook in 1931. Particularly interesting and useful was the information it gave on specific ingredients and where to source them. In her book *Italian Food* (see page 465), the writer Elizabeth David mentions finding the 1951 edition of the guide 'invaluable', and praises the motor industry for understanding that tourism could help to preserve the vast array of wonderful local ingredients and specialities across the country.

Among the consequences of both the guidebook and map was that regions such as Apulia, Basilicata and Calabria were lifted out of obscurity, so to speak.

Post-unification Writings

One of the most influential cookery books to be published between the wars was Ada Boni's *Il Talismano della Felicità* (The Talisman of Happiness, 1929). Furthermore, this book has stood the test of time. In comparison with other writers, not least Artusi, Boni probably covers more corners of Italy than anyone else has managed to do so far. The first edition had 882 recipes, rising to 2000 in subsequent editions, so it is perhaps not surprising that it has become a standard work of reference for both home cooks and professional chefs in Italy and beyond. I remember my relatives remarking that the book was often given to brides as a present during the 1950s and 1960s, almost becoming a tradition.

Ada Boni came from a well-off, upper middle-class family in Rome and was involved with food from an early age. In 1915 she founded *Preziosa*, a food magazine targeted at women, and wrote other books on regional cooking, including one dedicated to the food of Rome.

The first decade or so post-Fascism and the Second World War was still characterized by economic hardship for large sections of the population. The food distribution system remained underdeveloped, so, to a certain extent, people were still tied into local produce.

In 1950 the publishers of *Domus*, a magazine devoted to architecture and design, produced *Il Cucchiaio d'Argento (The Silver Spoon)*. The first edition had over 1000 recipes collected from all over Italy. In compiling the book, the editors had talked to both chefs and home cooks, and did a good job of organizing and presenting the results. Particularly ground-breaking was their precision with measurements and cooking times. As a result, the recipes were easier to follow and the book itself was ideal for translation. Editions were produced in several languages, and those in English were so successful that they started a trend for translations of country-specific cookbooks.

The first edition of *The Silver Spoon* included a chapter called 'Dieteca della Belezza' (Eating for Beauty). This is especially interesting for the light it throws on the messages then being targeted at women: how they should look and what body shape they should aspire to. This was at a time when the fashion and film industries in Italy were enjoying great success and therefore wielding a lot of influence.

Dietary Changes and Industrialization

It was also in the early 1950s that the American scientist Ancel Keys was conducting research in the Naples area for his major work on the Mediterranean diet. In this he expounded the idea that animal fats were an important contributory factor in causing heart disease, and that olive oil was far less damaging. His view has had a huge influence all over the world, and in Italy it is thought to have led to northern parts of the country shifting away from cooking with butter and other animal fats. With his wife Margaret, a biochemist, Keys wrote a number of best-selling books (see page 466), the first of which — *Eat Well and Stay Well* — was published in Italian in 1962. Keys lived to the ripe old age of 100, and spent most of his last 29 years in Pioppi, a village in Campania, where he apparently practised what he preached.

Key's hypothesis about the effects of eating animal fats has been contested by a number of scientists over the years. Here we are concerned not with the validity of the hypothesis, but with the influence it had on dietary habits in Italy. For many, the benefits are seen as self-evident, and it has certainly done no harm to the food and tourism industries in countries all around the Mediterranean.

The economic boom of the 1960s saw both the improvement of food distribution and major waves of

Prior to the 1950s inter-regional exchange had occurred mainly amongst the higher classes, who could afford to travel for pleasure, but now it was happening across all social classes.

internal migration, especially from the rural south to the more industrial centre and north. The movement of food and people allowed for regional and local specialities to become known in other parts of the country. Previously, inter-regional exchange had occurred mainly amongst the higher classes, who could afford to travel for pleasure, but now it was happening across all social classes.

The post-war economic boom saw many Italian food companies grow to achieve both national and international success. Some, such as Barilla (now the world's largest pasta-maker) and Illy (one of the world's best-known coffee brands) have remained in private hands, whilst others, such as San Pellegrino (at one time the largest beverage company in Italy) have been acquired by major multinational food groups, in this case Nestlé.

Another mighty oak that has grown from a tiny acorn is Parmalat. Started as a small pasteurization company in Parma in 1961 by Calisto Tanzi, it has grown into a diversified food multinational employing over 30,000 people in 30 countries and is listed on the Milan stock exchange. In 2002 it was valued at €3.7 billion. Following a well-publicized financial scandal, the company went into administration and was reconstituted and relisted in 2005. Today the majority shareholder is the Lactalis Group, a French food multinational, which owns 83 per cent of the company stock.

While Italy has undoubtedly had a global impact on people's eating habits, it too is subject to outside influences. This is clearly seen in the variety of modern fast food that has been imported — everything from burgers to instant coffee. Of course, indigenous fast food has also appeared, one of the latest developments being a type of sandwich-cum-pizza called *trapizzino* (see page 411). So-called fine dining restaurants have not been immune to global trends, succumbing to everything from nouvelle cuisine to the practice of serving sorbets between courses.

A positive side of Italy's economic success was that a number of chefs were able to travel and develop some of their skills and techniques in foreign kitchens before returning to open their own restaurants in Italy. This was not necessarily a new thing, but it became increasingly common for chefs and front-of-house personnel to learn and practise their profession in many of the finest restaurants in the world.

It is not unusual today to find Italian nationals leading a kitchen brigade or front of house in restaurants all over the globe. More recently, sommeliers have also beaten the same path. The best example of this 'foreign' education is Gualtiero Marchesi, the first non-French person to be awarded three Michelin stars (in 1985). He trained in Switzerland as a young man and also worked in some of the best restaurants in France, such as Ledoyen in Paris, Le Chapeau Rouge in Dijon and Maison Troisgros in Roanne. Marchesi's culinary education has been emulated by a number of other top Italian chefs, including Alajmo and Massimo Bottura who alongside Fulvio Pierangelini, are talked about as being amongst the best in the world.

Whilst fine dining is far from being the only measure of a nation's gastronomic health, it can be regarded as an indicator of how seriously food is taken. By the mid-1980s Italy could boast some of the finest cooking in the world; on the other hand, it also had some of the worst. In between the two extremes I would argue that there was a massive middle ground of wonderful local and seasonal food available in homes and simple restaurants.

Slow Food

During the 1970s and the first part of the 1980s, a combination of industrialized food production and socio-economic change led to increased urbanization and saw many agricultural and pastoral traditions come under threat. The threat produced a food and wine counter-culture that was to have an impact both in Italy and beyond. It began with Arcigola, an organization founded in 1986 by Carlo Petrini. Among its aims were the protection of the environment and the promotion of consumer rights. That same year Stefano Bonilli started *Gambero Rosso* magazine (see page 18) and helped spread Arcigola's thoughts and ideas.

Arcigola took its name from the left-leaning Italian Association for Recreation and Culture (ARCI) and its magazine called *La Gola*. The two elements of the name – *arci* and *gola* – translate as 'arch appetite', which was a happy irony when the organization protested against the opening of a McDonald's restaurant in Rome in 1986. Fast food subsequently inspired a change of name. Arcigola became Slow Food and its chosen symbol was the snail. In 1989 delegates from 15 countries met in Paris to sign the Slow Food Manifesto, and the international movement was born.

Slow Food's philosophy of food is based on three principles: good, clean and fair. It envisions a world in which all people can access and enjoy food that is good for them, good for those who grow it and good for the planet. The movement opposes the standardization of taste and culture, and the unrestrained power of food industry multinationals and industrial agriculture.

Today, Slow Food has over 100,000 members worldwide and millions of supporters. Headquartered in Bra, Piedmont, it is coordinated by an international council and steered by an executive committee, but also operates at national and local level. The local groups are known as convivia, and there are currently over 1500 of them worldwide. They coordinate activities and organize events in cities, towns and communities in many countries, including the UK, USA, Switzerland, Germany, Japan and the Netherlands. Carlo Petrini remains president of the organization as a whole.

To realize its projects and ambitions, Slow Food has created a number of subdivisions, including the Slow Food Foundation for Biodiversity, founded in 2003 to support Slow Food projects that defend food biodiversity and traditions. To preserve the wealth of domestic biodiversity, Slow Food created the Ark of Taste, which 'collects' plants, animals and food products (breads, cheeses, cured meats and so forth) that are at risk of extinction. The Ark of

Taste is basically a catalogue of products, but Slow Food has also started an initiative – the Presidia – that directly involves food producers. The Presidia are projects that take action to safeguard a traditional food (an Ark product), or a traditional technique (for fishing, farming, food processing or cultivation), or a rural landscape, or an ecosystem. In Italy alone, at the time of writing, there are 224 Presidia.

For those interested in discovering some of the best foods available in Italy (and elsewhere) it is certainly worth consulting the Slow Food list of Presidia on a regular basis. Of course, it is not infallible. From time to time you may find a product that has been overproduced, or declined in quality, or slid towards commodification.

In the case of Italy, I have been very impressed by the robust quality standards and ongoing monitoring conducted by the Presidia. In fact, in many respects there is more attention to quality than in, for example, the European Union schemes – Protected Designation of Origin (PDO), Protected Geographical Indication (PGI) and Traditional Specialities Guaranteed (TSG). These promote and protect the names of quality agricultural products and foodstuffs, ensuring that only those genuinely originating in a designated region are allowed to be identified as such. The emphasis is, therefore, more on provenance than quality.

Another initiative has been the Terra Madre (Mother Earth) Foundation, established in 2004 to support the growth of a global network of food communities, chefs, academics and young people working for a sustainable food system. Every two years it holds a conference in Turin at the Salone del Gusto, the largest food and wine fair in the world, and this event attracts people from all over Italy and the rest of the world.

Also in 2004 the University of Gastronomic Sciences (UNISG) was opened in Pollenzo, Piedmont, and Colorno, Emilia-Romagna, to educate future food professionals. I have had the pleasure of working with a number of very impressive graduates of this university, as well as the unrelated University of Parma Food Sciences Department.

Parma was chosen as the site for the European Food Security Authority (EFSA) that was set up in January 2002, following a series of European food crises in the late 1990s. EFSA is an independent source of scientific advice and communication on risks associated with the food chain. This body is a key component in European Union risk assessment regarding food and feed safety.

Although many people are heartened by the aims and activities of Slow Food, some regard the movement as elitist, something to which only the more affluent, mainly Western, middle classes can devote time and effort. Whilst it is true that developing knowledge of exceptional and often rare foods and then having the pleasure of consuming them are not options for everyone, these by no means represent the full scope and raison d'être of Slow Food. Indeed, the work it has undertaken since 1989 – promoting an alternative to fast food, whilst striving to preserve traditional and regional cuisine and encouraging the farming of plants and livestock characteristic of local ecosystems – is nothing short of remarkable.

It would be a mistake, though, to think that the problems posed by fast food and globalization have been overcome. Italy still has to deal with most of the food issues that one sees in, say, the USA and the UK. In terms of retail, large supermarkets and hypermarkets, many owned by pan-European or multinational groups with immense buying power, threaten the small independent and specialist retailers, just as they do elsewhere.

Italy is certainly not, as some people might expect, a country free of 'junk' or processed food. In *The Lost Art of Feeding Kids,* Jeannie Marshall, a Canadian journalist living in Italy, reveals that packaged snacks and junk foods are displacing natural, home-cooked meals in a place widely associated with a healthy Mediterranean diet. Italy's food culture, she asserts, is giving way to Americanized processed, packaged and industrially produced foods.

This certainly contrasts with issue four of *Fool Magazine*, which is dedicated to Italian gastronomy. Read that and you would conclude that Italy is a country dominated by superb designers, artisan food and wine producers, and stupendous chefs.

What the editors of *Fool* do recognize is that Italy is still a young country, and even today is more like a confederation of states than a unified nation. Regional differences are reflected in food, and there is a very rich food culture. Traditions are defended, but there is still much debate and disagreement about authenticity. The editors suggest that the rich food culture and tradition lead to a static status quo, obstructing development, curiosity and creativity. However, the history of Italian cooking before and after unification would suggest otherwise. Rather than atrophy, there has instead been, and continues to be, a veritable melting pot of influences on food. What has gone into the pot has arrived with invaders, expatriates returning home and, more recently, through the technologies that facilitate mass communication and media.

Clearly, Italians and Italian cooking are open to change, new ideas and new ingredients, but the strong national food culture is not so easily diluted as elsewhere.

Timeline of Post-unification Italy

1870 Italy becomes a unified kingdom under the House of Savoy. During the process of unification, soldiers spread some of their regional foods and traditions.

1891 Pellegrino Artusi publishes *La Scienza in Cucina e l'Arte di Mangiare Bene* (*Science in the Kitchen and the Art of Good Eating*).

1915 Italy enters the First World War against Austria and Germany. Many of the soldiers' rations, such as coffee, dried pasta and cheeses, become de facto necessities for the whole populace.

1917 Olindo Guerrini's *L'Arte di Utilizzare gli Avanzi della Mensa* (*The Art of Using Leftovers*) is published – a year after his death.

1922 Benito Mussolini and the Fascist Party take power.

1926 The National Agency for the Scientific Organization of Work is founded.

1929 *Il Talismano della Felicità* (The Talisman of Happiness) by Ada Boni is published.

1936 Mussolini proclaims economic self-sufficiency in Italy.

1940 Italy enters the Second World War, siding with Germany. Food is very scarce and the black market is buoyant.

1943 Mussolini is imprisoned and the King of Italy signs a truce with the Allies. Germany occupies Italy.

1946 Italy becomes a republic and an economic boom begins.

1954 Ancel Keys conducts research in Naples that will form a key part of his hypothesis about the Mediterranean diet.

1959 Ancel and Margaret Keys write *Eat Well and Stay Well*.

1963 Introduction of Denominazione di Origine Controllata (DOC), introduced for wines in Italy.

1975 Ancel and Margaret Keys publish *How to Eat Well and Stay Well the Mediterranean Way*.

1977 Gualtiero Marchesi opens his first restaurant in Milan and earns a Michelin star.

1985 Gualtiero Marchesi becomes the first non-Frenchman to earn three Michelin stars.

1986 *Gambero Rosso* magazine is founded.

1989 The founding manifesto of the international Slow Food movement is signed in Paris by delegates from 15 countries.

1992 The EU establishes Protected Designation of Origin (PDO) and Denominazione di Origine Protetta (DOP).

2002 Massimiliano (Max) Alajmo becomes the youngest chef to be awarded three Michelin stars.

2003 Parma is chosen as the seat for the European Food Security Authority (EFSA).

2004 The University of Gastronomic Sciences is founded in Bra by Carlo Petrini, the founder of the Slow Food movement.

2012 Umberto Bombana's Otto e Mezzo in Hong Kong becomes the first Italian restaurant outside Italy to be awarded three Michelin stars.

2013 Massimo Bottura's Osteria Francescana is ranked third at the San Pellegrino World's 50 Best Restaurants Awards.

Ingredients & Equipment

A List of Essentials

Before writing this section, I went and had a good look in my store cupboard and noticed that over 60 per cent of the foods it contained can best be described as Italian, or at least Italo-centric. If some of these foods or ingredients were not there, I wonder if I could actually sleep at night.

The list here is obviously very subjective, but I believe it provides the minimum requirements for cooking Italian dishes on a regular basis. Many of the items allow you to prepare a number of courses or one-plate meals in under 20 minutes. This proves that there is really no need to buy any of the 'Italian' ready-meals found in supermarkets when you can knock up something that is far more delicious and healthy with the contents of your store cupboard and fridge in the time it takes you to warm the ready-meal in a microwave or oven.

Store Cupboard

- Anchovies (Cetera or Noli, in salt or tins; and Colatura di Alice – refrigerate after opening)

- Beans (borlotti and cannellini, dried or tinned)

- Black peppercorns

- Capers (Pantelleria, in salt)

- Caster sugar

- Chilli flakes

- Flour ('0' and '00')

- Herbs (dried bay leaves and thyme)

- Honey (Italian)

- Marsala fortified wine

- Oil (the best and freshest extra virgin olive oil you can obtain; and flavourless oil, e.g. sunflower, rapeseed or grapeseed)

- Olives (in tins or jars)

- Pasta (dried spaghetti, linguine and penne, plus ditalini for soups – none of these contain eggs; also dried tagliatelle and pappardelle, which do contain eggs)

- Pine nuts

- Polenta

- Porcini (dried mushrooms)

- Raisins or sultanas

- Risotto rice (Carnaroli and Vialone Nano)

- Saffron strands

- Sea salt (e.g. Sale di Cervia)

- Semolina (Semolina di Grano Duro)

- Tomato purée

- Tomatoes (tins or jars, e.g. San Marzano PDO, Corbarina or Piennolo)

- Vinegar (balsamic tradizionale and a good *Essenza*; red wine vinegar)

Fridge

- Bottarga di Muggine

- Butter (Italian)

- Fresh herbs, especially basil and flat leaf parsley. (It's best to grow them yourself and pick as required)

- Guanciale

- Mascarpone

- Mostarda di Frutta (refrigerate once opened)

- Pancetta

- Parmigiano Reggiano

- Pecorino Romano

- Pecorino Sardo or Toscano

- Ricotta

- Salumi (e.g. Felino, finocchiona, Proscuitto di Parma, Proscuitto di Carpegna, or Proscuitto di San Daniele)

Kitchen Equipment

If you are already a keen home cook, it is unlikely you will need to buy any more equipment to prepare the recipes in this book or Italian dishes in general. However, there are a small number of items that are particularly useful and will often improve results.

Box grater

A good-quality box grater with four gradations of holes is perfect for grating cheese, nutmeg and bottarga.

Cast-iron mincer

Food processors and electric mincers tend to rip meat rather than mince it, so I prefer to use a manual mincer that clamps to the table. It can be hard to find this type in the shops nowadays, but second-hand ones are widely available.

Flywheel manual slicing machine

Many Italian families will have a slicing machine at home, especially if they live in a region noted for cured meats. Buying whole hams or salumi is usually more economical than buying ready-sliced, so if you travel to Italy on a regular basis, it's probably worth bringing some back with you and buying a decent manual slicer too. Electric ones in my opinion tend to generate too much heat, which damages the outside of the meat, and even imparts a slightly odd taste. Among the best makes, either new or vintage, are Berkel, Volano and Tamagnini, who produce small slicers that are perfect for home use.

ICE-CREAM MACHINE

If ice cream and sorbets will feature regularly on your menus, I strongly recommend that you invest in a good ice-cream machine with a capacity of at least 1.5 litres.

MEZZALUNA

This double-handled semicircular knife is excellent for chopping herbs, but may also be used for cutting gnocchi out of the potato and flour dough.

MORTAR AND PESTLE

I believe pounding by hand makes by far the best pesto or Creamed Salt Cod (see page 176). The food processor is often overused and does not produce the best texture for certain dishes.

PASTA MACHINE

If you are very adept with a rolling pin, there is no real need for a pasta machine as you can achieve the same results without one. However, if you plan to make fresh pasta very often, it is worth investing in a machine as it will help you to achieve the correct thickness of dough for whatever pasta you are making.

Pasta tongs

I find these invaluable for lifting long types of pasta out of boiling water and transferring it to other pans or individual serving dishes.

Pastry cutters

I use oval cutters of various size, mainly for the preparation of gnocchi (see page 116).

Truffle slicer

Rather like a cheese slicer, a truffle slicer consists of a single horizontal blade within a wooden or plastic frame. It is drawn across truffles to produce fine shavings. If you are lucky enough to obtain black or white truffles on a regular basis, this is an essential piece of equipment.

Vegetable mill

Known as a *passaverdure* in Italian, or *mouli* in French, this item is very useful for mashing potatoes when making gnocchi, and straining tomato sauce if you are looking for a particularly smooth version.

Regions & Ingredients of Italy

1. PIEDMONT
Nocciola Piemonte, Tartufo Bianco d'Alba, Riso di Barragia Biellese e Vercellese

2. VALLE D' AOSTA
Fontina Val d'Aosta, Val d'Aosta Lard d'Arnad

3. LOMBARDY
Gorgonzola, Tallegio, Mostarda di Cremona, Bresaloa dell Valtellina

4. TRENTINO-ALTO ADIGE/SÜDITROL
Speck Alto Adige

5. VENETO
Riso Nano Vialone Veronese, Radicchio Rosso di Treviso, Monte Veronese (cheese)

6. FRIULI VENEZIA GIULIA
Prosciutto di Sauri, Prosciutto di San Daniele

7. LIGURIA
Basilico Genovese

8. EMILIA-ROMAGNA
Prosciutto di Parma, Culatello di Zibello, Parmigiano-Reggiano, Aceto Balsamico Tradizionale, Sale di Cervia

9. TUSCANY
Cinta Senese (pigs), - Chianina (cattle), Lardo di Colonata, Miele della Lunigiana

10. UMBRIA
Prosciutto di Norcia, Faro di Montelone di Spoleto

11. MARCHE
Prosciutto di Carpegna

12. LAZIO
Pecorino Romano, Zafferano dell 'Aquila, Castagna di Vallerano

13. ABRUZZO
Santo Stefano di Sessanio Lentil, Mortadella di Campotosto

14. MOLISE
Conca Casale Signora (salami)

15. CAMPANIA
Colatura di Alici di Cetara, Mozzarella di Bufala Campana, Pomodoro S. Marzano dell'Agro Sarnese-Nocerin, Pomodoro Corbarino, Pasta di Gragnano, Limone Costa d' Amalfi

16. APULIA
Clementine del Golfo di Taranto Capocollo di Martina Franca

17. BASILICATA
Melanzana Rossa di Rotanda Peperone di Senise Fagiolo di Sarconi

18. CALABRIA
Cipolla Rossa di Tropea, Nduja di Spilinga

19. SICILY
Pistacchio di Bronte, Pomodoro di Pachino, Arancia Rossa di Sicilia, Sale marino di Trapani

20. SARDINIA
Bottarga di Muggine di Cabras, Miele Amaro di Corbezzolo, Zafferano di Sardegna, Pecorino Sardo

Pasta & Gnocchi

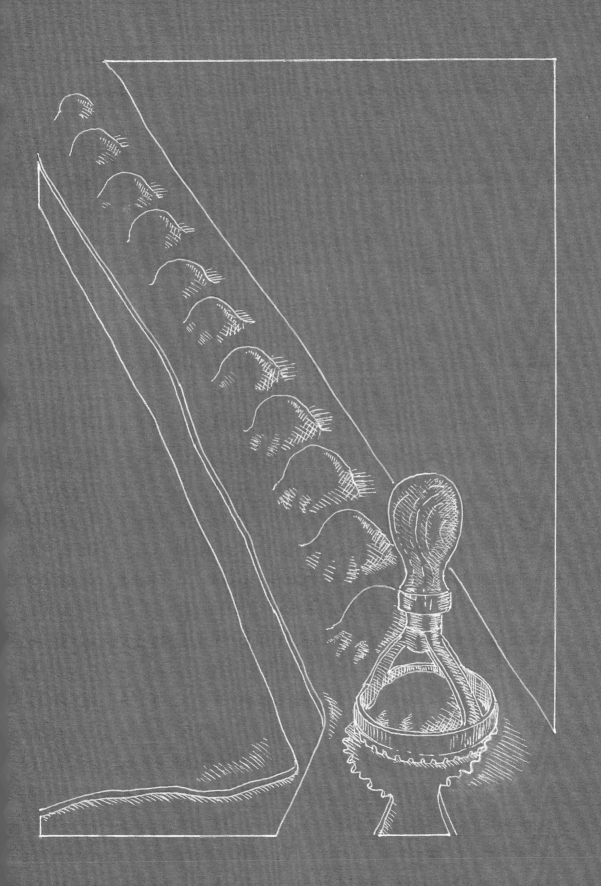

Pasta & Gnocchi

In the early 21st century no other single ingredient or food, with the possible exception of pizza, is more widely associated with Italian cooking than pasta. At its best, pasta is an amazing ingredient, needing only a little butter or oil and a sprinkling of Parmigiano to turn it into a delicious and satisfying dish. But it can also be lifted to gastronomic heights when combined with sauces that draw upon the finest tomatoes, oils, herbs, meat or seafood. It really is the most versatile and biddable of ingredients. Sadly, when in the hands of the misinformed or misled, it is also one of the most misunderstood and poorly prepared elements of Italian cooking.

According to the International Pasta Producers Organization, nearly 14 million tonnes of pasta are produced annually, of which Italy produces about 3.3 million and the USA 2 million. In terms of total consumption, the USA outstrips everyone else, eating 2.7 million tonnes, followed by Italy at around 1.5 million, but Italy has by far the highest per capita consumption, at 26 kg per annum. Other countries eat like birds in comparison — the USA on 8.8 kg, Argentina 7.9 kg, Canada 6.5 kg, Brazil 6.2 kg, Australia 4.0 kg and the UK a mere 2.5 kg.

The pasta used in Italian cooking can be broadly divided into two types: dried pasta (*pasta secca*, aka *pasta sciutta*) and fresh pasta (*pasta fresca*). The former is traditionally made with hard durum wheat, whilst the latter is made with softer grano tenero wheat, usually bolstered by the addition of eggs.

A key component of pasta is gluten, a protein network that forms when the durum wheat and water are made into dough. It is gluten that allows the compound to bind together. High-quality semolina (i.e. ground wheat with a high protein content – at least 14 per cent – and a high percentage of gluten) will create a network that will be able to retain gluten inside the starch of the pasta, and all the nutrients too. In order to ensure that all the nutritional components remain intact, the pasta must be dried slowly at a low temperature. (Drying at very high temperatures adversely affects the structure of the dough and greatly reduces its digestibility.)

Many countries around the world, including most of Europe, North Africa, the Middle East and Asia, have an ancient tradition involving pasta or something very similar. However, as Silvano Serventi and Françoise Sabban observe in their excellent book on the subject (see page 469), the homeland of pasta can be seen as both Italy and China because each has developed and spread its own culinary traditions in using it.

In Italy, there is an ongoing debate about the history, origins and diffusion of pasta, and many competing theories. Interested factions in this debate include historians, etymologists, sociolinguists and anthropologists, to name just a few, but speak to any Italian and you will get yet more heartfelt opinions. No one stands on the sidelines in the great pasta debate.

Trying to discover the precise origins of pasta is very difficult because it is such a simple product, combining just two ingredients – flour and water – and therefore also hard to distinguish from a plethora of other flour and water creations that we can generally call unleavened breads or cakes. These are mentioned in various ancient sources, but without offering much detail about the grain used or the cooking methods. It may therefore be wise to remain sceptical about the ancient forerunners of what we call pasta, the Greek *laganon* and the Roman *lagani*, for example, which were cut into strips. From an etymological point of view, these are thought to have been the antecedents for a number of pasta shapes. However, it must be stressed that there is no evidence that they were cooked in the way pasta is today (i.e. boiled), or that they were similar to dried durum wheat pasta.

Other ancient evidence is similarly doubtful. There are, for example, a number of Etruscan images dating as far back as 700 BC that show equipment that could have been used for cutting pasta, but none explicitly showing it being done.

Charles Perry, the Arabist, food historian and journalist, suggests that the Jerusalem Talmud (Judaism's book of laws) may have the first reference to what can be called boiled pasta. It is certainly different from how the Greeks, Romans and Etruscans cooked their combinations of wheat and water, which were most likely baked or grilled into unleavened breads. However, the authors of the Jerusalem Talmud, writing in Aramaic during the 5th century AD, merely debated whether *itriyah* (a type of flatbread, the name of which may be linked to the Greek word *itrion*), violated Jewish dietary laws. By the 10th century AD, *itriyah* had become an Arabic word for 'noodles', and it is the Arabs who are thought to have introduced them to various parts of southern Europe. This theory is supported by the Arab geographer Muhammad al-Idrisi (1100–66), who produced a map of the world for King Roger II of Sicily, and also noted that people in Palermo made strings of dough called *trii*, a word he assumed came from the Arabic *itriyah*. In view of both the Greek and Arabic occupations of Sicily, it could have come from either, as the plural of the Greek word *itrion* is *itria*. *Trii* remains the word for 'spaghetti' in Sicily, and is probably also the root for *tria*, the word used in Apulia.

Anthony Buccini, a linguistics expert and food scholar, argues that there is little hard etymological or historical evidence that the Arabs introduced pasta into Sicily. He points instead to the role of merchants in Genoa and Pisa trading pasta with Sicily and Piedmont.

Other scholars suggest that Persia may have been where early forms of pasta evolved and spread to both east and west. Old Persian manuscripts refer to *lakhshah*, thin strips of dough that may have been boiled. This name is thought to have links with the Yiddish word *lokshen*, and with the Indonesian *laksa* too.

There is a well-known story that suggests a possible direct connection between Italy and China when it comes to pasta, and it involves the explorer Marco Polo (1254–1324). After many years travelling in the Far East, he is said to have brought pasta home with him in 1298.

However, the city of Genoa archives contain a document dated 1279 listing the estate of a certain Ponzio Bastone, and it includes a basketful of 'macaronis'. Marco Polo was therefore 20 years too late to claim the credit. Indeed, other sources clearly indicate that types of pasta were being made in both Liguria and southern parts of the Italian peninsula well before Marco Polo was even born.

Much of the confusion is caused by attempting to fit forerunners into what is, in effect, a modern category, pasta. For example, in *The Decameron* (1352) the author Giovanni Boccaccio describes the mythical land of Begondi, where the inhabitants rolled 'macaroni' down a mountain of grated Parmigiano cheese, but we cannot be sure if he was talking about the curved pasta tubes that we today call macaroni. It could well have been something closer to a stuffed fresh pasta shape, such as agnolotti, or maybe even gnocchi.

The key point in relation to the pasta we eat today is that a few centuries after the invasion of Sicily by the Arabs, in the area around Naples, but also in Apulia, Liguria and Tuscany, durum wheat dried pasta was being produced for local sale and distribution. These locations may have been its traditional strongholds, but perhaps they were chosen for other reasons. Gragnano near Naples, for example, benefited from the Gulf of Sorrento breezes, which made it ideal for drying pasta, but also had the advantage of proximity to the main areas of durum wheat farming.

The Naples area benefited from technological innovation and the spread of railways to take an early lead in the production and distribution of pasta. The technology in question, developed in the late 19th century, involved separate machines for extruding, kneading and rolling the dough. Eventually, by the beginning of the Second World War, mechanization was replaced by continuous production lines.

At that time the dictator Benito Mussolini was in power, and his agricultural policies, which aimed to make Italy self-sufficient in food, contributed to Naples losing the lead to large industrial producers in the north of the country. Over time, this led to a reduction in the number of artisan pasta-makers, and those who did survive, especially in Gragnano, chose to focus on premium-quality products.

In the north of Italy, which is unsuited to farming durum wheat, the manufacturers had to make do with softer wheat, so they focused on making fresh pasta. Industrial production of fresh pasta continues there to this day, but home cooks and specialist shops still produce their own fresh pasta too.

Today few would argue that the best dried pasta is still produced in and around Naples, though Apulia and Abruzzo get honourable mentions. Similarly, most would agree that the best fresh pasta is found in the north, especially in Emilia-Romagna and, to a lesser extent, in Piedmont, Veneto and Lombardy. There are exceptions, of course, and you might find an excellent dried pasta in, say, Trentino, or superb fresh pasta made in a specific restaurant or household in the Naples area.

In many countries outside Italy, the UK being a good example, there seems to be a common perception that fresh pasta is somehow superior to dried pasta. This is absurd, and has probably been fuelled by a multitude of misinformed cookbooks and TV programmes. Large-scale manufacturers of fresh pasta, producing either under their own brand names or for supermarkets and shops, have added fuel to the fire. The very idea of mass-produced fresh pasta is a nonsense because it should be made in limited quantities that can be eaten within just a few hours of being prepared. Added to that, the mass-produced product is generally a total abomination, made of pasteurized dough and often filled with ingredients I would be reluctant to feed even to my cats.

Fresh and dried pasta both have their place in the kitchen: they each have their specific uses, and are normally associated with a specific sauce or ingredient. The great advantage of dried pasta is that it normally has a shelf life of years, so you can stock up with no fear of it going off. Fresh pasta, though, is quite a different matter. In my view, unless you make fresh pasta yourself with the best flour and eggs you can find, or have access to a shop or restaurant that makes its own, my advice is to avoid it completely.

I recently heard something very odd about an Italian restaurant chain. While their pizzas and pasta sauces are reasonably good, their pasta itself is a strange hybrid. It is basically dried pasta supplied in an undried state so that it can be cooked in just a few minutes. The reason for this is that, apparently, the British don't like to wait up to 15 minutes for their pasta to be cooked to order. In a way, this is an improvement on the practice of part-cooking pasta before service and then 'refreshing' it before sending it out to the tables. Neither habit, though, is desirable, and in my opinion, both are completely unnecessary.

My wife reminded me of an incident a few years ago in a London, Italian-run restaurant. I had ordered simple spaghetti with tomato, garlic and basil as a first course. When it arrived, I could see the pasta was overcooked, but tasted it just to be sure, and then called over one of the waiters. At this juncture, I was still calm and prepared to accept that a simple human error had occurred. However, my mood darkened when the waiter said I should have indicated that I was of Italian origin and knew about pasta, and they would have cooked it to order and so on. If my memory serves me right, the most polite word I used in responding was *vergogna* (shame), and within minutes, both the owner and most of the kitchen brigade visited me, apologizing profusely for the *incidente*. The point I am making is that, apart from the fact that a pasta course can be expensive and should therefore at least be cooked properly, if we settle for less, that will be what we end up getting.

The Italian food historian Oretta Zanini de Vita has spent years researching the history and varieties of fresh and dried pasta, and produced the comprehensive *Encyclopedia of Pasta* (see page 469). With Carol Field, who contributed the foreword to her book, she has developed a useful categorization of pasta, which I reproduce below.

General Categories of Pasta

Pasta Corta — short forms, such as penne or rigatoni, but also types such as handmade trofie.

Pasta Lunga — long forms, such as spaghetti and tagliatelle, plus handmade shapes, such as pici.

Pasta Ripiena — stuffed pasta, such as ravioli, and certain rare pastas layered with sauce and baked, such as vincisgrassi.

Pastina — tiny shapes that are cooked in broth.

Gnocchi/gnochetti — usually small, dumpling-like forms, but also some rustic long forms.

Strascinati — pasta squares, which are traditionally handmade and dragged (*strascinato*) across a wooden board before being shaped. Orecchiette are the most famous example.

Even Oretta Zanini's Herculean labours for her encyclopedia do not account for every shape and variety of pasta, past and present, in Italy. That is because new shapes continue to be developed, many specially commissioned from well-known industrial designers. One of the most famous is *marille*, designed by Giorgetto Giugiaro for maximum sauce retention.

Excellent dried pasta is available around the world, and it is widely accepted that the best comes from the town of Gragnano by the Bay of Naples. The Abruzzo region also has clusters of outstanding producers, and there are highly rated producers like Martelli in Tuscany and Mancini in Le Marche.

The firm of Felicetti, based in Trentino, not far from the Swiss and Austrian borders, also makes outstanding dried pasta, some made with ancient forms of wheat, such as Kamut, a trademark for khorasan wheat (*Triticum turgidum*), and farro wheat (*T. dicoccum*). People with mild wheat sensitivities (as distinct from coeliac disease) often find it easier to digest. One such person is Riccardo Felicetti himself, who told me that his own sensitivity, allied to his passion for eating pasta, drove him to work with these ancient and less common varieties of wheat.

People are always surprised when I tell them that supermarket own brands of pasta are often better than some of the more expensive and heavily marketed brands, and often half the price. It all depends on which manufacturer the supermarket has contracted to make its pasta. I try to speak direct to the best pasta-makers to find out who they are working for, but contracts come and go, so it is necessary to monitor things and make sure the high quality you enjoyed one week hasn't disappeared the next.

The fundamental point is that it really is worth getting the best. And remember that even the most expensive pasta will probably cost you no more than the cheapest hamburger in your local fast food chain.

Apart from working with supermarkets, pasta-makers such as Giuseppe di Martino and Riccardo Felicetti also work closely with high-profile chefs who understand that the pasta is as important as any other ingredient in the composition of a dish. I always find it heartening to see the pasta brand mentioned by name on their menus. However, I am also sad when some high-end chefs and restaurateurs, who should know better, use a commodity brand but charge superior brand prices. Sometimes this is due to a crude way of calculating their food margins, but sometimes it is because they are effectively 'sponsored' by those mass-market producers.

Based on extensive research and tastings, I recommend the following pastas as best in class from their respective areas of production.

Pastificio dei Campi
Gragnano

In much the same way that DOC connotes a fine wine, so the name Gragnano implies a superior pasta. Products allowed to be called *pasta di Gragnano* must be produced in a legally defined area in and around the Bay of Naples, and must be made by mixing durum wheat with the low-calcium water of the Lattari Mountains. The dough is forced through rough bronze forms (*trafilata al bronzo*) and dried at low temperatures in the mountain air. Depending on the shape, it takes 28–60 hours to dry – quite a contrast to industrial pastas, which are speed-dried in just a few hours. The result is a high-quality product with plenty of ridged surface area to hold on to the sauce with which it is served.

I have been fortunate enough to meet Giuseppe di Martino, who is president of Gragnano's society of pasta-makers, and owner of Pastificio di Martino, his family firm, and Pastificio dei Campi. The latter produces what is widely regarded as the Ferrari of dried pasta. Each pack is traceable to the original durum wheat used to make it, all of it grown in fields within 250 km of Gragnano. This high-protein grain represents less than 1 per cent of the total wheat production in Italy, so it is a pretty exclusive product.

Other top-notch pasta-makers in Gragnano include Faella, D'Apuzzo and Di Nola.

Pastificio Masciarelli

Abruzzo

I first came across Masiarelli spaghetti in various restaurants in Rome. Like Pastificio dei Campi, it is made in small quantities from top-quality wheat, then extruded through bronze dies to create the essential ridged surface, and slow-dried. Arcangelo Dandini, chef-patron of L'Arcangelo restaurant in Rome, rates this pasta as one of the best two from the Abruzzo region (the other being Verrigini).

Pasta Dishes

It is very difficult to select a limited number of pasta recipes as there are so many to choose from. I have tried to highlight some lesser-known recipes while offering others that may be well known but are either misunderstood or may have been corrupted during their travels. Note that other chapters in this book also feature pasta recipes, especially if they are a particularly good example of a dish that uses a specific ingredient covered in that section.

Finally, wherever ingredients include a type of pasta along with a place name, it is an indicator that the pasta itself is a star and should not be considered a bit part in the dish. This means you should not only try to make or source the very best pasta, but also take care not to drown it in other ingredients.

How to cook pasta

Top-quality pasta produced as described here is cooked in just the same way as homemade or shop-bought fresh pasta made with softer flours and eggs.

All pasta, fresh or dried, is best cooked in boiling water. Allow about 1 litre for every 100 g pasta, though very large shapes might need more. Salt should be added once the water boils, and the quantity depends to a certain extent on the saltiness of whatever sauce or cheese will be going on the pasta. As a rule of thumb, I would say to add at least 1 teaspoon salt per litre of water.

A cooking time is usually suggested on most packets of pasta, but the best way to know if it is ready is to taste it. With experience, many people develop the ability to tell simply by looking at the pasta and lifting it with a fork. Remember to factor in the time it takes to get the pasta to the plate and the plate to the table, as pasta will continue to cook once it has been drained. Aim to cook the pasta *al dente*, literally 'to the tooth', or, in the words of Giuseppe di Martino, until it has 'tenacious resistance and elasticity'. The slightly firm texture ensures better flavour and nutrient content, and also aids digestion because the starch and gluten remain bound. This allows the pasta to be digested slowly rather than giving a glycaemic peak (a quick but fleeting rise in blood sugar level). It is very noticeable when eating high-quality pasta that it feels much lighter on the stomach, and leaves you feeling ready to proceed to the next course. In Italy pasta is nearly always served as a first course — that is, after antipasto and before a main course. In this case, portions should be around 80–90 g (uncooked weight). If your meal consists of just a plate of pasta, you might consider cooking 100 g or so. Unless you are planning to run a half-marathon or ride a stage of the Giro d'Italia the next day, any more could be too much of a good thing.

Fresh Pasta Dishes

Inevitably, I must start this section with a recipe for making your own pasta, but I must also make a confession. I have to be honest and say I rarely do, but regular trips to Emilia-Romagna and other parts of Italy, where excellent fresh pasta is made in homes, shops and restaurants, tends to ensure I eat plenty of it.

Once you have had the best fresh pasta made by a sfogline or a relative in Bologna, it is difficult to motivate yourself to make your own.

Living in London, as I do, means that I often use dried, Italian-made egg pasta for dishes that require, say, tagliatelle or pappardelle. Filotea and La Campofilone, both artisan pasta-makers in Le Marche, make very good products that are exported to most of Europe and North America. Mario Musso's Casa dei Tajarin in Piedmont makes outstanding dried tajarin, the local version of noodles, which are made with and without eggs, but these are hard to find outside Italy.

My desire to eat only the best pasta has made me cheeky enough to call London-based Italian chefs who have become friends and ask them to make a little extra for me. I then either buy or barter the fresh pasta from them over an espresso.

When I do make fresh pasta, I use my hands. Machinery comes into play only for cutting, never for rolling. I find pasta kneaded in a food processor and/or rolled with a machine produces something that is too smooth. It is simply more difficult to control than when you use a rolling pin.

Homemade Pasta

The recipe below is the traditional one in my mother's family, but is also typical of Emilia-Romagna. Of course, there might be slight variations from home to home. Some add salt, for example, but I think it is unnecessary as you add salt to the cooking water. Others might add a little olive oil, but I see no value in that because even a small amount will add an unnecessary or unwelcome flavour, and not contribute to a better final product in any discernible way.

One ingredient you might have to play by ear is the number of eggs because, no matter how good, they can differ in richness and size. Once you find your favourite source, try to stick with it. As a general rule, use 1 large egg for every 100 g flour. As with eggs, try to find a flour you like and stick with it. My preference is for the soft flours from Mulino Marino in Piedmont: I use their '00' flour for fresh pasta.

Serves 8–10

- 1 kg '00' flour
- 10 large free-range eggs, preferably with very dark yolks to add colour to your pasta (avoid those from chickens force-fed extra carotene)

Method

Tip the flour on to a work surface or board. Make a well in the centre. Crack the eggs into the well and beat with a fork until frothy. Using your hands, start working in some of the flour from around the well. Continue doing this until a dough forms. Depending on the warmth of your kitchen and hands, you might need to add a little warm water if the dough does not come together. Knead for about 10 minutes, keeping your hands lightly floured, until the dough is smooth and elastic.

Cut the dough in half and place one piece on a lightly floured surface. Using a lightly floured rolling pin, roll out the dough to the thickness required for the pasta shape you are making. As a general rule, long pasta (e.g. spaghetti) should be perhaps 1–2 mm, while that used for stuffed pasta (e.g. ravioli) should be even thinner. The rolling is hard work because the dough is stiff, but it is well worth the effort.

If you want long strips, such as pappardelle or spaghetti, or big rectangles, such as lasagne, fold the pasta sheet several times and cut the size you want using a knife. When unfolded, you will have multiple strips. If making smaller shapes, use a pastry cutter or the cutting implement from a pasta machine to produce the shape you need. For simple round shapes you could use a glass or cup.

Keep the pasta on floured wooden trays in a cool part of the kitchen for no more than 3 hours or so before cooking it. The trays can be stacked, and the top one should be covered with a cloth.

Tagliatelle with Bolognese Sauce

Tagliatelle al Ragù Bolognese

As the name suggests, this dish originates from Bologna, and it combines two of the things the city is best known for in culinary terms: fresh pasta and bolognese sauce. In fact, 'sauce' might be a misleading term, as it could be argued that ragù bolognese is, in effect, a stew consisting mainly of meat, onion, celery and carrot, with only a hint of tomato purée.

The good thing about bolognese sauce is that you can make it and use it for a number of dishes throughout the week, and it can be frozen too. As always with Italian dishes, there is no single authentic recipe, but a fairly generic one with a few variables.

While 'spaghetti bolognaise' is a common version of this dish (the misspelling being just one way in which it has been bastardized), the perfect pasta for the sauce is actually tagliatelle, which, at around 1 cm, is wider than fettuccine, but not as wide as pappardelle. However, all three work well with the concentrated, slow-cooked meat sauce. In 1982 the Bolognese chapter of the Italian Academy of Cooking, 'having carried out long and laborious investigations and conducted studies and research', published an 'official' recipe and lodged it with the Bologna Chamber of Commerce. It is actually very similar to my family recipe, which I first took note of from my great-aunt, who lived in Bologna when I was a child. In fact, I remember recording her on a cassette player as she read the recipe out to me when I was 10 years old.

The choice of beef is important, and I would urge you to choose a specific cut and mince it yourself or get your butcher to do so. This is far better than ready-minced beef, which is normally a mixture of cuts and likely to be different each time you buy it. My personal approach is to combine thick skirt, which has a very good flavour, with short rib, which has more fat, the ratio of the former to the latter being 70:30.

Serves 4–6

- 200 g pancetta, chopped into small pieces
- 100 g onions, finely chopped
- 100 g carrots, finely chopped
- 100 g celery, finely chopped
- 1 kg beef (flank, chuck, short rib or thin skirt), thickly minced or finely chopped with a knife
- 1 glass (125 ml) red or white wine (optional)

- 3 teaspoons double-concentrated tomato purée
- 2 teaspoons sea salt
- freshly ground black pepper
- 500 ml water or veal stock
- 250 ml full-fat milk (optional)
- 500 g fresh handmade tagliatelle or top-quality dried tagliatelle
- Parmigiano Reggiano cheese, freshly grated, to serve

Method

Heat a flameproof (preferably enamelled) casserole dish, or a terracotta one like those used in Bologna. When hot, add the pancetta and stir over a high heat while the fat renders. When there is enough fat, add the soffritto (onions, carrots and celery), stirring until they start to brown. Transfer the contents of the dish to a plate and set aside.

Add the beef to the residue of fat in the casserole and fry, stirring until brown. When it starts sticking to the bottom of the dish, reintroduce the soffrito and gently stir together. When everything starts sticking to the bottom again, add the wine and wait until it has largely evaporated. Stir in the tomato purée, salt and pepper, and when everything starts sticking again, add a little water or stock. Repeat this process at least 4 or 5 times over 30 minutes, until all the liquid is used. Cover and cook the sauce on a low heat for at least 2 hours, checking often to ensure there is always enough liquid to avoid burning the meat. After 2 hours, fold the milk into the sauce. Check the seasoning and add more salt

continues over >

and pepper if required. Cover again and let it simmer for another 30 minutes, then leave it to rest off the heat for another 30 minutes.

Boil the tagliatelle as per the generic method suggested on page 77, making it a little more al dente than usual. Remember to factor in the time for completing the remaining steps and the time before the pasta will be served.

Place a large saucepan on a low heat, add one ladleful of the meat sauce per person, then warm slowly. Drain the tagliatelle, reserving 4 or 5 tablespoons of the cooking water, and add them both to the hot sauce. Mix well, using tongs or a wooden spoon and moving the pan back and forth.

Serve in deep pasta plates, spooning any sauce left in the pan on top of each portion. Serve with freshly grated Parmigiano Reggiano.

Lasagne

Cook the sauce as above and make a béchamel sauce (see page 87). Put a layer of cooked lasagne in a buttered ovenproof dish, then spread with some bolognese sauce and grated Parmigiano Reggiano. Repeat these layers 3 or 4 times, depending on the depth of the dish. Use the béchamel sauce as the final layer, sprinkle with more cheese and cook in an oven preheated to 180°C/gas mark 4 for 45–60 minutes.

Wild Boar Sauce (Ragù di Cinghiale)

Follow the same method as above, but omit the pancetta and milk, and use wild boar meat (always hand-chopped) rather than beef, and olive oil for frying. I also double the quantity of wine, preferring to use a simple medium- or full-bodied sangiovese, such as Chianti, and add a sprig of rosemary. Usually served with pappardelle.

Pork Sauce (Ragù di Maiale)

Make this in the same way as the wild boar sauce above, but use ordinary pork, which is easier to find.

Baked Pasta

Pasta al Forno

Oven-baked pasta is a very popular dish in central and southern parts of Italy. It should be made with dried pasta, which is used more al dente than usual as it will continue to cook in the oven. In the USA you might find a version of this dish called baked ziti, which is a staple of American-Italian family cuisine.

Variation using fried aubergines

Add 150 g Fried Aubergines (see page 269) cut to roughly the same size as the pasta shape you are using. The aubergine is added at the point you mix the cooked pasta with the meat sauce and Parmigiano.

Variation using other cheeses

Use other cheeses in place of Parmigiano, such as ricotta salata on its own or combined with fior di latte mozzarella or Mozzarella di Bufala Campana PDO.

Serves 4 as a one-plate meal, or 6 as a first course

- 500 g small tubular pasta from Gragnano, such as paccheri, penne, rigatoni or ziti, or even bucatini
- 200 g bolognese sauce (see page 82)
- 150 g Parmigiano Reggiano cheese, grated

For the béchamel sauce
- 80 g butter, plus extra for greasing
- 100 g flour
- 1 litre warm milk
- sea salt and freshly ground black pepper

Method

Cook the pasta in boiling salted water until extra al dente. Preheat the oven to 180°C/gas mark 4.

Meanwhile, make the béchamel sauce: melt the butter in a saucepan, add the flour and mix well. Pour in the milk a little at a time, beating well with a balloon whisk until it has all been used. Season and set aside.

Drain the pasta, then add a third of the bolognese sauce and a third of the Parmigiano and mix well.

Spread the remaining bolognese sauce in the bottom of a greased ovenproof dish. Cover it with the pasta, then pour all the béchamel sauce over it. Sprinkle with the remaining cheese and place in the oven for 35–50 minutes.

Vincisgrassi

While this dish has strong associations with Le Marche, the area from which it originates, for me it is also associated with Ann and Franco Taruschio, who for many years ran the Walnut Tree Inn near Abergavenny in South Wales. Franco, who hailed from Le Marche, cooked a version of this dish, and with his wife created a convivial restaurant serving outstanding food and wine in the type of informal environment rarely seen in the UK. It drew people from far and wide, even before the Severn Bridge opened in 1966, and was a favourite restaurant of many serious gastronomes, including Elizabeth David. Since Ann and Franco's departure, it has suffered a number of false starts, but it is once again in safe hands — this time with Shaun Hill, who ranks as one of the finest British chefs of the last 40-odd years.

Store the truffles and eggs to be used for all the elements of this dish in the same airtight jar. This will ensure that the truffle flavour permeates everything, and is much better than wasting money on truffle oil, which in most cases is not particularly good.

I first visited the Walnut Tree with my parents in the mid-1970s, and later tried to eat there at least a couple of times a year. In fact, between 1989 and 2000 I must have eaten there at least 300 times because during that period, I worked for a Canadian technology company that had a manufacturing plant in South Wales, and most weeks I would go down the night before a meeting and book myself into a hotel that was a cab ride away from the restaurant. I had many memorable meals, but the first course I probably had most often was vincisgrassi.

In simple terms, vincisgrassi is a lasagne in which the beef is replaced with air-dried ham and mushrooms. The story goes that it was named after General Windisch-Grätz, an Austrian who was based in Ancona in 1799, during the Napoleonic War. The Marche region has many versions of this dish, all using a variety of meat and offal. However, the recipe here, based on one of Franco Taruschio's, is the version I tend to make, and it brings back many happy memories of eating at the Walnut Tree.

Serves 4–6

- 500 g fresh handmade lasagne,
  or top-quality dried lasagne
  (the Filotea brand actually has
  vincisgrassi pasta sheets in its range)
- 150 g Parmigiano Reggiano cheese,
  grated
- 30 g white or black truffle

For the sauce

- 80 g butter, plus extra for greasing
  and dotting
- 100 g flour
- I litre warm milk
- 400 g porcini mushrooms, sliced
- 60 ml extra virgin olive oil
- 200 g Carpegna or Parma ham
- 200 ml single cream
- I tablespoon finely chopped parsley
- salt and freshly ground black pepper

continues over >

Method

First make the sauce, which is basically a béchamel with added prosciutto crudo and porcini. Melt the butter in a saucepan, add the flour and mix well. Pour in the milk a little at a time, beating well with a balloon whisk until it has all been used. Fry the porcini in the olive oil, drain in a colander, then add to the béchamel. Stir in the ham, cream and parsley, add seasoning and bring to the boil. Turn off the heat and set aside.

Boil the pasta sheets extra al dente, as they will cook further in the oven. After draining, you can add a little butter or oil to prevent them sticking together, but this won't be necessary if you work quickly enough and your fingers don't mind the heat.

Preheat the oven to 200°C/gas mark 6.

To assemble the vincisgrassi, butter a gratin dish and cover the bottom with a layer of pasta. Spread some béchamel sauce over it, dot with butter and sprinkle with some Parmigiano. Continue making layers in this way, finishing with the béchamel and a sprinkling of cheese. Place in the oven for 25 minutes.

Serve in deep pasta plates and shave the truffle over each portion.

Agnolotti Filled with Braised Beef

Agnolotti al Brasato

Here is a classic Piedmontese combination of fresh pasta with a meat stew based on the region's superlative beef and wine. Agnolotti are normally little square parcels, but smaller and shorter than ravioli. In the Langhe and Monferrato areas they are normally pinched together, so are called agnolotti al plin (plin means 'pinch'). In Emilia-Romagna and Lombardy the most common stuffed pastas are tortelli, which are square but usually bigger than agnolotti, and tortellini, which are ring- or navel-shaped and traditionally served in a meat or poultry broth.

This recipe works well with tortelli as well as either of the agnolotti variants, and is a wonderful way to use up leftovers. When making Braised Beef Cheeks (see page 212), I always make a little extra to fill my agnolotti or tortelli. You can also use Ossobuco alla Milanese as a filling (see page 216), something that chef Giorgio Locatelli has done with great success.

The main thing to remember with this recipe is that the cooked beef needs to have been kept in the fridge overnight. What I normally do is shred the meat and any vegetables and leave them in a covered bowl. The fat present in the juices will congeal, making it perfect for a pasta filling as it is easy to handle. The quantity of filling required is relatively small — about half a teaspoonful per parcel — and once the parcels are cooked, the filling will become liquid again, but will only run when you break the pasta with your fork. As most people will place an entire agnolotto in their mouth, the sauce and filling will explode when they start chewing. This is a great gastronomic experience, similar to eating the legendary broth-filled Shanghai meat dumpling called xiaolongbao.

In Emilia-Romagna and Lombardy the most common stuffed pastas are tortelli, which are square but usually bigger than agnolotti, and tortellini, which are ring- or navel-shaped and traditionally served in a meat or poultry broth.

Serves 4–8

- I kg fresh pasta dough (see page 80)
- '00' flour, for dusting
- 250 g Braised Beef Cheeks (see page 212), shredded and refrigerated overnight
- 2 eggs, beaten
- semolina flour, for dusting
- 5 g unsalted butter
- 150 g Parmigiano Reggiano PDO cheese, to serve

Method

Roll out the dough as thinly as possible. You should be able to see the filling through it but without any risk of it escaping during preparation or cooking.

Cut out 2 strips of dough about I metre long and 10–12 cm wide and lay these widthways on a work surface dusted with flour.

Using a teaspoon, form little balls of the braised beef and arrange them in a row along the leading edge of the first pasta strip. They should be about I cm from the edge, at least I cm apart and extend just halfway along the strip.

Using a pastry brush dipped in the beaten eggs, lightly moisten the pasta all around the balls but not the filling itself. Fold the empty half of the pasta strip over the row of balls and press down between them to squeeze out excess air and form a seal. Now press down along the front seam in the same way.

Run a rotary cutter along the front of the pasta, leaving a 5 mm border of pasta between the covered filling and the edge. Now cut between each one. When all the agnolotti have been cut, pick up each one and ensure that all the seals are tight. Place them on a wooden pasta tray or large dish in a single layer and dust with semolina.

continues over >

Repeat the process of filling, cutting and sealing until you have used up all your dough. If you run out of filling, use the dough to make some tagliatelle or other non-filled pasta shape.

You can cover and leave the agnolotti in a cool part of the kitchen for a couple of hours before cooking. Some people suggest you can freeze them, but I find that freezing pasta or pasta dough does not generally produce good results. In my opinion, fresh pasta should be eaten within a few hours of making it.

Cook your agnolotti in boiling salted water until slightly more al dente than usual. Remember to factor in the time needed for the steps below and up to the point of serving.

Melt the butter in a frying pan, then add the drained agnolotti (in batches if necessary) and move the pan to and fro to ensure they are coated in the butter.

Serve in individual pasta plates, with the Parmigiano grated on top.

Dried Pasta Dishes

When it comes to dried pasta dishes, most of my favourites come from central and southern Italy, including the islands. Spaghetti alla Bottarga, for example, is a wonderful island dish that has crossed over to the mainland and become very popular (see page 155).

In and around Rome there are four truly outstanding pasta dishes, three of which are sometimes called the 'holy trinity'. These are Spaghetti alla Carbonara, Spaghetti alla Griscia and Spaghetti con Cacio e Pepe. The fourth exceptional dish is Buccatini or Spaghetti all' Amatriciana.

Spaghetti alla Carbonara

There is no substitute for guanciale: it has the right flavour and fat profile to make the dish a success. When made properly, this dish is neither too wet or over-sauced; it has the perfect ratio of ingredients, each of them distinctive yet at the same time perfectly blended.

The origins of this dish and its place in Roman cooking are vague, but the anecdotal information is worth retelling.

Although thought of as a typical Roman dish, some say it originated in the Apennine Mountains of the Abruzzo, where woodcutters, who made carbone (charcoal) for fuel, cooked the dish over a charcoal fire. They also used penne rather than spaghetti because it was easier to toss with the eggs and cheese.

The second theory, perhaps obvious given that alla carbonara means 'coal worker style', is that the dish was eaten by coal workers. But it could also have stemmed from the dish's abundant use of coarsely ground black pepper, which resembles coal flakes.

Another story is that food shortages after the liberation of Rome in 1944 were so severe that Allied troops distributed military rations consisting of powdered egg and bacon, and the local populace used these to flavour their easily stored dried pasta.

There is also a theory that it is a refinement of a dish found in the province of Ciociaria, in the region of Lazio, about halfway between Rome and Benevento. It is said that middle-class Roman families, who escaped to this region following the German occupation of Rome during the Second World War, learnt a pasta dish seasoned in a Neapolitan style, with eggs, lard and pecorino cheese. They might deserve the credit for introducing it to the city after the war, and transforming it into carbonara.

Yet another story suggests that La Carbonara, a famous restaurant in the Campo d'Fiori in Rome, was named after its creation. While the restaurant does have carbonara on its menu, the owners deny being its originators, and claim that the name came about for other reasons.

A couple of years ago I had the pleasure of meeting the great Roman chef Arcangelo Dandini, and we discussed Spaghetti alla Carbonara. I was pleasantly surprised to find that we used exactly the same ingredients: spaghettoni, guanciale, pecorino Romano and egg yolks. Arcangelo actually wrote out his recipe for me on a paper napkin and passed on a useful tip — that the egg yolks should be fridge-cold before use.

One of my favourite, but highly unlikely, theories about the derivation of carbonara is told in the classic Italian cookbook *Il Nuovo Cucchiaio d'Argento (The Silver Spoon)*. This claims that the dish was originally made with black squid ink, and therefore acquired its name because it was as black as coal.

The simplest explanation of carbonara, and therefore the most likely, is that the dish had always existed at the family level and in humble eating places before traditional Roman cuisine became popular and made it famous.

Many people are tempted to use cream in this dish, but that is totally unnecessary because the yolks, fat, cheese and pasta water create a cream-like emulsion.

Serves 4

- 3 g black peppercorns
- 400 g spaghettoni (extra thick spaghetti) or vermicelli, preferably Pastificio dei Campi
- 100 g Lazio-produced artisan guanciale, cut into lardons 5 x 20mm
- 4 fridge-cold egg yolks, ideally from marigold-fed chickens for a beautifully rich colour
- 80 g pecorino Romano, preferably Brunelli, finely grated

Method

Place the peppercorns in a pan over the heat and roast for a couple of minutes, then crush to a medium-fine texture using a mortar and pestle. This brings out the aroma and oils of the peppercorns, and allows them to infuse the dish.

Cook the pasta in plenty of boiling, well-salted water until al dente. Drain, reserving a cupful of the pasta water for the sauce.

Meanwhile, fry the guanciale in a dry frying pan until crisp but not charred. Allow the fat and lardons to cool a little.

Beat the egg yolks with one-third of the pecorino and 1½ tablespoons of cooled guanciale fat.

Tip the pasta into a large bowl, then add the following, mixing well between each addition: the guanciale with the remaining fat; a little pasta water; the beaten egg mixture; the ground peppercorns; another third of the cheese. When properly combined, there should be a creamy emulsion on the sides and bottom of the bowl. Serve the pasta in deep plates and sprinkle each portion with the remaining cheese.

continues over >

Most of my friends in Rome will always have ingredients at home to make at least three of the following variations. All are superb as impromptu meals, or even as midnight snacks, as are the simple tomato pasta dishes described in chapter 6.

Spaghetti in Grisciano Style (Spaghetti alla Griscia)

Some people call this dish 'white all' amatriciana', which suggests that it originates from Grisciano, just down the road from Amatrice. I have spoken to many people who think that Spaghetti alla Griscia actually predates carbonara. To make it, follow the recipe, but omit the eggs, and you have something equally delicious but somewhat lighter.

Spaghetti with Cheese and Pepper (Spaghetti con Cacio e Pepe)

Again, follow the recipe, but omit the guanciale and eggs and you have delicious cheese and pepper pasta. In the absence of a hot frying pan, heat the mixing bowl by placing it over the boiling pasta pan. The warmth will help to produce the creamy emulsion, which is similar to those above.

Bucatini in Amatrice Style (Bucatini all' amatriciana)

Unlike the dishes above, which omit some of the basic
carbonara ingredients, this dish adds some new ones —
namely, tomatoes, possibly onions, and a touch of chilli,
depending on which version you try. In Amatrice, now
in Lazio but previously in Abruzzo, the dish is made with
guanciale, tomatoes and pecorino, whilst most Roman
versions include onions. I have heard many chefs and
citizens of the Eternal City say that this dish has nothing
to do with Amatrice: the name should actually be *alla
matriciana*.

I have tried pretty much every configuration of this
dish and have to say that they can all be delicious if the
tomatoes are particularly good and the onions are on the
sweet side. However, if forced to choose, I would side
with the principle of *semplice*. So to make this dish, follow
the quantities and method for carbonara (omitting the
eggs, of course) up to the point where the guanciale has
been cooked. Add ½ teaspoon fresh or dried chilli, 250
g freshly peeled and deseeded tomatoes and cook for
10–15 minutes, until broken down and mingled with
the guanciale and its rendered fat. At this point, add
the drained pasta, plus 3 or 4 tablespoons of its cooking
water and half the pecorino. Move the pan to and fro to
ensure everything is well combined.

Spaghetti alla Puttanesca

My father gave me a good piece of advice when I left home to go to university, and that was always to have the ingredients for this dish in the larder. I ended up spending nearly seven years as a student, including three as a postgraduate, so I think I must have cooked this dish at least once a week during that time.

Spaghetti alla Puttanesca (literally 'whore's spaghetti') is the best kind of fast food, perhaps the most famous and ubiquitous in Italy. The most common story about how the dish got its name is that it was a favourite among prostitutes because it was quick and easy to make, and gave them a second wind, which allowed them to 'entertain' more customers. However, the word puttanesca may well be unrelated to the oldest profession, as in some Italian dialects it can mean 'any old rubbish' (puttanata qualsiasi).

In view of the ingredients, it would be no surprise if this dish first evolved in parts of the country where tomatoes, olives, anchovies, garlic and capers were locally available. This would point to the Amalfi coast and nearby islands, including Sicily. It is certainly a 20th-century dish — there are no records of it before then — and it seems to have spread from the south to the rest of Italy by the 1980s.

Whatever its origins, here is the recipe I use and adore!

Serves 4

- 400 g dried spaghettini, fedelini or linguine (the sauce also works with short tubes, such as rigatoni)
- 3 tablespoons extra virgin olive oil
- pinch of red pepper flakes
- 10 Cetaro or Nola anchovies, rinsed
- 11 garlic cloves, 3 of them chopped
- 6 fresh San Marzano tomatoes, chopped and deseeded, or 1 x 400 g can San Marzano tomatoes, drained
- 15–20 Taggiasca olives, stoned and chopped
- 2 tablespoons Pantelleria capers, drained
- 1 tablespoon chopped flat leaf parsley

Method

Cook the pasta in a pan of boiling salted water until al dente.

Meanwhile, heat the olive oil in a frying pan. Add the red pepper flakes and anchovies, stirring and crushing them into the oil, and cook for 1½ minutes. Add the chopped garlic and fry until it begins to brown. Stir in the tomatoes, olives and capers, then simmer the mixture, uncovered, for 5–8 minutes. Add 2–3 tablespoons of the pasta water to the pan just before the pasta is ready.

Drain the pasta, then tip it into the pan of sauce and toss well. Serve in deep pasta plates, sprinkling a generous amount of chopped parsley on each portion.

Linguine with Prawns, Tomatoes and Capers

Linguine con Gamberi Rossi, Pomodorini e Capperi

I have had this dish many times in both Sicily and Campania, and it's a wonderful way to eat three superb ingredients — red prawns, tomatoes and capers. If you cannot get gamberi rossi, any good-quality, fresh, unshelled prawns, or even langoustines, are a worthy substitute.

Serves 4

- 4 tablespoons extra virgin olive oil
- 12 red prawns
- 2 garlic cloves, sliced
- 150 g fresh Pachino, Corbarini or
- Datterini tomatoes, or good-quality cherry tomatoes, halved
- 2 tablespoons Pantelleria capers
- 1½ teaspoons sea salt
- freshly ground black pepper
- 400 g Linguine di Gragnano
- 20 g fresh flat leaf parsley, finely chopped

Method

Heat 1 tablespoon of the olive oil in a frying pan large enough to comfortably hold double the quantity of the ingredients. Add the prawns and cook for 2 minutes on each side. They should be roughly half-cooked. Transfer to a plate and, when cool, peel all but 4 of the prawns.

Place the pan back on a high heat and add all the prawn shells. Cook for 5 minutes, then press down on the shells, especially the heads, to release any juices. Discard all the shells.

Now add the remaining 3 tablespoons of olive oil to the pan, add the garlic and fry over a medium heat without browning. Add the tomatoes, increase the heat, then stir in the capers, salt and pepper and cook for 5 minutes on a high heat, shaking the pan now and then.

Meanwhile, cook the linguine in boiling salted water until al dente. Using tongs, transfer the linguine to the pan of tomatoes, lower the heat and combine everything by moving the pan to and fro. Add the shelled prawns and keep shaking the pan for another 30 seconds to ensure they are warmed through.

Serve the linguine in pasta plates, sprinkle with parsley and place a whole unshelled prawn on each serving.

Paccheri, 'Nduja and Burrata

This dish can be described as a fusion of three iconic ingredients from three different regions: paccheri (large pasta tubes) from Campania; 'nduja (spicy and spreadable pork sausage) from Calabria (see page 274); and burrata (creamy mozzarella) from Apulia (see page 416). I am not sure this dish could have been created in Italy, as I have never come across it there. I first had it in the London restaurant L'Anima, cooked by Calabrian chef-patron Francesco Mazzei, whose menus tend to feature food from southern parts of Italy, where his wife comes from. A very good version of this dish is also on the menu at Tinello, another restaurant in London, which uses the superb paccheri made by Pastificio dei Campi.

The wonderful thing about this dish is how with each bite you have the heat from the 'nduja, the sweetness of the tomato and the wonderful cooling effect of the burrata.

Serves 4

- 3 tablespoons extra virgin olive oil
- 6 San Marzano tomatoes, chopped and seeded, or 1 x 400 g can San Marzano tomatoes
- 2 teaspoons sea salt
- 400 g paccheri from Gragnano
- pinch of sugar (optional)
- 4–6 teaspoons 'nduja, depending how much spiciness you like
- 80 g burrata
- 8 fresh basil leaves

Method

Heat the oil in a frying pan, then add the tomatoes and salt and cook, uncovered, on a high heat for 10 minutes.

Meanwhile, cook the paccheri in boiling salted water until al dente.

Taste the sauce and add a pinch of sugar if the tomatoes are not sweet enough. Pass the mixture through a mouli or passavedure, then return the sauce to the pan and stir in the 'nduja.

Drain the pasta, reserving half a cupful of the cooking water. Tip the pasta and reserved water into the sauce and mix well.

Serve each portion with a dollop of creamy burrata in the centre and sprinkle some torn basil leaves on top.

Norma-style Pasta

Pasta alla Norma

If you want to use basil in this dish, add it at the end, just before serving.

To prepare this dish you will need ricotta salata, which is a pressed, salted and aged cheese that is firm, bordering on hard, and almost brown. Versions of it are made outside Italy, but these are very soft and moist — much closer to everyday ricotta — and should not be used. If you cannot find the right type of cheese, do not make the dish. Parmigiano Reggiano or pecorino are just not the same.

The ideal pasta for this dish is short and tubular, such as penne or rigatoni, and the aubergines should be cut into pieces of a similar size.

Serves 4

- 2 medium-large aubergines
- 4 tablespoons extra virgin olive oil
- 2 garlic cloves, roughly chopped
- ½ teaspoon dried chilli flakes
- 400 g fresh or canned San Marzano PDO tomatoes
- 3–4 teaspoons sea salt (depending how salty the ricotta is)
- 1 teaspoon double- or triple-concentrated tomato purée (optional)
- 1½ teaspoons dried wild oregano or 8 torn fresh basil leaves
- 400 g rigatoni di Gragnano
- freshly ground black pepper
- 100 g ricotta salata, to serve

Method

Cut the aubergines into rounds about 2 cm thick. Wash them in a colander, then dry on a clean tea towel or kitchen paper and set aside. Heat 3 tablespoons of the oil in a large shallow pan and fry the aubergines (in batches if necessary) until they are brown and almost caramelized. Transfer to a plate but do not drain off any of the oil.

Add the remaining oil to the pan with the garlic and chilli, and fry until the garlic is almost brown. Add the tomatoes, salt, tomato purée (if using) and oregano. Cook for 10–15 minutes on a medium heat. Towards the end mash the tomatoes a little with a wooden spoon to create a rough sauce. Meanwhile, cook the rigatoni in boiling salted water until al dente.

Cut the aubergine slices into pieces that are a similar size to the pasta. Add them to the sauce and warm through. Taste and season. Pick out and set aside at least 8 pieces of aubergine. Drain the pasta, reserving a cupful of the cooking water. Add the pasta and a tablespoon of the reserved water to the sauce and mix by moving the pan back and forth.

Divide the pasta between 4 deep plates. Grate the ricotta salata over each portion and garnish with 2 or 3 pieces of the reserved aubergine.

Trenette with Pesto

Trenette al Pesto

Perhaps the most common way of eating pesto alla Genovese, this is also one of the most delicious. It's a lovely way of celebrating good-quality basil, and for me is very much a summer dish. Ideally, you should make your pesto as described on page 379 just before you cook the pasta. It makes a delicious first course or a one-plate meal, especially with the addition of French beans.

Serves 4

- 320–400 g trenette or linguine
- 4 basil leaves
- 200 g French beans, topped and tailed (optional)
- 10 tablespoons Pesto alla Genovese (see page 379)
- 60 g Parmigiano Reggiano PDO

Method

Cook the pasta in plenty of boiling, well-salted water until al dente. If you plan to add beans, put them in the water at the same time as the pasta. When ready, drain the pasta, then return it to the saucepan. Add 8 tablespoons of pesto and stir well so that the pasta is fully coated.

Serve in pasta plates and place a basil leaf in the centre of each portion. Grate some Parmigiano on top before eating.

Gnocchi

Gnocchi are little dumplings, often listed with pasta on menus, and generally eaten as a first course. This makes perfect sense because gnocchi were originally made with flour and water, and can be found in various forms all over Europe, most likely spread by the Romans. Other early versions of gnocchi were made with local ingredients, such as pumpkin and semolina. In fact, the latter is still used for the famous gnocchi alla romana. Potato gnocchi, the form we know best today, came about much later, after the potato was introduced to the Italian peninsula in the 16th century.

The word *gnocchi* is most likely related to either *nocca*, meaning 'knuckle', or perhaps *nocchio*, a knot found in wood, because the shapes are similar. The dish is popular throughout Italy though versions of gnocchi can also be found in countries where large numbers of Italians emigrated, and certain traditions have grown up around it. In Argentina and Uruguay, for example, gnocchi is commonly served on the 29th of the month (Dia del Ñoquis), when a coin is placed under the plate to bring prosperity and good fortune in the following month. Some makers of dried pasta also produce a shape called 'gnocchi'.

Gnocchi should not be confused with *gnudi* (nudes), which are little balls of the filling normally used in stuffed pasta, such as ravioli or tortelli. These are served minus the usual pasta wrapping with a variety of sauces, and are becoming more popular in Italy, as well as in some of the swankier Italian restaurants in London and New York. They have a long history dating back to the early 13th century, and you might come across them under different names. In Tuscany, for example, they are called *malfatti*, meaning 'ill formed' or 'badly made' because of their irregular shape.

Homemade Gnocchi

The recipe below is for classic potato gnocchi, best eaten as a first course with butter and sage, or pesto, or a simple tomato sauce. They can also be infused with saffron and served with fish (see page 170).

Some of the best gnocchi I have ever eaten were made by the chef Marco Canora. They also entranced the restaurant critic William Grimes, who described them in the New York Times as 'lightweight and butter-laden, each dollop an eye-rolling pleasure bomb'.

I have had the pleasure of meeting Marco, as well as eating his superb food, and the recipe below is based on his.

Serves 4–6

- 500 g starchy potatoes, such as King Edwards or Rooster in the UK, and Idaho in the USA
- 1 teaspoon ground white pepper
- 1 egg yolk
- 200 g '00' or '0' flour
- 40 g unsalted butter, diced
- 1 tablespoon chopped fresh sage
- sea salt and freshly ground black pepper
- Parmigiano Reggiano cheese, freshly grated, to serve

Method

Preheat the oven to 240°C/gas mark 9. Prick the potatoes with a fork and bake them until a knife penetrates them easily.

While still hot, cut the potatoes in half lengthways — you want to create as much surface area as possible so that the steam billows out.

Scoop the potato flesh out of the skin and pass it through a fine-holed ricer on to a large, clean work surface. Using the back of a large metal spoon, spread the potatoes into an even rectangle about 2 cm thick. Season with the white pepper and leave until cool enough to handle.

Beat the egg yolk and drizzle it over the potatoes, then sprinkle a small handful of the flour over the top. Using a pastry scraper, cut the flour and egg into the potatoes, chopping and folding the mixture together, until everything is well mixed and resembles a coarse crumble. Bring the mixture together into a ball.

Sprinkle another handful of the flour on the work surface. Place the dough on it and press down with both hands, flattening it into a circle. Dust the dough with another fistful of the flour and work it in with your hands. Add 2 dustings of flour to the work surface and dough and repeat the kneading. If the dough still feels sticky, repeat once more, this time dusting both the surface and the dough with no more than a small handful of the flour. Roll the dough into a compact log. Dust the outside with flour, then set aside to rest for about 5 minutes.

Dust the work surface lightly with flour. Cut the log into 8 equal pieces, then roll each into a long 'sausage' about 1.5 cm thick. Using a floured knife or pastry cutter, cut each sausage into gnocchi about 3 cm long.

Bring a pan of heavily salted water to the boil. Add about one-third of the gnocchi and cook, stirring occasionally, until they float to the surface (2–3 minutes). Retrieve the gnocchi with a slotted spoon and set them aside on a baking sheet or plate. Cook the remaining gnocchi.

Meanwhile, melt the butter in a large frying pan over a medium heat. Add the sage, season with salt and black pepper, and cook for about 4 minutes. Add the gnocchi to the pan, then take off the heat and move it to and fro until the gnocchi are coated and the butter starts to look creamy. Serve topped with the Parmigiano Reggiano.

Rice &
Polenta

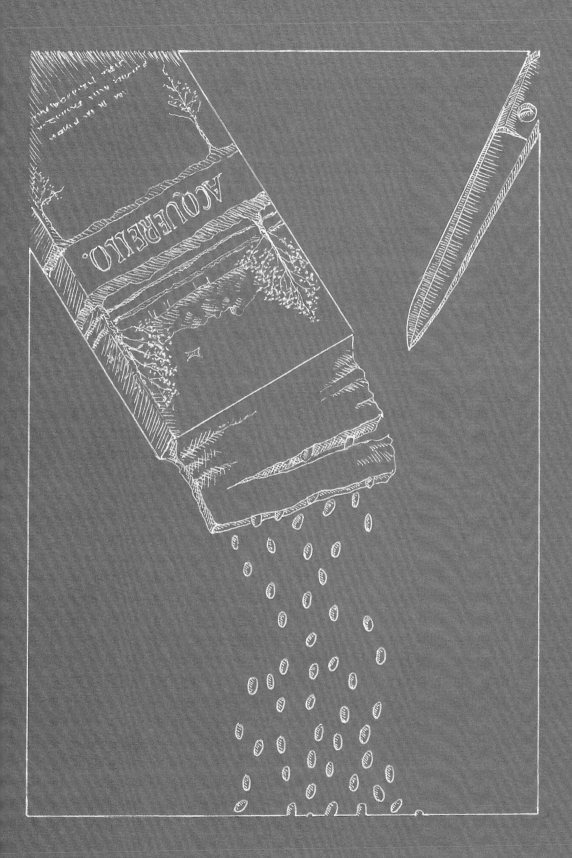

Rice & Polenta

Most people strongly associate pasta with Italian food and culture, but in many ways, rice and polenta are equally important, and in some regions are actually consumed as often as pasta and in similar quantities. On average, though, per capita rice consumption is less than a fifth of that for pasta.

When I travel around Italy I really enjoy crossing into parts of the country where either rice and/or polenta are more common, and watching dishes being slowly stirred with great reverence, skill and attention.

Rice

Riso

Significant quantities of rice are produced in Italy. The country is, in fact, the top producer in Europe, and among the top 30 producers in the world. Annual production is around 2 million tonnes, most of it cultivated on 200,000 hectares of land in Piedmont (in the triangle Vercelli-Novara-Pavia) and Lombardy, but also in Veneto, Sardinia and some parts of central and southern Italy. Of the 3000 varieties of rice known worldwide, Italy produces 150, and its National Rice Authority runs one of the most advanced research centres.

It is almost certain that rice came to Europe from the east, and records show that the Venetians traded it, along with spices. Entry points further south suggest that the Arabs introduced it to southern Italy, as they did to Spain. Both the Greeks and Romans treated rice rather like a medicine, serving it to invalids, and there seems to be a definite link between the rice pottages of the Romans and what we know today as rice pudding.

In Italy the earliest documentation about rice being cultivated dates from 1475, when Galeazzo Maria Sforza, Duke of Milan, wrote that from the one sack of rice he sent as a gift to the Duke of Ferrara, 12 sacks could be harvested, if properly cultivated. This impressive yield led to rice being grown throughout the region during the Renaissance.

Until the mid-19th century, just that one variety of rice (Nostrale) was grown. In 1839, however, a Jesuit priest called Padre Calleri, returning from the Philippines, brought 43 different rice varieties with him and it was from this stock that Italians began to experiment and learn what would be best suited to the temperate climes of northern Italy. This period became the most significant in terms of Italian rice cultivation, and was much helped when, at the instigation of the Count of Cavour (perhaps best known for his role in Italian unification), the farmers of Vercellese joined together to open a large and highly efficient irrigation system in 1853. This was further enlarged in 1866 thanks to the construction of the Cavour Canal, which allowed the 'transfer' of water from several rivers and Lake Maggiore to around 400,000 hectares of paddy fields. Thus did rice establish itself in Italian agriculture. Now let's look at its role in Italian cooking.

The origins of rice (Oryza sativa) are contested by historians, but genetic and archaeological studies strongly point to China and Southeast Asia being the places where it was first cultivated, maybe as far back as 7000 years ago.

I must tell you straight away that when it comes to cooking the great Italian rice dishes, such as risotto, there are no instant solutions or short cuts. Time and patience are necessary, but the results are well worth it.

It is also very important to use the correct type of rice — one that is able to absorb liquid and release starch — because many typical Italian rice dishes aim for a creamy consistency, which is created by the starch. This is exactly the opposite of cooking, say, pilau rice, when what you want are separate fluffy grains.

The principal rice varieties used in Italy are Arborio, Baldo, Carnaroli, Maratelli, Padano, Roma and Vialone Nano. I tend to use only Carnaroli and Vialone Nano because the former is more difficult to overcook, whilst the latter, being smaller, is faster to cook and better at absorbing both liquids and condiments. However, the variety of rice in itself does not guarantee a good end result. As with all ingredients, the dedication of the original producer is a key factor in its quality.

Carnaroli Rice

If using Carnaroli, I would strongly recommend the Acquarello brand, which has been produced by three generations of the Rondolino family on the Colombara estate in the heart of the rice-producing Piedmontese province of Vercelli. This organic rice is aged for a minimum of one year, and there is also a three-year-old version. The Rondolino family have developed their own milling and maturing process that gently polishes the rice, which not only allows the grain to retain most of its nutrients and flavour, but also to absorb more liquid than other brands made using different methods. Acquarello is exported to most of Europe and North America, and is used by some of the world's top chefs.

In Italy the designation superfino, semifino or fino is often seen on packets of rice. These terms refer to the length and width of the grains, rather than the quality. Choice depends on the type needed for a particular dish. I should also mention that I like to use high-quality risotto rice for desserts, especially rice pudding

Vialone Nano

If using Vialone Nano, look out for the Ferron and Riso Corte Schioppo brands, both of which are exported to Europe and North America. In Australia, Simon Johnson, who is a top-notch sourcer of fine foods from around the world, has a really excellent Vialone Nano that he sells under his own label in his stores and online.

The rice recipes that follow include some classics, and if you master them, you will find most rice-based dishes within your grasp.

White Risotto

Risotto Bianco

A popular dish in northern Italy, particularly in Piedmont and Lombardy, risotto bianco can be seen as the basis of all risotto dishes. The variables tend to be the wine and cheese used. If the wine is specific, it may be incorporated into the name of the dish — risotto al prosecco, for example, or risotto al franciacorta. The use of a quality sparkling wine adds a sense of luxury to the dish, but in my view it does not improve on using a still white wine. In terms of cheese, both Parmigiano Reggiano and Grana Padano can be used, and the latter is more common in Lombardy.

A heavy-based saucepan is best for risotto. I do not recommend using a shallow casserole dish or frying pan as the large surface area does not allow optimal absorption of liquid or release of starch. For stirring, you might like to use a girariso, which is a wooden spoon with a hole in it. This is not essential — an ordinary wooden spoon will work perfectly well — but it does come into its own in the final stages of preparation, when it's good to have the rice moving in two directions as you stir.

Risotto must be cooked to order, and the person cooking it will need to stand over it for at least 30 minutes, which explains why it can be expensive in many restaurants. Cheap versions often involve short cuts, such as pre-cooking and reheating, and the result is never good. In recent years it has become common to see risotto served quite liquid, which is not a bad thing, but it is sometimes a sign that a pre-cooked dish has been 'refreshed'.

With the exception of Ossobuco alla Milanese (see page 216), risotto is served as a first course instead of pasta or soup. And if you make a little extra or have leftovers, you can make delicious rice balls the next day to serve as an antipasto, first course or quick snack (see Supplì, page 128).

Serves 2–4

- 1 litre light chicken, vegetable or veal stock (avoid using stock cubes)
- 50 g unsalted butter (place half in the freezer)
- ½ onion, finely chopped
- 200 g Carnaroli rice
- 1 glass (125 ml) dry white wine
- 80 g Parmigiano Reggiano or Grana Padano cheese, freshly grated

Method

Bring the stock to the boil and keep it gently simmering throughout the cooking of the dish.

Melt the unfrozen butter in a heavy-based saucepan. Add the onion and fry until soft, not brown. This can take up to 8 minutes. Add the rice, then turn up the heat and stir thoroughly. This stage is sometimes called *brilliatura* (sparkling) because the rice becomes glistening and translucent, but it is more commonly known as *tostatura* (toasting). The point is that it ensures a uniform cooking of the grain.

When the rice is hot, add the wine and keep stirring until it has evaporated. Now start adding the stock, a ladleful at a time, and stirring each addition until nearly absorbed. The rice should remain 'wavy' and moist, never totally dry. Repeat this process until the rice begins to soften (about 13 minutes, but check by tasting), then add the stock in smaller amounts. Keep stirring and tasting, until it is to your liking.

To finish the dish, add the frozen butter and all but 1 tablespoon of the grated cheese, and stir with great gusto, until the risotto is rich and creamy. This stage is called the *mantecatura* (mingling).

Take the risotto off the heat and leave to rest for 2 or 3 minutes, then serve immediately with the rest of the cheese sprinkled on each portion. *continues over* >

White or Black Truffle Risotto
(Risotto al Tartufo Bianco/Nero)

At least 24 hours before you intend to cook this risotto, place your whole truffle in a sealed glass jar with the rice you are going to use and leave to infuse. Follow the recipe above, but omit the wine and cheese, and try to use veal stock. When ready, simply shave some truffle on to each portion just before serving.

Mushroom Risotto *(Risotto ai Porcini)*

If using fresh porcini (ceps), you will need about 100 g (half the weight of the rice). Fry them in a little olive oil and add to the basic risotto just before the *mantecatura* stage. This also applies if adding ingredients such as asparagus, courgettes or even radicchio di Treviso, as they do not take long to cook and should remain distinct but complementary flavours.

Saffron Risotto *(Risotto allo Zafferano)*

Add 20 strands of good-quality saffron to your stock when heating it up, and another 10 or so strands to the onions while they are cooking.

Marrowbone Risotto *(Risotto alla Milanese)*

Add 30 g veal marrow to the melted butter before the *tostatura* stage, then continue following the basic recipe.

Fried Roman Rice Balls

Supplì

Perhaps you are familiar with arancini, the fried rice balls very common in Sicily, but did you know there is a Roman version called supplì? Both are very popular bar snacks, but may also be served as antipasti.

I have to say that I am generally underwhelmed by both arancini and supplì, especially those sometimes offered for free in bars with aperitifs. However, some of the swankier restaurants in Italy, especially Rome, go to a lot of trouble to make something special, and use very good ingredients. Also, the best pizzerias in Rome often have excellent supplì.

It seems that the most innovation with fried rice balls occurs in Rome, where you will see versions that combine both the names and ingredients of classic pasta dishes: for example, supplì al gricia, which combines rice with guanciale, pecorino and black pepper.

One day I decided to enter into the spirit of innovation because I had some ossobuco left over from the night before. What I made turned out to be rather good, so I recommend you try it.

If you do not have any leftovers, you can simply cook some risotto rice using the Risi e Bisi method (see page 132) and make some of the variations below.

Supplì Margherita

Use a very reduced tomato sauce combined with mozzarella cheese and basil.

Supplì al Telefono

Use fontina or any other stringy cheese, which forms long strands like telephone wires when bitten into.

Makes 16–18

- 300 g leftover Risotto allo Zafferano (see page 216)
- 100 g leftover Ossobuco alla Milanese (see page 170), shredded
- 25 g leftover marrow, from the ossobuco
- 30 g Parmigiano Reggiano PDO, freshly grated
- 25 g gremolata (see page 216)
- '00' flour, for dusting
- 2 eggs, beaten
- breadcrumbs, for coating
- 100 ml rapeseed oil

Method

Take a heaped tablespoon of the rice and shape it into a ball. Using your thumb, make a hollow and fill it with the ossobuco, add a touch of the marrow, Parmigiano and gremolata, then reshape the ball so that the filling is covered. Shape the ball into an elongated croquette. Repeat this process until all the leftovers are used up.

Put the flour, egg and breadcrumbs on separate plates. Roll the supplì first in the flour, then the beaten egg and finally the breadcrumbs. Place them on a platter, cover with cling film and chill for at least 20 minutes. Take out of the fridge at least 10 minutes before you want to cook them.

Heat the rapeseed oil in a frying pan until hot but not smoking, then fry the supplì, turning them often, until golden brown. This should take no more than 5 minutes. Drain on kitchen paper and serve immediately as part of an antipasti selection. Alternatively, serve as a first course on small plates, offering 3 or 4 per person.

Asparagus Risotto

Risotto con Asparagi

During the asparagus season, you can make more intensely flavoured risottos by using a light poultry or meat stock mixed with some of the asparagus cooking water. Vialone Nano rice works best for this particular dish, but you can also use Carnaroli.

- 300 g green asparagus, cut into 4 cm pieces
- 1.5 litres light chicken or veal stock
- 80 g unsalted butter, diced
- ½ onion, finely chopped
- 250 g Vialone Nano rice
- 100 g Parmigiano Reggiano cheese, freshly grated

Method

Place the asparagus in a pan of boiling salted water and cook for 5–10 minutes, until al dente. Using a slotted spoon, transfer the pieces to a plate. Measure out 300 ml of the cooking water and keep it simmering. Bring the stock to the boil and keep that gently simmering too.

Melt half the butter in a heavy-based saucepan and put the other half in the freezer. Add the onion and cook gently, until it softens but does not brown. This can take up to 8 minutes. Add the rice, turn up the heat and stir to coat the grains with the butter.

Add a ladleful of the simmering asparagus water and stir until it has evaporated. Repeat until all the water has been used. Now start adding the stock a ladleful at a time, stirring until each addition has been nearly absorbed. The rice should remain fluid, never dry, moving in waves when stirred. Keep repeating this process of adding stock and stirring until the rice begins to soften – about 13 minutes, but check by tasting. Now add the stock in smaller amounts, testing the rice regularly until cooked to your liking.

Stir in the asparagus, then add the frozen butter and 80 g of the cheese, and stir with great gusto, until the risotto is rich and creamy.

Take the pan off the heat and allow to rest for 2 or 3 minutes, before serving with the remaining cheese sprinkled on each portion.

Rice and Pea Soup

Risi e Bisi

I first made this dish after discussing it with some friends from Venice, and it has always worked beautifully. The important thing to note is that it is not a risotto with peas. It is a thick Venetian soup that is eaten with a spoon rather than a fork.

Risi e Bisi is best made in springtime with freshly picked peas, so if you grow your own, as my wife and I do on our allotment, it is truly superb. It never works as well with those you buy from greengrocers or markets, as they have rarely been picked just a day or so before. For that reason, this is one of the few occasions when I recommend using frozen peas if you don't have access to really fresh ones.

If using your own home-grown peas, save the pods, but discard the inner membrane, to use in whatever stock you decide to make. I tend to favour a light stock, either chicken or vegetable, so as not to overwhelm the flavour of the peas, which should dominate the dish. If you do not have a decent stock, please don't resort to stock cubes. Simply cook something else.

I also prefer to use Vialone Nano rice for this dish as it is the most commonly cultivated in the Veneto, and doesn't seem to mind simmering without much attention.

Serves 2–4

- ½ onion, finely chopped
- 50 g unsalted butter
- 1.3 kg fresh peas (unshelled weight)
- 1 teaspoon sea salt (if the stock is not fully seasoned, you might need more)

- 1 litre light chicken, veal or beef stock, or vegetable stock made using the pea pods
- 200 g Vialone Nano rice
- 2 tablespoons chopped parsley (optional)
- 50 g Parmigiano Reggiano cheese, freshly grated

Method

Put the onion in a pan with the butter, and fry over a medium heat until pale gold but not brown. Add the peas and salt, and cook gently for 3–4 minutes, stirring frequently. Add 750 ml of the broth, cover the pan and simmer for 10 minutes. You can stir it from time to time, but there is no need to do so constantly.

Add the rice, parsley and the remaining stock, then stir, cover and simmer for another 10 minutes, or until the rice is al dente. Again, stir from time to time, and taste to see if it has enough salt.

Just before serving, stir in the Parmigiano. Serve in soup plates and eat with a spoon.

Polenta

Also known as 'cornmeal', polenta is a versatile product made from ground maize/corn, which was introduced to Europe during the 16th century. It can be boiled to make a type of porridge, but can also be baked, grilled or fried. It is thought to have originated from the Roman gruel or grain mush known as *puls* or *pulmentum*, which was made from ground chickpeas, spelt, farro, chestnuts or millet.

Polenta today is particularly popular in northern Italy and pockets of central Italy too. Southerners sometimes use the term *polentone* (literally 'big polenta') as an insulting name for a northerner. Northerners, in turn, use the much more derogatory *terrone* (literally 'from the earth') to refer to a southerner. My advice is never to use these words to an Italian unless you are absolutely sure the other person knows you are joking.

In the second half of the 17th century, Piero Gaioncelli imported corn to the region of Bergamo in northern Italy. Like the potato in Ireland, corn was soon seen as a much-needed way to feed the poor economically. In a surprisingly short time, it was well established as the daily fare of poor people across much of the north. In fact, the first part of the 18th century has been referred to as the 'Golden Age of Polenta'. However, the way it was prepared led to a serious illness called pellagra, which caused a deficiency in vitamin B3 (niacin). In South America, where corn had originated, the Aztecs were aware of the problem and had learnt to avoid it by boiling the corn in a lime solution, then washing it before grinding it.

Unfortunately, this vital information was not passed on when corn was introduced to Europe. Indeed, it was not until the 20th century that the problem was fully appreciated and corrected.

Once you have mastered the basic polenta recipe, you have a base for making the baked and grilled variants. The basic polenta can also be eaten with a number of stews or other ingredients, such as cheese, providing a delicious alternative to pasta, rice or even potatoes.

Basic Polenta

The soft, porridgey form of polenta is delicious with sausages and various stews, including the famous horsemeat stew of Verona and Braised Beef Cheeks (see page 212). It is also good when topped with strong-tasting cheeses, such as Gorgonzola.

It is still made this way in northern Italy on special family occasions or feast days, but some people prefer to use a casserole dish with a built-in electric stirrer. In fact, all you need to make a perfectly good polenta is a large, heavy-based saucepan and a wooden spoon.

Serves 4

- 300 g finely ground polenta/
  cornmeal, preferably by Mulino
  Marino (failing that, try to find a
  good-quality, stone-ground
- product, such as Pignoletto Rosso
  made by Mulino di Piova)
- 1.5 litres boiling salted water

Method

Let the cornmeal drop through your fingers into the boiling water and
start stirring straight away with a wooden spoon. Reduce the heat and keep
stirring in the same direction for about 40 minutes, until the mixture has
become a thick paste. When ready, serve with your chosen stew.

Soft Polenta with Cheese

In Lombardy I have had versions of soft polenta made with
Gorgonzola dolce and Gorgonzola piccante, both washed
down with a hearty red wine. Simply add 180 g of your
chosen cheese to the hot polenta, stir briefly and eat with
a spoon.

Set Polenta

To turn the polenta into cornbread, place the cooked
mixture in a lightly oiled baking tin about 2–3 cm deep.
Leave to get cold, then cut into diamond or oblong
shapes. These can be grilled, griddled or fried in olive oil,
and served with stews or sausages. They can also be used
instead of bread as the base for crostini and bruschette.

Most people think of white wine being added to risotto, but in the Veneto especially red is often used, and it produces wonderful results.

Risotto with Amarone and Radicchio

Risotto all'Amarone e Radicchio Trevigiano

This risotto with Amarone wine and radicchio di Treviso is pretty common in restaurants around Verona. Amarone can be pricey even when young, but the dish works well with a less expensive Ripasso di Valpolicella.

Serves 2–4

- 1 litre veal stock
- 50 g unsalted butter
- ½ onion, finely chopped
- 200 g Vialone Nano rice
- 2 glasses (250 ml) Amarone or Ripasso di Valpolicella
- 100 g radicchio di Treviso, chopped
- 80 g Parmigiano Reggiano cheese

Method

Bring the stock to the boil and keep it gently simmering throughout the cooking of the dish.

Dice half the butter and place it in the freezer. Melt the remaining butter in a heavy-based saucepan and gently fry the onion, making sure it softens but does not brown. This can take up to 8 minutes. Add the rice, turn up the heat and stir well.

Add a glass of wine and keep stirring over a high heat until it has evaporated, then repeat with the second glass. Over a medium-low heat, start adding the stock a ladleful at a time, stirring each addition until it has nearly all been absorbed. The rice should remain moist and move in waves when stirred. It must never become dry or sticky. When the rice begins to soften (after about 13 minutes, but check by tasting), add the stock in smaller amounts and test it regularly, until it is cooked to your liking.

Stir in the radicchio, then add the frozen butter and grate in 60 g of the Parmigiano. Stir with great gusto, until the risotto is rich and creamy. Take off the heat and leave to rest for 2 or 3 minutes, then serve immediately with the rest of the cheese shaved over each portion.

Fish & Seafood

Fish & Seafood

A glance at a map of Italy shows that the majority of the regions have access to a coastline or, if not, at least to rivers and lakes. It is therefore no surprise that fish and seafood in general are common components in the regional Italian cuisines. This has led to a huge number of recipes – in fact, so many, according to food writer Alan Davidson, that it is really difficult to make a selection. Nonetheless, I've done my best to choose dishes that make optimum use of the featured ingredient.

Let's begin by taking a brief look at the history of fishing in Italy. Forms of fishing are thought to have existed well before the Neolithic period (about 4000 years ago), and some of the techniques used began to spread worldwide. After those early beginnings, pictorial representations of fishing can be seen in Roman mosaics, which show men in boats using rod and line, as well as nets. They also depict a number of species that are considered delicacies today, including lobster, sea urchin, cuttlefish and octopus.

Tuna fishing, or *tonnara*, as it is known in Sicily and Sardinia, uses an ancient system of fixed nets to trap the fish, and then human muscle-power to haul them on to boats. Some scholars claim this method goes back more than 3500 years, but it is now in decline because of overfishing and faster modern methods.

It may come as a surprise to learn that fish farming, too, is an ancient practice. It is reliably documented that the Romans developed techniques to raise fish in artificial basins – probably to meet the demand for fish in places far from the sea.

Another historic factor which prompted increasing demand for fish was the spread of Christianity. It was symbolically important because Jesus was a 'fisher of men' but, as the church was formalized, it was decided that abstinence was good for the soul and the church ruled that Christians should eat fish rather than meat on Fridays. Consequently, more fish were needed, and freshwater species from lakes and rivers, especially in the north, became more important to both farmers and consumers.

Fishing continued at a sustainable level for many centuries after the Romans, but the industry suffered ups and downs, especially during difficult economic times. Following the Second World War, for example, when Italy suffered heavy bombing and severe hardship, fishing declined. But once the Italian economy began to grow again, so did the demand for fish, especially in some of the larger cities and towns which were a long way from the coasts. This brought about the creation of big fish markets. Milan, for example, has the Mercato Ittico, the largest fish market in Italy, but if you happen to be in Venice, the wonderful Rialto fish market is certainly worth a detour.

Nowadays, with demand for fish outstripping supply, fish farming is a growth sector in many Mediterranean countries, notably Spain and Greece, though not Italy itself. Part of the reason for this growth is that fish stocks in the Mediterranean are in decline, so only fish farming can fill the gap. Nonetheless, some of the much-reduced sea catch is still exported to places as far away as London and New York. In a quid pro quo, some of the finest Atlantic fish landed by UK fleets (and others) finds its way to fish markets in Italy.

Like most nationalities bordering the Mediterranean, Italians often eat much of their fish whole — and nose-to-tail eating is certainly possible, as some of the following recipes show.

And what about the types of fish and seafood that are actually caught in Italian waters? Very little of the catch, apart from prawns, is exported. Regional names and local varieties often cause confusion, and not just to foreigners: plenty of Italians get confused too. The anchovy, for instance, is called both *acciuga* and *alici*. Some argue that the way the fish is packed or preserved determines which word is used, or that *acciuga* is the favoured name in the north. In my experience, there are so many exceptions to these 'rules' that I end up using both terms. My feeling, however, is that *alici* is more commonly used in the south of the country.

The selection of recipes in this chapter has been made with the aim of including fish and seafood that are exceptional or unique to Italy, whilst also being within reach of home cooks who live elsewhere. If these key ingredients elude you, the dishes can be prepared with imported, high-quality preserved products. Failing that, ask your trusted fishmonger to suggest an equivalent fresh alternative from local waters.

In fact, cooking the fish whole tends to lead to better results for a home cook as there is less chance of overcooking. It is also common for whole fish, when served as a main course at home or in a restaurant, to be unaccompanied, apart from a drizzle of extra virgin olive oil and a wedge of lemon. That's because when the fish is really fresh, it does not need any vegetables or sauces. If you stick to the principles of this book, you will discover the truth of this for yourself.

Anchovy
Alici or Acciuga

Anchovies are one of those foods that divide opinion: you either like them or loathe them. I suspect, though, that a good proportion of those who do not like them have had a bad experience with poor-quality or badly prepared anchovies. In their preserved form — either packed in salt or oil — they undeniably have a big, strong umami flavour, which is not to everyone's taste, but they can also be eaten fresh, in which case they taste rather like whitebait.

There are many fish around the world called anchovies, but the type discussed here is the European anchovy (*Engraulis encrasicolus*), a small fish, usually no longer than 20 cm, which feeds largely on plankton. Around the Mediterranean, cured or preserved anchovies are strongly associated with Cantabria in Spain, where in fact Sicilian settlers started the industry, and Collioure in France. In Italy the fishing and preserving of anchovies is an ancient tradition and a major source of livelihood in villages such as Pisciotta, Pollica (Menaica anchovies) and Cetara in Campania, as well as Noli, Sportano and Finale Ligure in Liguria (Noli anchovies). Here anchovies are eaten fresh, but also preserved in oil or salt, and used as the basis of various condiments. Cetara also produces

anchovy water — *colatura di alice* (see page 150) — which is treated as an ingredient in its own right. This, along with Noli and Menaica anchovies, is a Slow Food product.

The ability of anchovies to boost and complement other ingredients has long been recognized. They are found in recipes by the great Renaissance chef Bartolomeo Scappi, for example, but they continue to be an essential ingredient in many Italian dishes today, from Spaghetti alla Puttanesca to Abbacchio (lamb) alla Cacciatora (see pages 102 and 226).

Anchovies Marinated in Lemon

Acciughe al Limone

I first had this dish when staying in Monaco for a trade conference but lunching across the border in Ventimiglia (Liguria). It was prepared with Noli anchovies that had been landed and purchased in the town's superb fish market 24 hours earlier. This simple dish was truly delicious and reminded me of great ceviche I have eaten in the USA and Peru, and some of the raw fish dishes prepared by Moreno Cedroni at his restaurant La Madonnina del Pescatore near Ancona in Marche.

Serves 4

- 400–500 g fresh anchovies
- juice of 3 good-quality Amalfi lemons

Method

Remove the anchovy heads and split the fish open down one side. Wash well, removing the guts and bones. Place the fillets flat in a shallow dish or plastic container. Bathe the anchovies with freshly squeezed lemon juice, ensuring you remove any pips. Cover the dish or container and place in the fridge for 24 hours. Take them out an hour before you want to serve them.

Truffled Anchovies

Acciughe Tartufate

This dish is something that you should try at least once in your life. I was very fortunate to do so in the perfect place at just the right time to sample it at its best. I was staying near Alba in Piedmont, it was the white truffle season, and my host was a very old and dear friend I had met in Paris when I was a postgraduate student. He had made the unusual career choice of leaving a senior position in the French civil service to work in the wine trade, and it was wine that had brought us both to the vicinity of Alba. My friend, who described the dish as 'umami lasagne', had first come across it in a book by Alan Davidson, probably Mediterranean Seafood, and he always sought it out on visits to the area. As it is a strongly flavoured dish and therefore difficult to pair with other dishes, I think it is best eaten as a one-plate meal for 2–4 with a good bottle of Barbaresco. However, it can be served as a small antipasto for 8, or a generous primo for 4 if you like.

Serves 2–8 (see above)

- 300 g salt-cured anchovies, rinsed in water
- 100 g white Alba truffle
- 80 ml delicate extra virgin olive oil (in the dish I tasted it came from Verona)

Method

Layer the anchovy fillets in a medium-sized baking dish, adding truffle shavings between each layer. Cover with the olive oil and cling film. Leave in a cool, dark place (not the fridge) for 48 hours.

Anchovy Water
Colatura di Alici di Cetara

The name of this ingredient is a little misleading. It's actually a fish sauce from Cetara, and is thought to be related to garum, the fermented fish sauce used in the cuisines of ancient Greece, Rome and Byzantium.

Colatura, meaning roughly 'filtering or leakage', refers to the amber-coloured liquid released from anchovies when they are macerated under salt — a process traditionally handed down from father to son. This concentrated liquid is highly sought after and is used mainly in salads or pasta, where just a few drops can transform a simple dish.

The anchovies used for the colatura are caught in the Gulf of Salerno from the end of March to the beginning of July. Once landed, they are beheaded and eviscerated by hand, then placed in a container and spread with a lot of sea salt to draw out the blood. After 12–24 hours, the anchovies are layered head to tail in another container, with more salt sprinkled in between. The container is covered with a wooden disc called a *tompagno*, and weights, usually sea rocks, are put on top. Maximum pressure is exerted for the first 48 hours, then it is reduced by decreasing the number and weight of the rocks. During this time, as the anchovies 'ripen', liquid starts to be released. This is poured off and filtered through special linen cloths called *cappucci* or *lambicchi*. The final result is an amber-coloured, limpid distillate, which may be filtered several times before considered ready for use. Altogether, the process lasts 2–3 months.

According to some scholars of local traditions, the maceration originally took place in an oak container called a *terzigno* (one-third of a standard barrel). However, varnished pots were also used. In this case, the quantity of colatura produced was very small. Today, although domestic production in pots and *terzigni* still exists, plastic food containers tend to be used instead, to comply with EU regulations.

The real colatura di alice di Cetara is a scarce product, but can be obtained in good delicatessens and online. It is beginning to find its way into Italian restaurants outside Italy, and I have come across it in London and Hong Kong. Once opened, the product needs to be kept in the fridge and consumed within a week at the most. For home cooks it is recommended to buy the smaller bottles.

As a general guideline, use colatura di alice as you would the finest balsamic vinegar. For instance, just a few teaspoons of the latter are needed to add a concentrated umami flavour to a salad of fresh tomatoes and capers. As with other fish sauces or anchovy-based products, it is important to balance colatura with the other seasonings in a dish, and you might need very little extra salt, if any.

Spaghetti with Colatura di Alice di Cetara

Spaghetti con Colatura di Alici di Cetara

Many restaurants along the Amalfi coast, especially in and around Cetara, serve this dish. It can be prepared from scratch in less than 15 minutes at home, and is normally a starter, but — like many pasta dishes — can be served as a one-plate meal or midnight snack. This dish, along with Spaghetti alla Puttanesca (see page 102), is one of my favourites if I get home late and have missed dinner.

Serves 4

- 350–400 g finest Gragnano dried pasta, either spaghetti or vermicelli
- 2 garlic cloves
- I small red chilli, deseeded and chopped, or ½ teaspoon dried chilli flakes
- I heaped tablespoon chopped flat leaf parsley
- pinch of Amalfi lemon zest (optional)
- 4 tablespoons extra virgin olive oil
- 2 tablespoons colatura di alice

Method

Cook the spaghetti in boiling unsalted water until al dente (no salt is needed because the colatura will provide enough).

Place the garlic, chilli, parsley and lemon zest (if using) in a large mixing bowl. Add the oil and colatura di alice and mix well.

When the pasta is ready, drain, reserving 2 tablespoons of the cooking water. Add the pasta to the parsley mixture and toss thoroughly. Add the reserved pasta water to create a little emulsion, toss again and serve.

Bottarga

Bottarga di Muggine

Bottarga is the naturally dried roe from grey mullet (*muggine*) or tuna and is thought to have been introduced to the coastal areas of Italy by the Phoenicians around the 8th century BC. With high levels of omega-3 fatty acids, a strong umami (savoury) flavour and a concentrated fishy aroma, bottarga tends to be either loved or hated.

The traditional method of producing it is to delicately extract the egg pouch from the female fish, then salt and press it until dry. The time allowed for this varies among both producers and countries. Some of the earliest records suggest that this method of producing and preserving fish roe originated in the Nile delta around the 10th century BC and eventually spread to areas that are now present-day Greece, Turkey, Italy and France.

The Italian word *bottarga* has its roots in Arabic. The grey mullet variety used here is known as *baterekh* in modern Arabic, *botarga* in Spanish, *poutarge* in French, and *avgotaraho* in modern Greek.

The main producers today are in Sardinia, Sicily and Tuscany. Excellent bottarga can also be found in Greece, where the avgotaraho from Messologiou has PDO status; in Turkey, whose *haviar* is listed in the Slow Food Foundation's *Ark of Taste*, a catalogue of excellence; and in Egypt, around Port Said, where outstanding baterekh is produced.

Sardinian bottarga di muggine from the small town of Cabras has become indelibly associated with fine Italian cuisine, which has contributed to the product's elevation to luxury status. Indeed, it is often referred to as the 'caviar of the south'. Bottarga di Orbetello, produced in the area around the Orbetello lagoon in the province of Grossetto, Tuscany, is listed as a protected product by the Slow Food Foundation. Historically, this bottarga was made mainly at home for personal use by the fishermen's families. Nowadays most of the grey mullet and its eggs are exported to Sardinia, where the bottarga 'industry' is all too well developed. Sadly, fish eggs from as far away as Florida find their way to the island to help meet global demand for the Sardinian product. Meanwhile, the Orbetello product is still produced on a very small scale, and can be found in a few upmarket delicatessens. Needless to say, it tends to be rather expensive.

Bottarga can be bought in good delicatessens or online. You will find that the Italian product is left in its natural casing, while the Greek and Egyptian products are coated in beeswax. The best examples tend to be firm but still tender, with colours that range from gold to dark amber. Always opt for vacuum-packed or beeswax-wrapped bottarga. Never buy the ready-grated product. In my view, the latter tends to be inferior quality and does not have the same intensity of flavour.

Bottarga can be grated, chopped, sliced or shaved, and will keep in the fridge for up to a year, as long as it is vacuum sealed or wrapped tightly in cling film.

Spaghetti with Grey Mullet Bottarga

Spaghetti alla Bottarga di Muggine

Particularly associated with Sardinia, this dish can be found in many of its restaurants. Also, most families on the island have their own recipe for it, so, like many dishes, it is the subject of heated debate. To add to the dispute, Spaghetti alla Bottarga has now 'crossed over', which means it is prepared and eaten all over Italy (and beyond). The great advantage of this dish is that it can essentially be made at any time as the majority of the ingredients can be kept in the store cupboard or fridge.

In my opinion, the main ingredient itself is so good and packed with multi-layered flavours that the number of other ingredients should be kept to an absolute minimum. For me, the addition of garlic, chilli and lemon juice or zest simply destroys the two core ingredients of this dish, namely the bottarga and dried pasta.

I have had variants of this dish for most of my adult life in Sardinian restaurants and homes, in other parts of Italy, and throughout Europe and North America. However, the best I have tasted, and the recipe that I tend to base my version on, was eaten in London.

I first ran into Roberto Pisano, a native Sardinian, when he was running front of house in one of London's better Italian restaurants. He later opened two of his own, whilst also running a restaurant group that had two other excellent Italian establishments. From the first time I met him, I noted that the Spaghetti alla Bottarga served in his restaurant was exceptional. After many requests over the years for the secret of his recipe, Roberto one day simply said to me, 'The spaghetti never touches water'. What he meant is that he boils his pasta in fumetto, a wonderfully intense fish stock made

with the bones, heads and trimmings of grey mullet or other white fish, such as sea bass or sea bream.

Roberto's dish, which I share with you here, is truly outstanding and perfectly balanced, but what I particularly like is that the limited number of ingredients allows the bottarga to be the star of the show.

Serves 4

- 3–4 litres fumetto (see page 158)
- 360–400 g best bronze die spaghetti (allow 100 g per person as a main dish, but 80–90 g as part of a multi-course meal)
- 4–5 tablespoons delicate extra virgin olive oil, probably from Sardinia or Liguria (avoid very fruity or pungent oils)
- 60–80 g bottarga di muggine (do not skimp)
- 2–3 teaspoons finely chopped flat leaf parsley

Method

Bring the fumetto to the boil. Add the spaghetti (no salt is needed) and cook until al dente.

Meanwhile, take a large frying pan and cover the bottom with the olive oil. Warm it slightly, then turn off the heat. Grate about a third of the bottarga into the pan. Cut another third of the bottarga into thin strips and set aside for garnish.

When the pasta is al dente, drain well, but reserve half a cupful of the fumetto. Add the pasta to the frying pan and toss with the bottarga, moving the pan to and fro. Now add 2–3 tablespoons of the reserved fumetto and keep mixing until the oil and starchy stock create an emulsion. You can add more olive oil if necessary to get the right emulsification.

Serve the spaghetti in deep pasta dishes, grating the remaining bottarga over each portion, then decorate with the reserved bottarga strips and a little parsley.

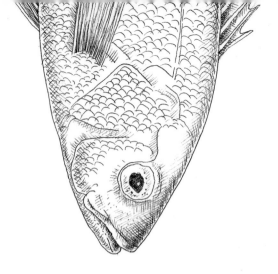

Fish Stock

Fumetto de Pesce

Fumetto is a concentrated fish stock that is used to enhance the flavour of a number of dishes, including seafood-based risotto, soups and pasta. If you have a good relationship with your fishmonger, you'll probably be given the fish heads, bones and trimmings for free, but you might have to request them if the fish is already filleted.

Some recipes recommend adding wine and various herbs to the basic liquid, but I tend to avoid this when making a large quantity of stock for multiple uses as it could add unnecessary flavour to a given dish. Seasoning and other flavours can be added on a per dish basis.

Makes 2–3 litres

- 4 carrots
- 4 celery sticks, with leaves
- 2 onions
- 2 tablespoons olive oil (optional)
- 15–20 black peppercorns
- 1 sprig of thyme and 1 sprig of parsley (optional)

- 4 kg white fish (grey mullet, john dory, sea bass, sea bream or sole), including heads, bones and trimmings
- 5 litres water
- 4 heaped teaspoons sea salt

Method

The vegetables can be left whole and placed straight in a stockpot, but if you prefer, they can be chopped and cooked for 5 minutes in the oil before being placed in the pot. Add the peppercorns, herbs (if using), fish and water. Bring to the boil and simmer for 10 minutes. Skim off any scum, then add the salt and simmer for a further 50 minutes, skimming the surface every 15 minutes or so.

Set the stock aside to cool, then strain through a sieve, discarding the fish and vegetables. Pass the liquid at least twice through a muslin-lined sieve to remove any impurities.

This stock will keep for 3 days or so in the fridge, and can also be frozen, so it is worth making a large quantity once a month so you always have some at hand.

Clams

Vongole

The *vongola verace*, literally 'true clam' (*Venerupus decussata*), is the most prized bivalve mollusc used in Italian pasta and soup dishes. In the UK it is known as the carpet shell clam, but tends to be sold under its French name, *palourde*. Excellent ones are cultivated in Dorset, and are widely available live (as they should be) from good fishmongers. In North America, Italian restaurants and home cooks tend to use Manila clams (*V. philippinarum*), which are cultivated on the west coast, but originated in coastal waters from Siberia down to Malaysia. People on the east coast of North America tend to use the hard-shell clam (*Mercenaria mercenaria*), sometimes called the Venus clam (*Venus mercenaria*), which is found from Prince Edward Island in Canada down to the south-eastern Mexican coastline.

Like most molluscs, clams feed mainly on plankton, which they filter out of the water by means of siphons and their gills. For this reason, the cleanliness of clams is therefore very dependent on the quality of the waters they feed in. When preparing clams, be they cultivated or wild, the cleaning process is crucial to avoid potential food poisoning.

When you buy clams from your fishmonger, they should be live. Once you get them home, place them in a bowl and cover with wet newspaper, piercing a few holes in it to allow air to flow in and out. The clams are best eaten on the day of purchase.

In Italy the process of cleaning the clams, almost a ritual, is called *spurgare le vongole*, literally 'purging the clams'. This involves placing them in a large bowl of water with a handful of sea salt and leaving them to soak for at least 20 minutes. During this time, the clams expel any sand, grit or impurities and take in the clean water. When ready, drain and rinse them under running cold water. Always check them before cooking by knocking each one on a hard surface and listening carefully — you may be able to detect that something loose is moving inside the shell, which often means it is full of grit or sand and should be discarded. Do a final check after cooking, discarding any unopened clams.

Clam Soup

Zuppa alle Vongole

I have had variants of this soup in Lazio, Tuscany, Liguria, Campania and other parts of southern Italy, but this recipe is based on a version I had in a small restaurant overlooking the port in Maratea, Basilicata.

The classic dish has just a few ingredients, but, eaten with some grilled sourdough, is a delightful first course or even a one-plate meal. I was lucky to have it with superb pane di Matera that a relative of the restaurant owner had baked. The bread is made with a sourdough starter and durum wheat flour. Before being baked, the dough is shaped and then scored, which results in a loaf that looks like a model of a small mountain range.

The finished soup will have at least 800 ml liquid, and half the clams will remain in their shells.

Spaghetti alle Vongole in Rosso

This dish can be turned into a version of Spaghetti alle Vongole in Rosso (or 'red sauce' as Americans call it). The quantities are the same as those given here, but omit the wine and tomato purée, and cook the spaghetti as in the next recipe. I have seen some recipes that use basil instead of parsley, or a mixture of the two, but I prefer flat leaf parsley on its own.

- 4 tablespoons extra virgin olive oil
- 3 garlic cloves, thinly sliced
- 1 teaspoon red chilli flakes or ½ fresh red chilli with seeds in, chopped
- 500–600 g carpet shell or palourde clams, cleaned
- 200 ml dry white wine
- 200 g fresh ripe tomatoes, e.g. San Marzano, deseeded and chopped, or 1 x 400 g can San Marzano tomatoes, drained
- 1 teaspoon tomato purée
- 2 tablespoons chopped flat leaf parsley
- sea salt and freshly ground black pepper

Method

Heat 3 tablespoons of the olive oil in a cast-iron pan. When hot, add the garlic and chilli and stir without browning. Add the clams, stir briefly, then add the wine and allow the alcohol to evaporate. This process takes about 2 minutes on a high heat. When all the clams have opened, take out about half, remove from their shells and return them to the pan. Add the tomatoes, tomato purée and seasoning, and cook on a high heat for 2–3 minutes.

Take the pan off the heat and add half the parsley, mixing it into the soup. Allow to rest for 2 minutes, then serve in soup plates, heaping the unshelled clams in the centre and sprinkling with the rest of the parsley.

Spaghetti with Clams

Spaghetti alle Vongole Veraci

Having eaten this glorious dish many times, and been lucky enough to watch a master cook it from scratch in less than 12 minutes whilst explaining each of its finer points, I am delighted to pass on the secret of the perfect Spaghetti alle Vongole to you.

This is one of the most popular pasta dishes in Italy and a feature on many Italian restaurant menus around the world. The version given here is in bianco (white) because it contains no tomatoes.

Spaghetti alle Vongole also led me to become friends with the London-based Calabrian chef Francesco Mazzei. The recipe here is based largely on his and is published here in his honour. In September 2009 I went to L'Anima, where Francesco is chef-patron, with American food writer and restaurant critic Daniel Young, food writer Rejina Sabur and my friend and gonzo video maker Eddie Vassallo, who produced eight videos showing Francesco cooking this dish. We launched each video on Twitter and invited people to enter a competition saying why (in 140 characters) they loved Spaghetti alle Vongole. The prize was a sumptuous dinner for two in the private dining room of L'Anima, and the menu included Francesco's magnificent dish. The videos can all still be viewed on YouTube.

Perhaps I should say here that what I love about Spaghetti (or linguine) alle Vongole is that, like many Italian dishes, it appears to be very simple — boil some pasta and throw in a few ingredients — but it is actually much more subtle than that. In reality, when you deconstruct this dish, you start to understand Italian cooking, the importance of good-quality ingredients and how they combine to produce a perfectly executed dish.

Like many other Italian dishes, Spaghetti alle Vongole provokes fierce debate because it transcends regionalism and can be found in all corners of the country. Every aspect is contested. Rosso or bianco? Chilli or no chilli? White wine or none? Fine or coarsely chopped parsley? Which is the best pasta? How long should it be cooked?

Serves 4

- 320–400 g best bronze die
  spaghetti from Gragnano or
  Abruzzo (for a first course as part of
  a four-course meal, 70–80 g pasta
  per person is enough, but if having
  only two courses, 100 g each is the
  recommended amount)

- 6 tablespoons extra virgin oil
- 2 garlic cloves, thinly sliced
- ½ red chilli with seeds in, sliced
- 600 g palourde clams
- ½ glass (75 ml) dry white wine
- 3 tablespoons roughly chopped flat
  leaf parsley

Method

Cook the pasta in a large pan of boiling salted water until a little more al
dente than usual.

Meanwhile, heat a wide frying pan on maximum heat and, when it
starts smoking, add the oil, garlic and chilli. Stir for less than a minute
without browning, then add the clams. Shake the pan to and fro, then
add the wine and heat until the alcohol evaporates and all the clams are
open; if necessary, briefly cover the pan to ensure the shells open. It
is important to allow the evaporation to occur before the clams start
opening so that you get the right level of acidity, and the flavour of the
wine remains in the background to the clams.

Drain the pasta, reserving a cupful of the cooking water. Add the pasta
to the pan of clams and start shaking it back and forth, adding 2 or 3
tablespoons of the pasta water. This process of mixing the olive oil, clam
juices and starchy water creates a wonderful emulsion, which can be seen
at the bottom of the pan.

Add half the parsley, shake back and forth for a final time, then serve in
deep pasta plates, sprinkling the remaining parsley on each serving.

Red Mullet

Triglie

Also known as surmullet, this fish has historically been one of the most prized in the Mediterranean. In Italy it is generally called *triglie*, but is also known as *tregghia* in the south (*trigghia* in Sicily). It has a very fine and delicate flavour, with a firm flesh which is similar to cod. A member of the goatfish or Mullidae family, it is found not only in the Mediterranean, but also in the North Atlantic and Black Sea.

There are two main types of triglie landed in Italy: the triglia di fango (literally 'mud mullet' – *Mullus barbatus*), which lives and feeds in sandy or muddy waters, and the triglia di scoglio (literally 'mullet of the rocks' – *Mullus surmuletus*), which lives in clear, deeper waters and feeds on other fish and crustaceans. The latter species is generally bigger and can be distinguished by the stripes on its first dorsal fin, its darker red colour and its more curved head profile. It is considered to be a superior fish for eating because, thanks to its diet, it has a more complex flavour. Triglia di fango can also be excellent, but is less reliably so because of its muddy environment.

The Romans were very partial to red mullet and kept them in pools to fatten them artificially, not only to meet demand but also to profit from the high prices they could command. Pliny mentions that *Apicius* (a collection of Roman recipes) recommended that red mullet was best when drowned in garum (fish sauce), one of many ingredients that have been considered aphrodisiacs at one time or another.

Those familiar with the TV series featuring Inspector Montalbano, Italy's most famous fictional detective, will probably have noticed that red mullet is one of his favourite foods.

My late father was very particular about red mullet and I remember as a teenager, when we were on holiday in Liguria, he was persuaded by a local restaurateur (against his better judgement) to order grilled triglia 'blind' (without inspecting the fish first). It was, the man assured him, as fresh as a daisy and the apotheosis of red mullet. After the meal, when asked how he found the fish, my father replied, 'The best thing about that triglia was the boiled potato'.

In Italy triglie are generally fried, grilled or baked whole, but may sometimes feature in fish soups. However, they are rarely eaten poached. Triglia di scoglio, when very fresh, can be cooked without being gutted, and the liver is considered a great delicacy.

Try to buy red mullet from a good fishmonger and, if possible, eat on the day of purchase. Look for firm shiny skin, clear eyes and bright red gills. Like most fresh fish, mullet should be stored at temperatures close to, but not below, 0°C.

Oven-roasted
Red Mullet

Triglie al Forno

When you have beautiful fresh red mullet — or sea bass, sea bream or sole, for that matter — one of the best ways to cook it at home is roasted whole in the oven. I have had fish cooked this way in many homes around Naples.

Some people score the skin before cooking, but I don't see any point. Others cook the fish with parboiled seasoned potatoes in the same dish, allowing them to get a head start of around 10–15 minutes. (The potatoes need 40 minutes in total, so you need to calculate the parboiling according to the time needed for the fish.) I would be happy to have potatoes with this dish if my previous courses do not include carbohydrates such as rice or pasta, but I prefer them steamed or boiled separately from the fish, then dressed with a touch of extra virgin olive oil and parsley. Grilled courgettes or wilted spinach are good accompaniments.

Serves 4

- 2 red mullet, 350–500 g each (ask your fishmonger to scale and gut the fish, but keep the liver if you wish)
- 1 sprig of thyme or rosemary
- 2 tablespoons extra virgin olive oil
- sea salt and freshly ground black pepper
- 1 or 2 Amalfi lemons, cut into wedges, to serve

Method

Preheat the oven to 180°C/Gas 4.

Season the fish on both sides with salt and pepper and place a sprig of thyme or rosemary in the cavity. Lightly coat both sides of the fish with some of the olive oil and place in a heavy baking dish. Pour in 4–5 tablespoons water.

Roast the fish for about 20–25 minutes, basting it with the juices halfway through the cooking time. If larger than specified, it might need another 5–8 minutes. The easiest way to check for doneness is to insert a knife near the dorsal line on the upper side of the fish. If the flesh is still pink and adhering tightly to the bone, pour a spoonful of the juices over the incision and return the fish to the oven for a little bit longer.

Serve the fish in its dish, dissecting it at the table. Drizzle a touch of the remaining olive oil over each portion and serve with lemon wedges on each plate.

Fillet of Red Mullet
with Saffron Gnocchi

Filetti di Triglia con Gnocchi al Zafferano

The combination of red fish, golden gnocchi and bright green spinach just happens to be the colours of the Italian flag.

I have eaten this dish many times in Sardinia, and also had gnocchi with a red mullet sauce on the island of Elba. However, I first cooked the version given here by chance, as I was informed at short notice that our guests, who were due to join us for lunch, could not bear the sight of whole fish with the head on. I therefore decided to pan-fry it, whilst using the bones and head to make a stock.

Serves 4

- 2 red mullet, 350–500 g each, filleted (keep the bones and heads)
- 1 quantity gnocchi (see page 116)
- extra virgin olive oil, for frying and drizzling
- pinch of saffron, ground in a mortar
- 600 g spinach, to serve
- sea salt and freshly ground black pepper

Method

Use the mullet heads and bones for making stock (see page 158).

Cook the gnocchi as described on page 116, then drain, reserving the cooking water.

Meanwhile, heat 2 tablespoons olive oil in a large, heavy-based frying pan. Season the fish with salt, then fry, skin-side down, for 3–4 minutes. Turn and cook for a further 1–1½ minutes, depending on the size and thickness of the fish. Set aside to rest on warm white plates.

Deglaze the pan with some of the fish stock and a little of the reserved gnocchi water, then dissolve the saffron in the liquid. Add the gnocchi and a drizzle of olive oil whilst mixing with a spoon to ensure they are fully coated. This process takes about 1½ minutes. In another pan, wilt the spinach in a little extra virgin olive oil.

Serve the fillets and gnocchi with wilted spinach seasoned with a touch of salt and pepper and a drizzle of olive oil. Although generally served as a main course, this dish can also be served as a first course. In this case, allow 70 g fish per person. Flake the cooked fillets in the pan, then add the gnocchi as described above. Sprinkle the finished dish with a little chopped flat leaf parsley.

Red Prawn

Gambero Rosso

Red prawns (*Aristaeomorpha foliacea*), sometimes called Sicilian red prawns, are blood-red, wild Mediterranean prawns. As in Spain, where they are called *carabinero* or, more correctly, *langostino moruno*, they are very sought after.

My friend Mat Couchman, who is both a fish scientist and fishmonger, tells me that prawns should be eaten as soon as possible after they have been caught because they suffer from melanization (black spotting) shortly after they die. Although harmless, it makes for a very unattractive shell. So unless you happen to live very close to a port or market where the prawns are landed, buying frozen ones is a good option. In fact, most of the Italian boats that fish by net for red prawns in deep waters actually freeze and pack them immediately on board. The resulting luxury product, with a price to match, is sent to some of the best restaurants around the world.

In London, until recently, red prawns would appear only occasionally in just a few high-end Italian restaurants, but were very hard to get from fishmongers. In 2010 I actually worked with Mat Couchman to source a reliable supplier, and it's good to see that the prawns are now available from the best fishmongers, in restaurants and also online.

Red prawns are so sweet and delicious that you can eat them raw or simply marinated in a fine extra virgin olive oil, adding a squeeze of Amalfi lemon juice to each one before you eat it. They are also delicious simply poached for 90 seconds, or fried in their shells in olive oil with parsley and garlic.

The red prawn is the antithesis of the myriad farmed prawns on the market today, so if you get the chance, do try them as they are really a world-class food. Of course, the price is prohibitive for most people: 4–5 of these superb prawns will set you back the same amount as 3 pints of run-of-the-mill beer, but are a far superior experience.

If you want to make the ultimate version of Linguine with Prawns, Tomatoes and Capers (see page 104), be sure to use these red prawns.

Salt Cod and Stockfish

Baccalà e Stoccafisso

Although Atlantic cod (*Gadus morhua*) is not present in the Mediterranean Sea, it is a very important fish in Italy and neighbouring countries partly because of religious obligations to have meatless days. In fact, as the writer Mark Kurlansky suggests in his superb book on cod (see page 466), it is a fish that changed the world.

In Italy there are enough recipes involving salt cod and stockfish to fill several volumes. Indeed, legend has it that in and around Naples alone there are more recipes than there are days in a year.

When fresh or frozen, cod is called *merluzzo*; when preserved in salt, it is known as *baccalà* (salt cod); and when air-cured, it is called *stoccafisso* (stockfish). The word 'baccalà' is likely to have originated from Spain, whilst the roots of 'stoccafisso' are thought to come from Flemish or German. The products themselves have a strong association with Norway and the Vikings, whose fishermen seemed to follow the Atlantic cod and are thought to have been the first to cure it.

In Italy baccalà is sometimes used as a generic name for both salt cod and stockfish — at least that is the case in the Veneto and Friuli-Venezia Giulia. However, I will never forget a meal I went to in neighbouring Bolzano, which was hosted by a Neapolitan who had married a local and been living there for over 20 years. It became the scene of a heated debate when he and two of his guests (from Vicenza and Udine) could not agree about recipes involving baccalà and/or stoccafisso. It eventually became clear that the root cause of the disagreement was the lack of clarity about which type of preserved cod was being referred to.

The finest salt cod and stockfish still come from Norway, where the artisan Sørøya Island stockfish and Møre og Romsdal salt cod remain scarce and much sought after. Unfortunately, the majority of what can be found on the market is produced from fish caught by trawlers or boats with long lines operating 24 hours a day during the season. Catches are frozen and delivered to large-scale producers, who use advanced industrial processes to salt and dry the fish.

Once you have your product, it is important to soak it for several days, changing the water four or five times a day. The general consensus seems to be two days' soaking for salt cod, and at least four for stockfish. I remember as a child, when visiting big cities such as Rome, Milan and Naples, that food shops would have large buckets of the preserved fish with hoses constantly circulating running water over them to produce ready-soaked fish for their customers.

Note that some producers use much more salt than others, so it is important to taste salt cod after soaking to gauge how much extra salt might be required for seasoning a specific dish.

Creamed Salt Cod

Baccalà Mantecato

This dish is from the Veneto region, and is often found in Venetian bàcari (wine bars), where it is served on grilled bread or polenta as one of the cicchetti (small bites) on offer. The concept of bàcari (something like Spanish tapas bars), has in recent years become popular in big cities such as London, and you may well find this dish on the menu. The Venetians call it baccalà, but in most cases they mean stockfish. The dish is certainly related to the French classic brandade de morue, which is very similar and normally has a touch of lemon added at the end. There is some debate about which of the dishes is the oldest.

When made properly and served on small pieces of grilled bread, this dish is an excellent accompaniment to sparkling or still white wines, or some of the local aperitifs. At home, it can be served in the same way as antipasti, but a slightly larger portion works well as a first course with grilled polenta. In this case, allow 100 g fish per person.

The liquid used to poach the fish is very important: some people use milk, while others use water. I prefer the latter because it is neutral. Similarly, the method of mixing (mantecare means 'to mix') makes a crucial difference. Some recipes recommend a food processor, but, as with pesto, I find that using a mortar and pestle produces the best result.

Remember to taste the fish before seasoning because the amount needed will vary, depending on whether salt cod or stockfish is used. With the latter, you will certainly need to add more salt.

- 500 g pre-soaked salt cod or stockfish (see introduction for times)
- 1 litre water or milk
- 250 ml extra virgin olive oil
- 2 garlic cloves, finely chopped or crushed
- sea salt and finely ground black pepper
- 1 tablespoon chopped parsley, for sprinkling
- capers and/or stoned olives, for garnish

Method

Place the fish and water or milk in a pan. Bring to the boil, then simmer for 25 minutes. Using a slotted spoon, transfer the fish to a plate and set aside to cool. Reserve the cooking liquid.

When the fish is cool enough to handle, remove the skin and any pin bones. Lay the fish out on a wooden board, cover with a clean cloth or cling film, then beat with your fist or a wooden mallet until the fish breaks into pieces. Place the fish in a mortar, season with salt (if necessary) and black pepper. Using one hand, start working the mixture with the pestle while using the other hand to add a small drizzle of olive oil, followed by a little of the poaching liquid. Keep repeating these additions, pounding constantly, until a creamy consistency is achieved. The garlic can be added halfway through the mixing, but the important thing is to ensure it is completely crushed and evenly combined.

The dish is finished when the fish can absorb no more oil or liquid. It should look similar to tinned tuna that has been mixed with mayonnaise – creamy but the fish texture is still visible.

Serve at room temperature or cold on grilled pieces of bread with a sprinkling of chopped parsley, and a couple of capers or a stoned olive.

Bolzano-style Stockfish

Stoccafisso alla Bolzanina or Bozner Stockfischgröstl

This dish is very common in and around Bolzano, which is close to the Italian–Austrian border, hence its dual Italian and German names. It is fairly heavy but delicious, so ideal for when you are snowed in on a cold winter's day and buying fresh fish is not easy. Again, both salt cod and stockfish can be used, even though I suspect the original recipe was made with the latter. To ring the changes you can add a couple of chopped anchovies to the garlic and onion, if you wish.

Serves 4

- 500 g pre-soaked salt cod or stockfish (see page 174)
- 500 g potatoes, unpeeled
- 60 g butter, for frying
- 1 onion, chopped
- 1 garlic clove, finely chopped
- 1 bay leaf
- 200 ml double cream
- sea salt and finely ground black pepper
- 1 tablespoon chopped parsley, for sprinkling

Method

Poach the fish for 25 minutes, then set aside until it has cooled to room temperature. Remove the skin and any pin bones. Flake the flesh into similar-sized pieces.

Meanwhile, boil the potatoes in their skin until soft to the point of a knife. Drain and set aside. When cool enough to handle, remove the skin and slice the flesh.

Heat the butter in a frying pan and fry the onion and garlic until starting to colour. Add the sliced potatoes and flaked fish to the pan, and fry until brown. Season with salt and pepper, add the bay leaf and cream and stir everything together. Serve directly from the pan, sprinkling a little of the parsley on each serving.

If you wish, the finished dish can be placed in an oven preheated to 180°C/gas mark 4 and baked for 10 minutes, so it resembles a fishy gratin dauphinois.

Sea Bass

Branzino or Spigola

In Italy wild sea bass (*Dicentrarchus labrax*) has two principal names: *branzino* in the north and *spigola* in the south, though I have also seen it called *lupo* and *ragano*. Sea bass has historically been one of the most sought-after Mediterranean (and Atlantic) fish. This member of the Serranidae family was, after salmon, one of the first fish to be farmed in Europe, but with less success. While I have had a few very decent farmed salmon (from the Faroe Islands and a couple of Scottish and Irish fish farms), I have yet to encounter a farmed sea bass worthy of note.

Primarily an ocean fish, sea bass does venture into fresh water, and can certainly be found in estuaries. The Romans, as noted by the scholar Pliny, preferred to eat those fished from rivers, but it's probable that their opinion would be different today.

Wild sea bass has firm flesh, is relatively free of bones and holds its shape when cooked. In Italy it is usually grilled or oven-cooked, but it may also be poached. I would advise home cooks to avoid grilling, especially large fish, as the risk of uneven cooking or overcooking is high.

The fish has a wonderful flavour and requires very little intervention or enhancement. Always buy from a trusted fishmonger who can give you an idea when the fish was caught and who (ideally) buys directly from where the fish was landed rather than through a large wholesale market, where days can be added to the supply chain.

Squid

Calamaro

Squid (*Loligo vulgaris*) is eaten all over the Mediterranean, and the Italian word for squid (*calamari* in the plural) has to a certain extent been adopted by the Greeks, Turks, French and Spanish. Those from the Mediterranean are often smaller than those from the Atlantic, and the very small ones — known as *calamaretti* in Italian or *chiperonnes* in Spanish — are much sought after.

Squid belong to a particularly successful group of molluscs called the cephalopods, which have been around for about 500 million years. They are mentioned in Greek and Roman texts, and in *Apicius* it is suggested that they should be cooked with pepper, lovage, coriander, celery seed, egg yolks, honey, vinegar, broth, wine and oil.

The general rule with squid is that to avoid a rubbery or chewy consistency they need to be cooked very quickly over a high heat or stewed for an hour or more.

It is best to buy squid fresh from a fishmonger, especially if you plan to cook something other than fried calamari. I've found that frozen squid rings can sometimes be decent, but the same cannot be said for whole frozen squid.

I rarely have to clean squid as my excellent fishmonger and his team will do it for me in seconds. If you do need to clean them yourself, see the tip alongside.

Cleaning and preparing squid is a fairly simple process that simply requires a very sharp knife. First, cut off the end of the head with the tentacles attached and set aside, as these make good eating. Grasp what is left of the head and pull it out of the body. Make a slit along the body and clean out any innards. Finally, rinse and dry the squid flesh and tentacles, and cut into strips or squares or whatever shape is required for the dish you are planning to cook.

Sea Bass Baked in Salt

Spigola al Sale

Here's the perfect dish for a dinner party or family meal, which can also often be found on the menu in Italian restaurants around the world. It provides a sense of theatre, as the whole fish is brought to the table, the salt crust is carefully removed, and the fish dissected into portions for each guest. I will never forget a restaurateur in Positano, who always performed this ritual whilst singing verses of 'Funiculì funiculà'. Fortunately, both his voice and his spigola were top notch.

Serves 4

- 1 large sea bass, 850 g–1 kg, or 2 smaller fish, 500–600 g each
- 3 sprigs of thyme or rosemary
- 4 tablespoons extra virgin olive oil
- 2 kg coarse sea salt (see opposite)

- 200 ml water
- sea salt and freshly ground black pepper
- 1 or 2 Amalfi lemons, cut into wedges, to serve

Method

Preheat the oven to its highest temperature.

Open the cavity of the fish and push in enough of the thyme or rosemary to half-fill it. Add a tablespoon of the olive oil and season with fine sea salt. Generously season just the outside of the fish with black pepper.

Mix the coarse salt and water together in a bowl, then stir in the leaves from the remaining thyme or rosemary. Take a baking dish large enough to accommodate the fish and make a 2 cm layer of the salt mixture in the bottom. Sit the fish on top. Cover with the remaining salt, patting it around so that the fish shape is still visible.

Bake the large fish for 25–30 minutes, or the two smaller fish for 20–25 minutes. Set aside to rest for 5 minutes or so, until cool enough to handle. Break open the salt crust with your hands or a serving fork and spoon, then divide the fish into portions (singing while you do so is optional). Drizzle some of the remaining olive oil on each portion and serve with a lemon wedge.

Serve this dish with boiled or steamed potatoes dressed in olive oil and chopped parsley. The perfect accompaniment is Grilled Vegetable and Parsley Salad (see page 298).

Squid Stewed in Red Wine

Calamari in Umido

There are many variants of this dish all over Italy, and the further south you go, the spicier it can be. I have tried it with both red and white wine, but I find that a full-bodied red works best. I also like to use Tropea onions (see page 329) as their sweetness provides a perfect balance. Adding spicy 'nduja sausage to the dish is optional, but I highly recommend it, even though I originally did so only because I ran out of chillies. It was a fortuitous accident, and now I always add 'nduja.

In my view this stew is best served with a few slices of grilled polenta (see page 137), but it's also good with grilled sourdough bread rubbed with a little extra virgin olive oil.

Serves 4

- 4 tablespoons extra virgin olive oil
- 150 g Tropea onions, roughly chopped
- I kg fresh cleaned squid and tentacles, body cut into thick rings
- 30 g 'nduja (see page 274)
- 2 glasses (250 ml) full-bodied red wine (in keeping with the Calabrian theme, go for a youngish 100 per cent Gaglioppo; drink the rest with the meal)
- 450 g fresh ripe tomatoes, peeled and chopped, or I x 400g can San Marzano tomatoes
- 2 tablespoons double- or triple-concentrated tomato purée
- 3 teaspoons sea salt, plus extra for seasoning
- 2 teaspoons wild dried oregano
- freshly ground black pepper

Method

Heat the oil in a large flameproof casserole dish. Add the onions and allow them to soften but not brown.

Add the squid and cook over a high heat until coated in oil and sealed. Add the 'nduja (if using) and the wine and keep over a high heat until the alcohol has evaporated. Stir in the tomatoes, tomato purée, salt and oregano. Cover and cook on a low heat for I hour.

When ready, the squid should be tender and the sauce thick and reduced. Taste and adjust the seasoning with pepper and salt as necessary. Serve in soup plates with grilled polenta or toasted sourdough.

Grilled Squid with Salsa Salmorigano

Calamari alla Brace con Salsa Salmorigano

If you can find good fresh squid during the summer, they are delicious grilled on the barbecue and served with a simple Sicilian oil and lemon dressing called salsa salmorigano. (The name is a contraction of its three main ingredients — sale/limone/origano — but in Sicilian there are many variations to the spelling, including sammurigghiu and sarmuriggiu. The dressing can, in fact, be used with a variety of grilled fish and meats, and I have had versions that included garlic and red chilli flakes instead of black pepper.

Serves 4–6

- 1 kg cleaned squid, including tentacles (keep the body tubes whole)
- 1 tablespoon extra virgin olive oil

For the salsa salmorigano

- juice from 2 Amalfi lemons and zest from one half
- 2 teaspoons Trapani sea salt (see page 446)
- freshly ground black pepper
- 1 teaspoon dried wild oregano
- 4 tablespoons chopped flat leaf parsley
- 5 tablespoons extra virgin olive oil

Method

First make the salsa. Put the lemon juice and zest into a bowl with the salt, pepper, oregano and most of the parsley. Stir to combine, then mix in the oil (do not whisk). Set aside.

Coat a cast-iron griddle pan with a little olive oil and place over a high heat. Brush the squid all over with the tablespoon of olive oil and griddle it for 4–6 minutes on each side.

Place the grilled squid on a serving dish and dress with spoonfuls of the salsa salmorigano. Decorate the top of each squid with the remaining parsley.

Meat, Game & Poultry

Meat, Game & Poultry

The aroma of a long, slow braise of meat or game, a roasting chicken or a steak sizzling on a grill can be intoxicating, and in Italy can often replace the need for an aperitif.

One of the patterns seen when a country undergoes economic development is that the consumption of fresh meat tends to increase. This was certainly the case with Italy in the post-war period, when rising income and lower meat prices (brought about by industrialized production methods) led to much more meat on the table. That pattern eventually started to dip, and levelled off at the beginning of the 21st century, but national production and imports of fresh meat and poultry have followed the same upward trajectory as patterns of consumption.

As noted by historian John Dickie, 'Italian eating habits show only residual traces of the religious norms that shaped them until as late as the 1960s, when the Vatican did away with the prohibition of meat on Fridays.' Nowadays just a tiny minority adheres to the church calendar divided between lean and fat days, but those who do might have noticed that some of the dishes traditionally served on lean days are actually quite delicious.

Italians, like people in many other countries, tend to purchase meat and poultry mainly from supermarkets. This has led inevitably to a decline in the number of *macellerie* (butcher's shops). Nonetheless, it is still possible to find a good one, and many people prefer to shop there as they know the value of having a good relationship with their butcher. To eavesdrop on conversations between shoppers and their butcher is always entertaining, but also very informative about cuts of meat and cooking methods.

In Italy, butchers can be very specialized, perhaps selling only fresh meat, while others may stock cured and cooked meats as well. Many also incorporate a *rosticceria* (rotisserie), where cooked poultry and meat are available, and some even sell fully prepared dishes. Freshly spit-roasted chicken, for example, tends to be available around lunchtime and at the end of the day, and it's well worth trying. In fact, some of the best-cooked chicken I have had in Italy has been from a *macelleria* that has a large rotisserie.

Despite the fact that Italy is one of the countries strongly associated with the Mediterranean diet, which is big on locally grown vegetables, pulses and fruit, it also has a huge repertoire of recipes involving meat, poultry and game. However, when served as a main course or part of a multi-course meal, meat is often prepared fairly simply and served without any accompaniments.

In this chapter I focus on dishes involving beef, pork, veal, lamb, goat, poultry and game, all of which can be prepared by a home cook with ingredients that are fairly easy to source. Where applicable, I suggest complementary dishes from other chapters.

Italian Methods of Cooking Meat

There are a number of traditional ways to cook meat, and the method used is often incorporated into the name of the dish.

Bollito – placed in boiling water and cooked

Lesso – placed in cold water, then brought to the boil and cooked

Arrosto – roasted

Brasato – braised (meat is seared first) until very tender

Stufato – braised (without searing first) until very tender

Stracotto – braised (without searing first) until it starts to break apart

Grigliare – grilled

The process of sealing meat is known as the Maillard reaction, one of the most important flavour-producing steps in cooking. It was first identified by the French chemist Louis-Camille Maillard in 1912, when he discovered that the reaction between amino acids and sugars at high temperatures causes browning, which is the visual alert for the intensification of flavour and associated aromas.

Beef and Veal

There are different terms for beef, depending on the age of the animal. Strictly speaking, *manzo* is the word used for meat from a heifer (young female cow), or from a steer (castrated male cow) under the age of four; when the steer is over that age, it is called *bue*. A bull (non-castrated male) is normally called *toro*, whilst a female cow that has had one or more calves is called *vacca*.

Historically, Italy has imported fairly large quantities of beef from South America, notably Argentina, Uruguay and Brazil, because that is where some of the Italian diaspora settled. This imported beef is necessary to meet demand in Italy, and has introduced non-indigenous cattle, such as Angus and Hereford cross-breeds, into the fresh and processed food-supply chain. Beef is also imported from EU countries, including Spain, Germany and eastern Europe. So substantial are beef imports that some of the Italian importers and wholesalers end up re-exporting a proportion to other parts of Europe and beyond.

If you eat beef in Italy, especially in a major city, it is likely to be imported meat, unless otherwise indicated. Sometimes, though, as in the case of Argentinian beef, the place of origin is highlighted because it has a premium connotation. Of course, the provenance alone tells the consumer very little. What is really needed is information about breed, husbandry, feed, age at slaughter and length of ageing.

Italy's Domestic Animal Information System lists 61 breeds of cattle, but 19 of these are now extinct. All are distant relatives of the auroch (*Bos primigenius*), the ancestor of most domestic cattle. Among the remaining breeds in Italy today, there are several that are highly prized for their beef. These include the five indigenous *razze* (breeds) known as the '5R' – the Chianina, Marchigiana, Maremmana, Romagnola and Podolica. Beef from 5R cattle is sold by name at premium prices by approved butchers, and the receipt details the breed, birth and slaughter dates, identification number and other data of the animal in order to guarantee its origin. All 18 principal cuts are branded with the 5R symbol.

A glance at the herd books shows that, at the time of writing, there are fewer than 15,000 Maremmana, Romagnola and Podolica cows being reared in Italy, whilst Chianina and Marchigiana number 47,000 and 50,000 respectively. These relatively low numbers are part of the reason why Italy needs to import so much beef.

In culinary terms, the Piedmontese or Fassone is also a very important breed, and listed in the Slow Food Foundation's *Ark of Taste*. It lacks the hormone myostatin, so it grows larger than usual muscles, and therefore yields more meat, less fat and fewer calories per gram. Its promoters claim all this is achieved with no loss of flavour, but I am not convinced. In my experience, it has a less interesting flavour than, say, a well-marbled, grass-fed Black Angus, Highland or Galician Red when eaten as a medium-rare steak. Where it does come into its own is served raw, as in a tartare or battuta recipe (see page 210).

Given the scarcity of good home-grown varieties of beef, it's useful to know that the recipes given in this section can be prepared with any top-quality beef from wherever you happen to be.

While there are exceptions, Italians generally prefer their beef fairly lean and fresh (as opposed to aged), so the indigenous breeds, which may be raised as draught animals, as well as for beef and milk, tend not to produce very marbled meat. The majority of Italian trade and retail customers at O'Shea's butchers in London, for example, continually ask for beef that has not been dry-aged for more than three or four weeks, whilst the non-Italian clientele fight over the prime cuts dry-aged on the bone for 38–45 days or more. The beef most commonly available tends to have been aged for about 30 days, but to ensure a good flavour, I aim to buy meat that has been aged for an average of 35 days. After that, it comes down to personal taste, as the flavour will change, becoming stronger and, in some cases, gamier.

VEAL

Vitello is the Italian word for 'veal', the meat that comes from very young calves. In Italy it usually refers to the meat from milk-fed calves, whilst *vitellone* comes from older animals that have cut their first two permanent incisors and have already progressed to feeding on grass and maybe grain too. Vitello is a light pink colour with a very mild flavour, whilst vitellone (known as rosé veal elsewhere) is much darker and with a fuller flavour. In Piedmont there is a traditional variant of veal called *sanato*, where the animal continues to be fed milk after it has been weaned and up to the age of 12 months. Its diet is supplemented with egg whites, which makes the meat particularly pale in appearance and delicate in flavour.

Veal is very popular in Italy, so locally reared animals are supplemented by imports mainly from the Netherlands, where there are many specialist producers of veal at all quality levels. In my experience, though, the local vitello and vitellone generally have much more flavour.

Lamb and Goat

Most sheep and goat farming in Italy is focused on milk production for cheese-making, just as it has been since the Middle Ages. This is not to imply that the meat is not seen as worthy for the table. It is, in fact, commonly eaten, especially in central and southern regions of the country. Indeed, the traditional *transumanza* (migration of sheep from highland to lowland, or vice versa) dates back to pre-Roman times, when flocks were moved between the northern Apennines and the southern plains of Apulia. The practice continues to this day, but on a much smaller scale.

The term for milk-fed lamb (the type most sought after) is *agnellino da latte*, but *abbacchio*, the name used for it in and around Rome, is now common parlance all over Italy. The animals are normally fairly small and the meat is pale and delicate, with a mild taste. Strictly speaking, abbacchio should be no more than a month old when slaughtered. Lambs allowed to continue growing are weaned after a month or so, and given a mixed but milk-centric diet until, aged 6–10 months, they become *agnello* (lamb). Milk-fed lamb is especially plentiful in Italy around Easter because of a surplus from milk-centred sheep farming. An older, fattened, castrated male sheep that would still be considered lamb in the UK is known as *castrato*. It has a strong flavour and is used mainly for braising and slow cooking. What constitutes lamb in the English-speaking world is very confusing. A simple rule of thumb would be to say that a sheep older than 12 months and that has one or more permanent incisors is really no longer lamb but either hoggett or mutton, both of which have a much stronger flavour.

GOAT

Known as *capra* in Italian, goat is particularly valued for its milk production, mainly for cheese-making, and can be reared in much sparser environments than sheep. The adult meat is an acquired taste and can be fairly tough, so lends itself to very slow-cooked stews. *Capretto* (kid), on the other hand, is much better for eating, and some people consider the milk-fed variety to be superior to the finest milk-fed lamb or suckling pig.

There are too many breeds of sheep and goat in Italy to cover here, but some of the 'indigenous' rare breeds have virtually disappeared or are under threat. The Altamurana sheep of Apulia, for example, graze on wild herbs such as thyme, mint, sage, rue, borage, fennel and beet leaves, giving the meat a unique flavour, but their numbers have fallen from over 100,000 in the 1970s to just a few hundred today. This decline has had an impact not only on meat consumption, but also on some of the oldest cheese-making traditions, which have relied on the unusually flavoured milk. A similar pattern can be seen with goats. Fortunately, the Capra di Cilento from Campania is still reared, not only for its excellent kid meat, but for its milk, which is used to make sublime cacioricotta cheese.

Many of the recipes which are usually associated with young lamb are interchangeable with kid.

Pork

Suino is the generic Italian word for 'pig', but *maiale* is the most common word for the animal and its meat, pork.

As in other European countries over the years, Italy has replaced its traditional, often regional, breeds of pig — the so-called rare breeds — with the likes of Large White and Landrace. These latter breeds are better for large-scale farming, producing leaner but rather bland pork for both the fresh and cured meat markets. The lack of flavour is due mainly to the feed they are given and to their natural lack of fat. It has to be noted too that some mass-produced pork is not reared humanely, but in cramped indoor environments, where it is subjected to fairly high levels of antibiotics.

The rare breeds, on the other hand, which are gradually being reintroduced in Italy, tend to be farmed on a much smaller scale and have a lot to recommend them, not least flavour. Fresh and cured pork from these breeds can be found in some good shops and restaurants, but the scale of production still makes it difficult to find quality pork in all parts of the country. Outside big cities the tradition of keeping a few pigs still continues, and for many people they provide a good proportion of all the fresh and cured pork they need.

In the early part of the 20th century there were over 20 breeds of 'indigenous' pigs being farmed or kept semi-wild in Italy. Nowadays, with some help from universities, the Worldwide Fund for Nature and the Slow Food Foundation, the Mora Romagnola, Casertana, Cinta

Senese, Calabrese, Sarda and Sicilian (Black of Nebrodi) breeds are still being farmed. The Nero di Parma, which started being revived in the mid-1990s, is also beginning to appear on the radar in a region dominated by Landrace, Large White and Duroc pigs. Native breeds remain a tiny niche, but if you have a chance to try the fresh or cured meat produced from them, it should be something very special. (As cured pork is such an important part of Italian food culture, it is discussed in more detail in the Cured Meat chapter.)

Game

Writing in the early 1950s, Elizabeth David noted that 'Italian game is not equal in quality to our own, but there is a great deal of it'. I am not sure that this statement holds true today. Italian wild boar and hare, for example, are among the best to be found. The former is, to my knowledge, only back in the UK after being more or less accidentally reintroduced 400 years since its extinction, but numbers are thought to be less than 1500. When you try to procure wild boar in the UK, it is always either farmed or imported. I have certainly had some reasonable hare in the UK, but it has never been on a par with its Italian or French counterpart. Woodcock in Italy is, in my opinion, as good as, if not better than, any you can find elsewhere in Europe.

However, it is undeniable that the UK management of game is more advanced than in Italy, and that British grouse, pheasant and partridge (along with culled venison) can be exceptional. In Italy, as well as other

Mediterranean countries, a wider range of what can be called game is eaten. This includes several varieties of songbird (known collectively as *osei*) that are trapped illegally during migration. The appetite for polenta e osei is such that millions of birds are killed to satisfy demand. It is also common for legal game-hunting quotas to be exceeded. In a nutshell, what has happened since the 1950s means that there is not a lot of game in Italy any more.

Grilled T-bone Steak Florentine Style

Bistecca alla Fiorentina

One of the most famous dishes in Tuscany, Bistecca Fiorentina (as it is often called) can now be found on restaurant menus all over Italy, be they Tuscan or not. The cut used should always be a thick T-bone, preferably from the Chianina or Maremmana breeds, both of which are generally very large animals, so the steak will be large as well. It is traditionally cooked over a wood fire (often olive wood).

The word bistecca is a corruption of 'beef steak', which, along with the T-bone, is said to have been introduced by the English, who settled in the city of Florence in the early 19th century. However, I'm pretty sure that long before then, people in the region were enjoying the grilled cut, as there are plenty of references to carne alla brace or griglia among the local dishes.

I have been lucky enough to have eaten a Bistecca Fiorentina where every element of the dish, except the salt, was from the closed farm system of the Fontodi estate, near the town of Panzano. The estate is known mainly for its superlative wines, but also produces a superb organic extra virgin olive oil made from a blend of Correggilo and Moraiolo olives, and this was used to finish the dish I enjoyed. Of course, accompanying it with a bottle of Flaccianello, one of the finest Italian red wines, was an added bonus.

Both the wine and olive oil are available in the UK and USA, but probably not the Chianina beef, as the small quantities available tend to be taken by the Manetti family, who own the estate, and the famous local butcher/ restaurateur Dario Cecchini at the Antica Macelleria Cecchini. However, even he uses beef from elsewhere, and to witness him running around and shouting while serving huge cooked T-bones and bone-in rib-eyes is a remarkable sight.

The popularity of Bistecca alla Fiorentina with tourists and visitors to Florence and Tuscany generally means that it is actually fairly hard to find a really good version using top-class Chianina, or any other beef for that matter.

Serves 4–6

- 2 T-bone steaks, 800 g–1 kg each, cut at least 3 fingers thick
- 2 teaspoons sea salt
- freshly ground black pepper (optional)
- 2 sprigs of rosemary
- 1 tablespoon extra virgin olive oil

Method

I don't like grilling top-quality meat over charcoal as I think it tends to mask the subtle flavours, so I strongly recommend you use a non-resinous wood, such as oak, juniper, chestnut, grapevine cuttings or, if you can find it, olive wood. However, excellent results can also be achieved by cooking with a flameproof cast-iron pan and an oven. Whatever method you employ, the main thing is to avoid blackening the meat because it destroys flavour and is also widely believed to be carcinogenic. The aim is to produce meat that is varying shades of brown, from light to dark.

About an hour before cooking, take the T-bones out of the fridge and allow them to come up to room temperature. There is a debate about whether seasoning should be done before, during or after cooking: my preference is to add sea salt and black pepper before cooking and, if necessary, to add more while the cooked meat is resting.

continues over >

If using a cast-iron pan, place it over the heat until very hot. Trim off some of the fat on the T—bones, then place the steaks in the hot pan and cook until the fat renders and the meat starts to brown and caramelize, at least 7—8 minutes on each side (see note below). When the meat is completely sealed and showing a good char on the outside, you can either finish cooking it on the hob, or transfer the whole pan to an oven preheated to 180°C/gas mark 4. The time required depends on the weight of the steaks, but as a guide, a 900 g T-bone will take around 25 minutes.

If cooking the meat on a wood-fired barbecue, the timing is a bit looser because it depends on the type of wood and the heat being generated. As a guide, I would say a 900 g T-bone will take 10—12 minutes per side.

Transfer the steaks to a warmed plate, place a sprig of rosemary on each one and leave to rest in a warm place for at least 10 minutes. This will ensure you have medium or rare steaks that are warm in the centre. Meanwhile, if you have used a pan, add a little water and deglaze it, scraping up the bits in the bottom to produce some meat juices.

Once the steaks have rested, remove the rosemary and drizzle a little olive oil over the meat. Cut around the bone to release the meat. Note that one side is fillet and the other is sirloin, so keep them separate. Cut into slices at least one finger thick, aiming for a uniform thickness.

Arrange the meat on a serving platter, again keeping the fillet and sirloin separate so that people can have some of each. Decorate with the rosemary and spoon some of the meat juices around the edge.

In Tuscany this dish is traditionally served with a side dish of local toscanelli beans, which are cooked in a flask or old wine bottle filled with olive oil and garlic and placed in the dying embers of the hearth for several hours. This is a truly delicious and simple dish, but I find it rather heavy, especially if using Angus, Hereford or Longhorn beef, which are more marbled than Chianina. In many restaurants outside Italy, especially those in 'Anglo-Saxon' countries, which have to cater for meat and two veg aficionados, it will be served with roast potatoes and spinach. My own preference is to serve it simply with rocket and cherry tomatoes, a drizzle of olive oil and a wedge or two of lemon.

Sliced Steak (Tagliata)

Usually made with sirloin or rib-eye off the bone, you can cook it in a pan as above (no need for the oven) and simply lay the slices on top of some rocket and cherry tomatoes. In parts of Italy, especially the north, shavings of Parmigiano Reggiano or Grana Padano are added to the rocket and tomatoes. For me that is an unnecessary addition of flavour and protein.

Mixed Boiled Meats

Bollito Misto

The English name of this recipe does not do justice to what is one of the great Italian meat dishes. It might be better described as a delicious soup — like a pot au feu — containing a rich assortment of fresh and cured meats.

The sauces and condiments served alongside Bollito Misto vary in different parts of Italy. The most common accompaniments are mostarda di Cremona (available from most Italian delis), Salsa Verde (see page 237) and salsa di rafano (horseradish sauce).

Bollito misto originated in northern Italy, particularly around the Po valley, but today can be found in many parts of mainland Italy and the islands too. There are numerous variations of the recipe, but the version that follows is fairly similar to the ones typically found in Piedmont, Lombardy and Emilia-Romagna, and was passed on to me by my relatives in Bologna.

References to bollito misto first appear in Maestro Martino's Libro de Arte Coquinaria (The Art of Cooking), written around 1495. It obviously became very popular because 17th-century gastronomic texts produced by Antonio Latini discuss 38 different ways of preparing it. Similar dishes that involve boiling and simmering mixed meats, poultry and vegetables can also be found elsewhere in Europe, the French pot au feu, the Spanish cocido, and the Portuguese cozido being the best examples.

Bollito misto is found on menus in a wide range of restaurants, from the simplest to the smartest. In the grandest it is often served with great theatre from a trolley that has a number of wells for the different meats and vegetables in their own broth, as well as for the various accompanying sauces. For this reason, it is rarely cooked at home because it is just too much food for most families.

Serves 6–10 people

- 5 litres water
- 4 sprigs of thyme
- 1 bay leaf
- handful of flat leaf parsley
- 10–15 black peppercorns
- 4 large carrots, cut into pieces
- 4 celery sticks, cut into pieces the same size as the carrots
- 2 large onions, each studded with 2 cloves
- 1 large leek
- 1 whole veal tongue or ½ ox tongue, preferably unbrined (if brined, cook alone in water, simmering for 2 hours)
- 2.5 kg beef brisket (shin or thick flank are good substitutes, or all three cuts could be combined)
- 1 whole cotechino, fresh or pre-cooked

- 2 kg beef or veal silverside, left in the piece (if brined, cook it alone in water, simmering for 1 hour before draining and adding to the meat mixture)
- 1 very large chicken or capon, at least 2 kg
- 1 whole shin of veal or 4 pieces thick-cut veal shin
- 1 pig's trotter, carefully trimmed and washed
- 2 big pieces marrowbone, wrapped in muslin (to avoid any marrow leaking into the stock)
- sea salt and freshly ground black pepper
- fresh vegetables to finish the dish, same quantities and preparation as above, or at least enough to cater for the number of people eating

Method

My advice is to prepare this dish 24 hours before eating it and ensure you have a big enough casserole to accommodate all the meat and liquid. Even if serving fewer than six people, it is better to make this dish in at least the quantities listed above. It will keep well for 4 or 5 days in the fridge, and the stock itself can be frozen.

continues over >

Bring the water to the boil, then reduce it to a simmer. Add the herbs, peppercorns, salt and vegetables. If using unbrined tongue, add it now and cook the mixture for 1 hour.

Add the brisket, cotechino (only if fresh) and silverside and cook for another hour. If using brined tongue that you've cooked separately, drain and add to the beef mixture after the first 30 minutes.

Add the chicken, cotechino (if pre-cooked), veal shin, pig's trotter and marrowbone, and simmer very gently for a further 1½ hours. The chicken needs to be checked after 1 hour and carefully set aside if it shows signs of falling apart.

When the dish is ready, discard all the vegetables, peppercorns and herbs, and drain the stock into a bowl or plastic container. Separate the meats – they should be tender enough to be eaten with just a fork – placing each type in its own container. Once cooled, cover all the containers and keep in the fridge for 12–24 hours.

When you are ready to use the stock, remove the layer of fat that will have formed on top during refrigeration.

To reheat the dish, bring the stock to the boil, add the fresh vegetables and simmer for 30 minutes. Taste and add seasoning (the amount required depends on whether you used cooked or uncooked tongue and cotechino). Now add all the meats and simmer until they are hot: this should take no more than 20 minutes or so.

Place the meats and vegetables in a large, shallow serving dish, drizzle with some of the stock (the remainder can be frozen in batches and used in other dishes), and serve with your chosen sauces.

Chopped Raw Meat

Battuto di Carne Cruda

There are various raw chopped beef or veal dishes in Italy, with a variety of names. Those starting with battuto tend to originate in Piedmont and may be followed by the name of the breed — Fassone, for example. In Tuscany, also famous for its beef, I have seen menus with similar dishes called 'sushi di carne cruda'. A more accurate 'translation' from Japanese might be sashimi, which are entirely raw and (unlike sushi) do not contain rice.

In parts of Italy, such as in and around Rome, battuto means soffritto (mirepoix in French), the sautéd mixture of onion, celery and carrot that forms the basis of many dishes.

In my travels around the world I have generally found that restaurants serving steak tartare, the classic French dish of raw beef, use fairly poor or bland meat, which they try to disguise by adding lots of other ingredients. Sadly, some do this even if using really good beef, and that's a pity because, again, the flavour will be masked. It is usually a brave chef or host who will offer this dish with just three or four other ingredients, but if the beef or veal is of good enough quality, the bravery is justified.

Chopped raw meat is often made with horsemeat, especially in the north of Italy, and prepared in a way that closely resembles steak tartare. If you have some good beef or veal, especially a whole fillet, this recipe is a good way to use the tail and/or trimmings that are removed before the steak itself is cooked. Other cuts that can be used but will require a little more work and cleaning are rib-eye and even thick skirt. In fact, the latter will give the most flavour. Whatever cut you opt for, it is better to use beef that has not been dry-aged for a long period — say, more than 28–30 days. If using veal, I recommend rose veal or vitellone, as it generally has much more flavour, especially when raw, than younger purely milk-fed veal.

Serves 4 as a generous first course, or 6–8 as an antipasto

- 400 g beef or veal fillet (see introduction)
- 2 teaspoons sea salt
- 4 tablespoons freshest extra virgin olive oil you can find
- 30 g white Alba truffle or 2 teaspoons colatura di alice (optional)
- 2 tablespoons coarsely chopped flat leaf parsley
- sourdough or ciabatta, sliced and toasted, to serve
- lemon wedges (optional)

Method

Using a very sharp knife, chop the meat and place it in a mixing bowl. Add the salt and oil and mix with your hands or a spoon until the oil emulsifies.

Divide the mixture between individual plates and shave the truffle or drizzle the colatura over the top. Sprinkle some of the parsley around the edge and serve with the toast alongside. Lemon wedges and a pepper mill can be offered to guests if you or they wish, but these are things I would not personally choose to add.

Braised Beef Cheeks

Brasato di Guanciale di Manzo

There are many braised meat dishes in Italy, but the best ones I have eaten were generally in regions where both meat or game are exceptional, and the wine too. In northern Italy perhaps no region better fits those specifications than Piedmont. It is therefore no surprise to see many recipes for various cuts of beef braised in Barolo or other notable but less expensive Piedmontese wines.

Of course, many excellent dishes of beef braised in wine exist in other countries, most notably boeuf Bourguignon and daube à la Provençale in France. I have to say that the dishes I have eaten in Lombardy, Piedmont and Emilia–Romagna are much closer in style and taste to the French ones than some of the versions in central and southern Italy, where tomatoes may be part of the mix.

I sometimes cook this dish with a combination of beef cuts, normally cheek, oxtail and shin, all three of which are perfect for long braising, but if I had to pick only one, I would choose the cheek. You can use pork or veal cheeks if you prefer, but cook the latter for about 30 minutes less than the beef.

This recipe deliberately makes a large amount as the leftovers can be used in other fantastic dishes. They make a great filling for Agnolotti (see page 92), or can be served with tajarin.

Serves 8

- 1.5 kg beef or ox cheeks
- 1 x 75cl bottle Barolo or Barbera d'Alba red wine
- 2 onions, preferably Curregio and Fontaneto (if unavailable, use another sweet variety)
- 4 carrots
- 4 celery sticks
- 3 garlic cloves, unpeeled

- 3 tablespoons rapeseed oil or light olive oil
- 3 teaspoons sea salt
- 1 bay leaf
- 8–10 black peppercorns
- 8–10 juniper berries
- 1 sprig of rosemary or 3 sprigs of fresh thyme
- 500 ml veal stock
- freshly ground black pepper

Method

Some versions of this dish suggest marinating both the meat and vegetables overnight in half a bottle of wine. I think only the meat requires this, as I do not believe that onions, celery and carrots are enhanced in any way by this process. If anything, they become more acidic, which probably explains why some recipes include sugar.

Trim the cheeks of any excess fat, but do not remove all of it. Place them in a large earthenware bowl or plastic container, add half the wine, then cover and leave in a cool place (7–8°C) for 12–24 hours. If you can't find such a cool spot, you can put them in the fridge.

When you are ready to cook, lift the meat out of the marinade and dry it on kitchen paper. Set aside, and reserve the marinade for later use.

Chop the onions fairly thickly but keep the carrot and celery whole, as they will be discarded later.

Heat half the oil in a large, cast-iron casserole dish (an enamelled one is ideal). Add the onions, carrots and celery and garlic and stir them every now and then over a high heat to ensure they are coated in oil. Just as the onions begin to colour, take all the vegetables out of the dish and set aside.

Add the remaining oil to the casserole dish. Sprinkle the cheeks with the salt, then place in the dish and brown thoroughly. Return the vegetables to the dish and add the bay leaf, peppercorns, juniper berries and rosemary. Mix with a wooden spoon, then add the marinade and remainder of the wine. Taste and adjust the seasoning, if necessary.

Increase the heat to deglaze the dish and evaporate the alcohol. Now add the stock, ensuring it is level with the meat but not above it. Bring to the boil, then cover and simmer on the hob for 30 minutes. Meanwhile, preheat the oven to 160°C/gas mark 3.

Transfer the casserole to the oven for 3 hours, turning the meat every 20 or 30 minutes. If the liquid reduces too much and there's a danger of the dish drying out, add any remaining stock or some water. By the end of the cooking time, the liquid should have reduced by about half.

When the meat is cooked (it should be tender enough to cut with a fork), discard all the vegetables. Strain the liquid through a sieve, then return it to the casserole.

The dish can be served with boiled or mashed potatoes, or polenta (see page 136), assuming your previous course is not heavy on carbohydrates. If you want to have vegetables with this dish, discard all those in the casserole 15 minutes before the end of the cooking time and add some freshly sliced carrots.

Braised Shin of Veal

Ossobuco alla Milanese

This classic Milanese dish is thought to have originated in the city's restaurants during the 19th century. It uses a cut or thick slice from the veal shank, which, if not on display in your butcher's, can usually be ordered on request.

Bizarrely, one of the best versions of this dish I have ever eaten was at Ribot, one of my favourite restaurants in Milan, which actually specializes in Tuscan food but has a few Lombardian daily specials. The meat they used was vitellone from Fassone cattle and had a much deeper flavour than usual. If you want to try this dish in its hometown and be certain it is on the menu, head to Antica Trattoria della Pesa, which first opened in 1880.

As always, there is much debate about the authentic recipe for ossobuco, such as whether or not it should include tomatoes or gremolata. More unusual is that it is the only example I can think of where a meat course is served with risotto. For that reason, when ordering it in a restaurant, it is advisable not to have a pasta or rice dish as a first course.

I always make enough ossobuco for eight people even when cooking for four because the leftovers are delicious. Slipped off the bone, the meat can be mixed into tagliatelle or used as a stuffed pasta filling. The latter is an idea first used by Giorgio Locatelli, I think, to wean 'ladies who lunch' on to ossobuco as they found the traditional way of serving it unappealing.

Serves 8

- 150 g unsalted butter, plus extra for thickening if you wish
- 6–8 medium or large slices of veal shank at least 3.5 cm thick
- 2 teaspoons sea salt
- freshly ground black pepper
- 1 large onion, finely chopped
- 150 g chopped carrots
- 150 g celery, chopped
- 400 ml dry white wine

- 1½ teaspoons double-concentrated tomato purée
- 1 bay leaf
- 250 ml veal stock
- Risotto Milanese, to serve (see page 126)

For the gremolata
- finely grated zest of 1 Amalfi lemon
- 1 garlic clove, finely chopped
- 4 tablespoons finely chopped flat leaf parsley

continues over >

Method

Preheat the oven to 180°C/gas mark 4.

Melt the butter in a large flameproof casserole dish and brown the veal. Add the salt and pepper to taste, then transfer the meat to a plate and set aside.

Add the onion, carrots and celery to the fat remaining in the casserole dish and fry over a high heat for 5–10 minutes, until the onions begin to brown. Return the veal to the dish, placing it with the bones upright to prevent the marrow falling out.

Lower the heat and add the wine. When the alcohol has evaporated, carefully stir in the tomato purée and cook for another 5 minutes. Add the bay leaf, then taste and adjust the seasoning before adding the veal stock. Cook for another 5 minutes over a high heat.

Cover the casserole and place in the oven for 2 hours. The meat is ready when it simply comes off the bone with a fork.

To make the gremolata, just combine all the ingredients for it in a bowl and set aside for later.

Transfer the meat to a large serving dish or arrange on individual plates. Using a wooden spoon, squash the vegetables remaining in the casserole dish to make a rough sauce, adding a little butter to thicken it if you wish. Pour the sauce over the veal and sprinkle the gremolata on top. Serve with the Risotto Milanese.

Roast Veal Shank

Stinco di Vitello Arrosto

Veal shank is a wonderful cut for long, slow cooking and is eaten in many parts of Italy. In Alto Adige and Friuli-Venezia Giulia I have had it with local versions of sauerkraut called cavolo cappuccio acido and capuzi garbi o crauti respectively. In central Italy it is often simply roasted in the oven with a few vegetables and red wine.

Roast pork shank is also very popular, especially in the north, and the recipe below works well with both veal and pork. I had this simple dish in an agriturismo in Umbria a few years ago.

Serves 4–6

- I veal shank, about 2.5 kg
- 3 teaspoons sea salt
- freshly ground black pepper
- 2 red onions, chopped
- 4 carrots, chopped
- I celery heart, chopped
- 3 tablespoons extra virgin olive oil
- I bottle Orvieto white wine
- 2 sprigs of rosemary
- Roasted Fennel (see page 326), to serve

Method

Preheat the oven to 180°C/gas mark 4.

Heat a shallow cast-iron dish over a high heat, then add the veal shank and render the fat on the outside of it. Continue frying until the shank is browned and sealed all over. Transfer the meat to a plate, season with the salt and pepper to taste, then set aside.

Put the chopped vegetables into the empty dish, coat them with the olive oil and brown for 5–10 minutes.

Place the veal shank on top of the vegetables, pour in one-third of the wine and add the rosemary. Cook, uncovered, in the oven for 30 minutes, then turn the shank, add a little of the remaining wine and reduce the temperature to 160°C/gas mark 3. Repeat the turning and adding a little wine every 30 minutes for a total cooking time of 2½ hours. When the meat is ready it will literally be falling off the bone. Remove it in portion-size pieces or rough slices, transfer to a warmed serving dish and keep in a warm place.

Scoop or scrape the marrow out of the bone and drip it into the caramelized vegetables remaining in the dish. Pass the mixture through a mouli or passaverdure.

Deglaze the dish with the remaining wine and add these juices to the vegetable mixture. Pass everything through a fine sieve until you have a thick, smooth brown sauce. Reheat if necessary.

Pour the sauce over the pieces of veal shank and serve with roasted fennel.

'Dressed' Milanese Veal Cutlet

Costoletta alla Milanese con Camicia

To clarify butter, melt it very gently over a low heat, then allow to rest for 20—30 minutes before using.

This dish has crossed over from its place of origin, and is now cooked throughout Italy, and in Italian restaurants all over the world. In Argentina and Uruguay it is called 'Milanesa Napolitana', and may also have crossed into Austria hundreds of years ago and 'given birth' to Wiener schnitzel, but that remains (if you'll pardon the pun) a bone of contention. The Wiener schnitzel differs in that the cutlet is dipped in flour as well as beaten eggs and breadcrumbs, then fried in oil or lard (not butter) off the bone.

In claiming the provenance of this dish, the Milanese point to a 12th-century reference in St Ambrose's archive. Lumbolos cum panicio (which translates as 'little chops with breadcrumbs') appears in a document specifying the menu to be served for the feast of Ambrose's brother, San Satiro. Whatever its origins, this dish offers an effective way to seal in the flavour of the veal, whilst also providing contrasting texture and complementary flavour.

Of course, such an iconic dish carries the usual baggage about how it should be prepared and cooked. Most of the debate centres around whether the cutlet should be beaten to make it thinner and flatter, as well as the number of times it should be dipped into the beaten eggs and breadcrumbs. In my view, the thickness debate cannot be resolved: it is largely a matter of taste, so if you like your veal cutlet medium-rare or pink, as I do, beating it until very thin is not required.

I have always liked this dish as a main course with rocket and small tomatoes lightly dressed in olive oil and lemon juice because the rocket adds a touch of bitterness and the lemon and tomato add slight acidity, both of which cut through the butteriness of the cutlet and add contrasting textures.

Serves 4

- 4 veal cutlets on the bone, about 300 g each, trimmed of any excess fat
- 2 eggs, beaten in a soup plate
- 100 g fine breadcrumbs mixed with 2 teaspoons fine sea salt on a flat plate
- 100 g clarified unsalted butter (see Tip opposite)
- lemon wedges, to serve (optional)

For the camicia

- 200 g wild rocket
- 100 g Datterini or cherry tomatoes
- 2 tablespoons extra virgin olive oil
- juice of 1 lemon
- pinch of sea salt
- freshly ground black pepper (optional)

Method

Holding the bone, dip each cutlet in the beaten eggs, allow the excess to drip off, then press into the breadcrumbs to form a consistent crust. Place on a plate, then cover and refrigerate for at least 30 minutes. Remove from fridge at least 45 minutes before cooking.

Heat the clarified butter in a frying pan until it just begins to bubble, then cook the cutlets until medium golden brown on both sides, turning once.

When the meat is ready, combine the camicia ingredients. Put a cutlet on each serving plate and place the camicia on top. Alternatively, you can dress just the cutlet in oil and add half a lemon to each plate, allowing people to squeeze it over both the camicia and the cutlet.

Lamb or Kid in Egg and Lemon Sauce

Abbacchio o Capretto Brodettato

This dish is associated with the area in and around Rome and can be made with milk-fed lamb or kid. If you cannot get either, very young spring lamb will work too. Brodettato means 'little broth', which is a good descriptor of the reduced sauce that accompanies the meat. Versions of this dish are strongly associated with the Sephardic Jews of Rome, who might also add artichokes, as they tend to be in season around the time that young lamb and goat are available.

I believe that shoulder of milk-fed lamb or kid is the best cut for this dish. If you have to use older lamb, be sure to trim off any excess fat as this will make the dish too heavy and adversely affect the taste.

The dish may also be described as in fricassea rather than brodettato, fricassea being a term associated with thickening using egg and lemon. In fact, the use of egg and lemon to thicken or finish soups and sauces is widespread around the Mediterranean. Examples include the Greek avgolemono soup and the similar Turkish terbiye. The difference between these dishes tends to lie in the herbs, meat or vegetables used.

I tend to cook this dish in a cast-iron enamelled casserole, but it is traditionally cooked in a lidded, deep terracotta dish. Some recipes include chopped onion, but I side with those who simply add a few garlic cloves. One school of thought also advises dipping the lamb in flour before browning, but I see no value in that — it just adds an unnecessary flavour and hinders browning. As for it contributing to thickening the sauce, the egg and lemon do that, so I consider flour totally superfluous.

Some versions of this dish use fat rendered from pancetta or guanciale, but a little olive oil and the fat present in the lamb should be all you need.

The trickiest part of the dish is when you add the egg and lemon. It is essential to achieve a smooth, creamy sauce, so you must not let the egg scramble.

Hunter's-style Lamb

(Abbacchio alla Cacciatora)

Another renowned lamb dish associated with Rome and Lazio can be cooked in a very similar way. I add white wine vinegar and rosemary instead of white wine and parsley, and for the finish I take 2 or 3 garlic cloves from the casserole, place them in a bowl with a little of the sauce, add a few chilli flakes and 2 anchovy fillets, and mash these ingredients to a paste. I then blend the paste into the casserole and cook for a further 10 minutes.

Serves 4

- 2 tablespoons olive oil
- 5 garlic cloves, unpeeled
- 1 milk-fed lamb or kid shoulder, cut into small pieces including the bone
- 4 small or medium artichokes (optional)
- 2–3 lemon slices
- 1 large glass (250 ml) dry white wine (I like to use Verdicchio)

- 3 teaspoons sea salt
- freshly ground black pepper
- 1 bay leaf
- 400 ml hot chicken stock or water
- 2 egg yolks
- juice of 1 lemon
- 50 g flat leaf parsley, chopped

Method

Heat the oil in a deep flameproof casserole dish and add the garlic.
Fry briefly, but before it starts to colour, add the meat and brown on
all sides.

Meanwhile, peel off and discard the tough outer leaves of the
artichokes. Trim what is left, then cut into 4 and place in a bowl of cold
water with the slices of lemon.

Add the wine to the meat and stir over a high heat until the alcohol has
evaporated.

Drain the artichokes and add them to the meat, then stir in the salt,
pepper and bay leaf. Add half the stock, stir well, then cover and cook
for 45–90 minutes, checking from time to time that at least three-
quarters of the meat is above the liquid. If the liquid falls lower than
that, top up with the remaining stock or water. The cooking time
depends on the age of the meat used. It is ready when the meat falls off
the bone when poked with a fork. Set aside to cool for 10 minutes or so
– this is to prevent curdling in the next step.

Place the egg yolks in a small bowl, add the lemon juice and beat well.
Add this mixture and half the parsley to the meat, stirring constantly.
The result should be a custard-like creamy sauce that coats the meat and
artichokes.

Serve on individual plates or in a large dish at the table, sprinkling the
remaining parsley on top.

Roast Shoulder of Lamb

Spalla di Agnello Arrosto

Shoulder of lamb is ideal for a long, slow roast. There tends to be more fat than on, say, a leg roast, but it serves to baste the meat and make it really tender. When cooked properly, the lamb will practically fall off the bone.

In Italy this dish is cooked pretty much everywhere, but the choice of herbs may vary, as will whether garlic and sometimes anchovies are inserted into the meat.

Serves 6

- 1 x 3 kg shoulder of lamb, at room temperature
- 3 tablespoons extra virgin olive oil
- 3 teaspoons sea salt
- freshly ground black pepper
- 20 g chopped dried thyme or rosemary

Method

Preheat the oven to 180°C/gas mark 4.

Coat the meat with the olive oil and massage it in with your hands for a good 10 minutes. Set aside to rest for at least 20 minutes, then add the salt, pepper to taste and your chosen herb.

Place the joint in a roasting tin with 50 ml cold water and roast for 2 hours. Transfer to a warm platter and set aside to rest in a warm place for a good 15 minutes.

Meanwhile, dispose of all the fat in the roasting tin, then deglaze the pan over a high heat using a little extra hot water and adding any juices from the meat plate. This will produce a delicious jus.

Cut the meat off the bone in ad hoc slices and chunks and serve.

Pork with Roast Fennel

Maiale con Finocchio Arrosto

Pork and fennel are a perfect match. They are famously paired in salumi and in Lazio's famous porchetta joint, but are also great served side by side. This recipe uses pork chops, but fillet may be used instead. A slow-roasted shoulder of pork is also very good.

Serves 4

- 4 Florence fennel bulbs, fronds chopped and reserved
- 3½ teaspoons sea salt
- 4 tablespoons extra virgin olive oil
- 4 pork chops
- 2 sprigs of thyme or rosemary, chopped
- freshly ground black pepper
- 30 ml chicken or veal stock

Method

Preheat the oven to 180°C/gas mark 4.

Cut the fennel bulbs in half lengthways and place in a baking dish with a splash of water. Sprinkle with 2 teaspoons of the salt and 2 tablespoons of the oil, then bake for 20–30 minutes, until the fennel has caramelized.

Meanwhile, heat the remaining 2 tablespoons of oil in a heavy-based frying pan. When piping hot, salt the chops with the remaining salt on both sides and add them to the pan. Cook each side for 8–10 minutes, until nice and brown. Transfer them to a baking dish, sprinkle with half the chopped herb and add pepper to taste. Set aside to rest for 5 minutes in a warm place.

Discard the fat in the pan, then pour in the stock. Place over the heat and stir well to deglaze the pan and make a sauce for the pork.

Serve each chop on a plate with a few spoonfuls of the sauce on it and the roast fennel beside it. Decorate the fennel with some chopped fennel fronds, and sprinkle the remaining thyme or rosemary over the chops.

Poultry

The Romans are thought to have been the first Europeans to breed poultry, as evidenced in both ancient art and literature. In fact, pigeoncotes dating back to about the 8th century BC can still be seen today in parts of Tuscany.

Popular breeds of chicken include the Leghorn (known as the Livorno in Italy), which was reared in large enough numbers to be exported to the USA as far back as 1828. The very same breed was introduced to the UK from the USA in 1870. Although more suited to egg-laying, it led the way for exports of other breeds to the rest of Europe and the Americas. The Livorno today is one of the breeds used to produce hybrids that are good for meat production.

Various rare breeds are now being revived and are worth looking out for when visiting Italy. The meat from the Tuscan Valdarno, for example, is truly delicious, comparable to the French Poulet de Bresse, the Spanish Castellana Negra or the Canadian Blue Foot. Its eggs too are fantastic; they have a very deep orange yolk and are perfect for making fresh pasta. The Piedmontese Blonde Hen is also highly rated, as is the Morozo Capon, which comes from the same breed. Capons (castrated cocks) are important ingredients in many dishes, either on their own, or boiled with other meats to produce an intense stock. They are also roasted, especially around the turn of the year, and I think the meat is far superior to that of turkey.

I remember a few years ago, when on a short break in Antibes, being invited to dinner in a private home near St Paul de Vence. The host was a French journalist and epicurean, and the coq au vin he served was the best I have ever had. I assumed that the bird was local or at least French, but later found out that our host had driven over the border into Italy to purchase a Gallo Nero della Val di Vara (Vara Valley Black Cock). I have to say that this bird was certainly worth the journey.

Like France, Italy is a country still blessed with plenty of alternatives to the horrors of mass-produced poultry. There are many producers of free-range chicken, turkey, geese, duck, quail and guinea fowl, and the general quality is often at least on a par with the French Label Rouge quality. Often, though, even better quality is available from Italian butchers, food markets and supermarkets. There is no labelling as such, but the seller will vouch for the provenance and quality of the birds. Outside urban areas many families continue the ancient habit of raising 'courtyard' birds for their own meat and egg consumption, and the quality of these is often excellent. Given these things, it is little wonder that many Italians are shocked at the generally poor quality of poultry when they visit countries such as the UK and USA.

If you want to get hold of decent birds in the UK, I recommend you buy French Label Rouge, Sutton Hoo, Fosse Meadows or Packington. The USA has its own superior free-range and organic birds, such as Poulet Rouge, Ashley Farms, Chatham County, NC or Zimmerman Farms.

Roast Chicken

Pollo Arrosto

A good roast chicken is one of the joys in life, but the problem, especially in the UK and USA, is finding a decent chicken to roast. I have eaten roast chicken in most parts of Italy, both in simple restaurants and in private homes, and they have nearly always been a delight. Perhaps that's because they used good free-range birds that had been allowed to grow slowly and naturally.

The simple truth is that no amount of seasoning or other 'tricks' will disguise an inferior bird. But good chickens are not cheap, so I think this dish deserves to be celebrated and eaten, perhaps, in lieu of other roasts made with prime cuts of beef, pork or lamb.

Ideally, try to buy a chicken that has not been packed in plastic. If it has, unwrap it at least half a day before cooking. The best chickens still have their heads and a few feathers on, plus their giblets tucked inside, but it's rare to find them like that in the UK or USA. You need to seek out the best possible bird wherever you may be (see page 233), or perhaps consider rearing your own chickens.

Note that a good slow-grown, free-range chicken should have enough fat to effectively self-baste, so there is no need to use any additional butter or oil.

Roast Capon or Guinea Fowl

Follow the recipe, but note that the cooking time will differ. Capon, being 3–4 kg on average, will need 3–3½ hours in total, while guinea fowl (about 1 kg) will need 1 hour and 20 minutes.

Serves 4

- 1 top-notch chicken, about 1–1.5 kg
- 2 teaspoons sea salt
- freshly ground black pepper
- 1 large Amalfi lemon or 2 of heads garlic (not both)
- sprig of rosemary
- a little hot chicken stock or hot water, for deglazing
- top-quality extra virgin olive oil, for drizzling (optional)

Method

Make sure the chicken is dry on the inside and outside. Preheat the oven to 240°C/gas mark 9.

Cover the inside and outside of the bird with the salt and black pepper. Roll the lemon (if using) on a hard surface, pressing it down a bit to release the juices, then make a dozen small holes in it with a toothpick or fork. Put the lemon (or garlic) and the rosemary in the chicken cavity and place the bird in a roasting tray.

Give the chicken a good blast in the oven for 10 minutes, then lower the heat to 180°C/gas mark 4 and roast for a further 50–80 minutes, depending on size. It's ready when there is no sign of blood when the leg is pulled away from the body. Transfer to a warmed serving plate and set aside to rest for 5–10 minutes.

Meanwhile, deglaze the pan with the hot stock or water over a high heat, scraping up all the bits in the bottom.

Cut the chicken into 4 pieces – 2 legs and 2 breasts – then cut each in half so each plate will have both dark and white meat. Drizzle the roasting juices on 4 serving plates and place pieces of chicken on top. If you like, you can also drizzle some very good olive oil on the chicken just before serving.

Grilled Spatchcocked Chicken with Green Sauce

Pollo alla Brace con Salsa Verde

To spatchcock a chicken, place it on a board breast-side down, with the legs towards you. Using poultry shears or a strong pair of scissors, cut right along the backbone and through the ribs on either side of the parson's nose. Lift out the backbone, open out the chicken and turn it over. Now press down with the heel of your hand so that the meat is all one thickness. Insert two skewers diagonally through the breast and thigh meat to secure the legs and keep the bird flat.

Grilled chicken is a staple in many Italian homes and restaurants. It is not only a nice alternative to roast chicken but allows you to cook a whole chicken in half the time.

Typically, I dress the chicken with salsa verde or Salsa Salmorigano (see page 186), which I use for most grilled meats and fish. I like to keep salsa verde ingredients to a minimum, and use only fresh flat leaf parsley. However, the ingredients used in this sauce vary all over Italy. The only consistent characteristic is that it is green. In Sicily and Calabria I have had versions with a touch of chilli, but you may also come across eggs, mustard and myriad green herbs and leaves in the mix. On one memorable occasion I even had a version that contained brains. Prepared by Leopoldo Bolomini, an Italian chef who worked in the Ritz hotel in London, his version, he told me, was very typical in the borderlands between Lombardy and Piedmont.

The recipe here works well with nearly everything, though I tend to use it mostly with Bollito Misto (see page 216, grilled or baked fish, and roast or grilled chicken.

The key to a successful sauce is to use a sharp knife rather than a food processor. A mezzaluna is the perfect implement.

Serves 4

- 1 medium-large spatchcocked chicken (see tip opposite)
- 6 tablespoons extra virgin olive oil
- 2 teaspoons Trapani sea salt

For the salsa verde

- 1 large bunch of fresh flat leaf parsley, ideally grown outdoors in a hot country; it should be full flavoured with fairly large leaves
- 4 Nola or Cetara anchovy fillets
- 2 garlic cloves, crushed
- 1 teaspoon sea salt
- 2 tablespoons capers
- 1 tablespoon red wine vinegar
- freshly ground black pepper
- 150 ml extra virgin olive oil

Method

Coat the chicken with the olive oil, sprinkle with the sea salt, then allow it to rest for 30 minutes.

The meat can be cooked on a barbecue, under a grill or in a griddle pan, so preheat as necessary. Cook the chicken, skin-side down first, for 15–20 minutes, depending on the size of the bird, then repeat on the other side. When it is ready, you should be able to easily pull it apart with your hands into 4–6 pieces.

While the chicken is cooking, make the salsa verde. Cut off and discard three-quarters of the parsley stalks. Place the remaining parsley on a wooden board and chop it using a mezzaluna. The texture (rough or fine) is up to you, depending how you like your salsa verde. I opt for a rough chop if it's going to accompany roast or grilled chicken or fish, but I prefer an almost paste-like version for serving with bollito misto. *continues over* >

Add the anchovy fillets, garlic and salt to the parsley and continue chopping until they are combined.

For a loose, rough-textured salsa, put the chopped ingredients into a large bowl, add some pepper and pour in the oil slowly whilst stirring constantly with a wooden spoon. The finished salsa should look like very wet chopped parsley with specks of anchovy and garlic still being visible.

For a paste-like consistency, put the parsley mixture into a marble mortar, add the chopped capers and vinegar, and pound together, using a light circular movement of the pestle against the sides. When the parsley drips bright green liquid, add the pepper and a thin layer of olive oil, and mix very lightly. Keep drizzling in the oil and pounding until you have used all the oil and achieved a paste-like consistency.

Both versions are best prepared just before you plan to eat. I do not recommend keeping it in the fridge. Instead, make as much as you need and eat it all.

Place the chicken pieces in a serving dish and dress it with the salsa.

Chicken with Salsa 'Nduja

Put 50 g 'nduja and 2 tablespoons extra virgin olive oil in a bowl and mix to form a rough paste. Smear olive oil all over the chicken and sprinkle with 2 teaspoons sea salt. Now rub the 'nduja paste all over the chicken. Grill for 15–20 minutes on each side. If you wish, you can place about 8 Tropea onions around the chicken while it cooks; these will take only 10–15 minutes, so need to be removed before the chicken is ready. Transfer the bird to a serving dish and drizzle a little olive oil over it before serving.

Cured
Meat

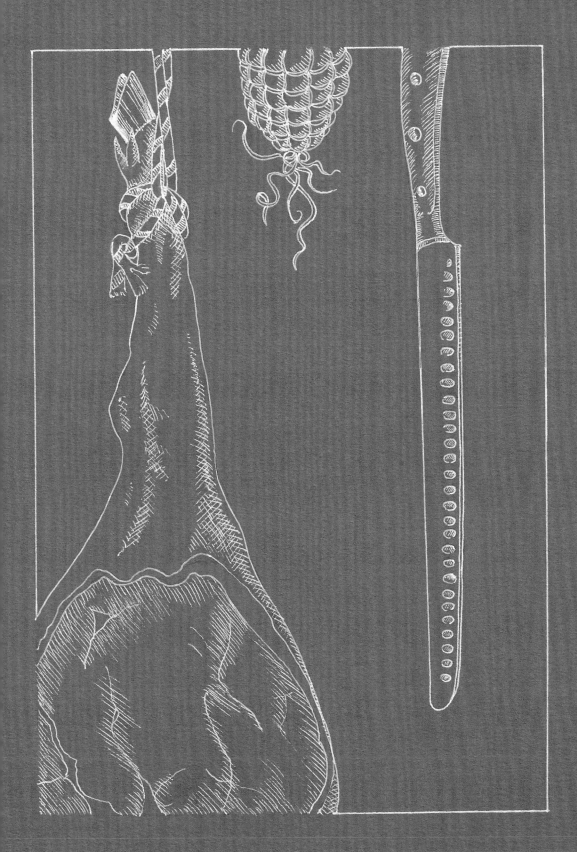

Cured Meat

As they keep and travel well, cured meats are a wonderful way to taste the best of Italy wherever you may be. Most Saturday mornings when I visit the Ham & Cheese Company in London and they start slicing the amazing finocchiona from Carlo Pieri, the aroma of the fennel seeds and pollen transports me, if only for a few minutes, to the Tuscan hills.

The methods for preserving and curing meat, as we know them today, were first devised by the Celts around 200 BC, and then further developed by Germanic cultures. In times before refrigeration, meats were cured out of necessity — so they kept well and could be saved for times of the year when fresh food was limited. In inland areas such as Salsomaggiore, near Parma in Emilia-Romagna (arguably the epicentre of Italian cured meats, as my relatives keep reminding me), the Celts found ways to extract salt from the soil to make their favoured meat (pork) last longer.

However, preserving meat is known to have started long before the Celts. There is evidence from about 5000 BC of the Sumerian and Akkadian peoples in Mesopotamia (present-day Iraq) using salt to preserve meat, and Jews are thought to have done the same around 3000 BC, using salt from the Dead Sea. In China, all evidence points to salt being used to cure and preserve meat as far back as 1300 BC.

The Romans and Greeks were curing meat with salt around 200 BC, the former having learned the method from the latter. It is also thought that the Romans saw the benefits of pig herding to produce pork with higher levels of fat, which improved both the flavour of the meat and the curing process itself. This was in contrast to the nomadic populations who tended to consume much leaner, almost wild, pigs.

Historically, pigs were raised all over Italy, apart from the coastal regions of Tuscany, Liguria, Lazio and Apulia. These areas have long been associated with the cultivation of olive trees and the production of olive oil, which probably explains the absence of any famous cured meat products.

The generic Italian word for 'cured meat' is *salume* (plural *salumi*) and should not be confused with *salame* (plural *salami*), a particular category of salume made with seasoned minced pork. A *salumeria* is a shop or business that sells a wide range of salumi, amongst other foods, which they either make themselves or buy from producers and wholesalers. It's also quite usual for butchers to make salumi. In San Angelo Scalo, near Montalcino in Tuscany, for example, Carlo Pieri makes arguably the best finocchiona and salame Toscano from pigs he raises in his smallholding.

Salumi can be divided into two types. The first are produced from a whole cut of meat, usually a shoulder or thigh (prosciutto di Parma, for example). The second are made from *insaccato* — minced or chopped meat, fat and herbs stuffed into a casing — and include fresh sausages, such as mortadella (which is cooked), and a variety of dry, aged salumi, such as salame di Felino.

Rural populations in Italy and across Europe still slaughter their pigs in the autumn and consume more or less every part. The bits that are not eaten roasted or grilled are made into sausages, blood sausages, salami and a variety of cooked and cured hams.

As discussed on page 4, Italian migrants took many aspects of their food with them, so it is no surprise to see versions of regional Italian salumi made locally in the countries where they have settled. Other incentives for making their own arose from the logistical difficulties of importing these products and from restrictions imposed on them by food safety agencies. During the 1960s, for example, the US Department of Agriculture (USDA) imposed a ban on Italian cured meats after traces of swine vesicular disease were found in them. This ban was not rescinded until 2000, and then only partially, when mortadella and prosciutto from Parma and San Daniele were allowed into the USA again. It was another 13 years before restrictions were lifted on cured meats from the regions of Lombardy, Emilia-Romagna, Veneto and the provinces of Trento and Bolzano. What this actually means is that producers from these parts of Italy can apply to receive importation certification. Unfortunately, this process is expensive, with estimates starting at $100,000, so it's likely that only large-scale producers will be able to afford it.

The current US regulations still prevent a number of products being imported: for example, lardo di Colonnata, finocchiona and various wild boar salumi from Tuscany, as well as other wonderful products from all over the Italian mainland and islands. In the UK, there are currently no restrictions on imports.

Wherever salumi are produced, there are artisans producing superb products, as well as large-scale food groups churning out ordinary, often poor products. Among the best in the USA are Salumi Artisan Cured

Meats in Seattle, Washington; Fra' Mani and Boccalone in Oakland, California; La Quercia in Norwalk, Iowa. Another interesting development is Creminelli Fine Meats in Salt Lake City, Utah, where salumi are produced using the long-established artisan methods of the Creminelli family in Piedmont. Added to this, an increasing number of chefs focused on Italian food, both in the US and beyond, are following Paul Bertolli and Chris Cosentino's example of adding salumerias to their restaurant operations.

In the UK, Jacob Kenedy makes a large proportion of his own salumi for his restaurant Bocca di Lupo in London; and Trealy Farm in Monmouthshire produces a number of Italian-style salumi within its range of cured meats. Cannon & Cannon have recently emerged as leading wholesalers of British artisan charcuterie and salumi, which they also sell in markets and through their own shop in Brixton, south London.

In many ways, charcuterie and salumi are following the pattern set by the artisan cheese-making revival that has evolved in the UK, Ireland and, to a lesser extent, in the USA over the last 30 years. Both, of course, are typical exemplars of 'slow food'. Also, many of the locally produced versions of salumi are better than those of the very large Italian producers. However, I have not yet tasted examples that can match those made by the very best artisan producers in Italy. Perhaps that's because they often raise their own rare-breed animals and, in some cases, have unique advantages, such as a microclimate or a specific animal feed.

Salumi are, in my view, the perfect start to a meal as an antipasti eaten with bread or combined with fruit. But some, such as cotechino, can also be a main course, while others, such as guanciale and pancetta, can be used as an ingredient in other dishes.

This chapter does not provide any recipes or instructions for curing your meats at home. If you would like to venture into curing territory, consult Michael Ruhlman and Brian Polcyn's excellent book *Salumi: The Craft of Italian Dry Curing* (see page 469).

The following pages discuss a selection of what I consider to be the best Italian salumi — and there are certainly enough varieties and producers to choose from. My recommendations are intended to save you the challenge of sourcing top-notch products, but don't be afraid to strike out on your own and do your own taste tests.

The raw salumi discussed here would probably all feature in my dream selection for an antipasto of *affettati di salumi*. When in Italy, look out for that term on restaurant menus as it is rare that the nearest locally cured meats do not feature among the selection. Outside Italy, numerous restaurants and gastropubs serve what they call 'charcuterie boards', and these will most likely include some of the same selections.

Raw Salumi

The majority of salumi consist of raw ingredients that are dry-cured, which means hanging them in an airy place to dry out. While this process obviously draws out the moisture, it also intensifies the flavours. The best examples are discussed below.

CULATELLO

It is generally accepted that Culatello di Zibello PDO is the king of salumi. Indeed, many would argue that it is the greatest cured meat in the world – superior even to the best prosciutto crudo and jamón Iberico.

It is made using meat from the muscular inner thigh of the pig, which is skinned, deboned, wrapped in a natural casing (a pig's bladder, which is thoroughly washed and cleaned), then tied with twine into its traditional pear shape. The meat is then salted and seasoned by hand with black pepper, and often white wine and/or a touch of garlic. After a week of dripping, the product is subjected to initial drying, which can take one or two months, depending on the weather, and must take place in a natural, temperate but not air-conditioned environment. After that comes the maturing process, which normally lasts 16–18 months, but can be up to 30 months.

The cured meat is then brushed under running water to remove mould. After that, the string and casing are removed and the culatello is scrubbed and rinsed. It is then wrapped in a cloth, which has been dampened in dry, non-aromatic white wine. Care is taken to cover the leanest and driest part first, namely the pointed end.

The word 'culatello' means 'little backside or bum', and the product is named after the cut of pork from which it is made. According to the Consortium of Culatello di Zibello (founded in 2009), the product was already being made as far back as the 14th century. The first official record, though, seems to be in documents dated 1735, which are housed in the municipality of Parma. The first literary references date back to the 19th century, when the local poet Giuseppe Callegari and the sculptor Renato Brozzi exchanged views on culatello with the famous poet Gabriele D'Annunzio, who along with the composer Giuseppe Verdi, a native of the region, were great aficionados of the cured meat.

The flatlands around the river Po in the province of Parma, where winters are cold and foggy and summers are hot and steamy, are the heartland of culatello production. The municipalities of Polesine, Busetto, Soranga, Roccabianca, San Secondo, Sissa, Colorno and Zibello form the designated area for PDO culatello, all of them sharing the necessary microclimate, local knowledge and traditions to produce this exquisite salumi.

In Italy, food retailers simply hang whole culatello alongside other salumi. Once started, though, they are transferred to glass-fronted refrigerated counters. The product is often exported in vacuum packs, and sometimes sold in halves. It is also available sliced and packaged, like prosciutto di Parma, but I don't recommend buying it this way. Culatello should be purchased as close as possible to the time of being eaten; better still, invest in a manual slicer (see page 57) and cut it yourself minutes before eating. Culatello is much smaller than a whole prosciutto crudo, so is perfect for slicing at home.

A whole culatello will keep for up to 12 months if refrigerated at 4–8°C, or if hung in a dry place where the temperature range is 17–20°C. However, many environmental health agencies recommend refrigerating the ham after it has been started. My own recommendation is to vacuum-pack it at the end of each use and consume it within two weeks. Wrapping it tightly in cling film is no substitute, I'm afraid. That will preserve it for only a couple of days. It is for this reason that the product is usually found only in retail outlets where turnover is fairly rapid, or in restaurants.

In the area where culatello is produced, it is normally sliced a little bit thicker than prosciutto crudo and served with excellent local bread and butter, and sometimes with fresh pasta tossed in butter and Parmigiano Reggiano. When eaten with bread and butter, it is often served with a glass of low–alcohol, lightly sparkling red wine – perhaps one made from the Fortanella grape.

If culatello is the king of salumi, Massimo Spigaroli and his brother Luciano are the kings of culatello-making. Operating from the 14th-century Antica Corte Pallavicina estate in Polesine, they produce one of the finest cured meats in the world. Both the Slow Food-listed Culatello di Zibello PDO 'Oro Spigaroli' aged for 24–40 months and the version produced with the rare breed Parma Black Pig during the 'cold' months from October to February are, in my view, amongst the very best cured meats in the world.

Watching the staff wash their hands in white wine and rub sea salt into the raw, deboned pork rump is a remarkable sight. What happens afterwards is truly magical: the rumps are wrapped in a thin pig's bladder and cured for up to 40 months in a 15th-century, custom-made cellar with two open windows at either end. One window is for the local fog to penetrate and the other is for air circulation. The 1000 identified friendly bacteria and the unique humid and foggy microclimate produces one of the wonders of the gastronomic world.

The Spigaroli brothers produce a range of world-class salumi, including strolghino and coppa, as well as wine, jams and condiments from the fruits of the estate. There are two restaurants, one formal, the other more simple. Massimo is a renowned chef in his own right, and if you are going to eat culatello only once in your life, this is the place to do so. I would be amazed if you leave without buying some culatello and other salumi to take with you.

Felino Salame PGI

Another classic salumi from Emilia-Romagna, Felino salami is made from fine to medium minced pork formed into a sausage shape, with one end slightly larger than the other. When well made, this salami leaves a soft and lingering flavour on the palate.

The salami is made in the town of Felino (which has a museum celebrating this cured meat and its history) and also in a few neighbouring municipalities. While there are producers outside the designated area, they have to call their product 'salami tipo Felino' (Felino-style salami).

Felino Salame PGI is produced exclusively with fresh pork meat from a traditional breed of animal raised in Emilia-Romagna, Lombardy, Piedmont, Veneto and Tuscany. It is made mainly with prime cuts of pork that have had all connective tissues removed, and contains about 25 per cent fat. After salting, it is usually seasoned with herbs, black pepper, white wine and crushed garlic. These are the key ingredients that create the salami's characteristic aroma and flavour. Some recipes include other herbs and spices, and these vary from producer to producer. In my experience, a good producer using the best-quality pork will tend to keep the seasoning to a couple of herbs, salt, pepper and white wine. A stuffing process, very similar to sausage-making, then follows after which the salami is tied with string at regular intervals along its length, and a loop is left at one end. The salami is then hung in a controlled environment for 29–51 days.

The Oxford Companion to Italian Food notes that Giovanni Ballerini, who has written extensively about both the history of the pig in Italy and salumi, suggests that there may be a link between Felino salami and Felsina, the ancient Etruscan name for the city of Bologna. In the beautiful baptistery of Parma (1196–1307) is a plate depicting the zodiac sign of Aquarius, and it clearly shows two salami draped over a saucepan. The shape and size of these salami suggest they could be early examples of the traditional Felino product.

If you buy Felino salami from a retailer who slices it for you, it should be stored in the fridge and eaten on the same day. If you buy a whole salami, it can be kept out of the fridge for a few weeks in temperatures that do not exceed 28°C, but, once started, wrap the cut end in cling film and store it in the fridge for up to a week. Generally speaking, I find this particular salami best eaten within a week of purchase.

Most Italian delis will have either a Felino or 'tipo Felino' salami as part of their offering, and it can often be found in other delis or food halls that stock a range of salumi and charcuterie from around Europe. Again, avoid buying it pre-sliced and vacuum-packed as it is neither economic nor particularly good to eat. Traditionally, it should be cut at a 60-degree angle with a sharp knife to highlight the grain of the meat and to avoid any crumbling.

Felino salami is best eaten on its own with bread or as part of a selection of salumi. In and around Felino and Parma, people will usually drink Lambrusco or a Malavisa-based sparkling wine with it.

Finocchiona

As the name suggests, finocchiona is a fennel-flavoured salume. It comes from Tuscany, where it is made by artisan butchers as well as large-scale producers. When made well, it is wonderful and moist, with the distinct aroma of wild fennel, which can be detected even before it enters your mouth.

Individual producers may vary the ingredients slightly, but generally speaking, the key cuts used are pancetta (pork belly) and shoulder, plus pork fat, which the better producers take from the back. Sometimes guanciale (pig cheek) may be used as well as or instead of pancetta. The meat is chopped either by hand with a knife, or passed through a mincer to produce a medium to fine grind, Salt, pepper, crushed garlic, wild fennel seeds and sometimes their pollen are mixed in. The seasoned meat is then set aside to absorb the flavours for 24 hours. After that, it is stuffed into a natural casing, tied with string and hung in a cool, dry and well-ventilated environment for a minimum of five months.

Among the legends circulating about the origins of finocchiona, the most popular is that it was created by a thief who stole a salume in the city of Prato and hid it in a cart full of wild fennel. When he came to collect it some time later, the fennel had apparently infused its flavour into the stolen salume. It is actually more likely that fennel was purposely added in the Middle Ages to replace the black pepper, which was imported and much more expensive.

In light of the legend about the thief, it is interesting to note that the word finocchio (fennel) has led to the verb infinocchiare, meaning 'to cheat or fool someone'.

The following day, based on the information he gave me, I headed to the shop belonging to artisan butcher Carlo Pieri in Sant Angelo Scalo, close to Montalcino. Carlo not only makes superb salume from his own pigs, but also very decent Sangiovese wine and olive oil from produce grown on his own land. He eschews cultivated herbs, and seasons his finocchiona with fennel seeds and pollen that his mother collects from the hedgerows around the village every September. It is these things that give his finocchiona their unique aroma and flavour. Elliott John, one of the people behind the Ham & Cheese Company in London, and (as far as I'm aware) the only UK importer of Carlo Pieri's salumi, says it smells like a mild curry. My own view is that it has an eastern aroma, but I would not go so far as to say it is curry-like.

I am delighted that I can find this finocchiona in London, but there are several other good producers who have found importers in the UK. These include L'Antica Macelleria Falorni based in Greve in Chianti, which has an excellent range of salumi made with both pork and wild boar. At the time of writing, Tuscan salumi cannot be imported into the USA, so consumers there will have to find the best versions made locally.

The best finocchiona I have ever tasted was when I was sampling some wines on a well-known estate near Montalcino. I remember that the wines were underwhelming, but all the salumi that was served with them was really top notch, especially the finocchiona. I'm fairly sure I upset the wine-maker when I quizzed him about its origins, rather than asking him about his wine.

Lardo

Lardo is very different from all the salumi discussed so far, as it is essentially composed entirely of pigs' back fat. It should not be confused with lard, which is *strutto* in Italian, and is used for pastry and general cooking purposes. The best lardo is lardo di Colonnata, a unique product that combines two of Tuscany's most famous products – the pig and the famous marble of Carrara, which is mined in Colonnata.

The fresh back fat is trimmed of any remaining meat until it is just a perfect white slab. It is then layered with salt, pepper, fresh rosemary and sage and a mixture of spices, such as nutmeg, cinnamon, coriander and cloves (the combination may differ between producers). The layers fit perfectly inside specially carved marble troughs known as conche, and are left to cure for six months. There is no need for preservatives or refrigeration as the process is done only in the colder months of the year. Added to that, the caves in which the porous marble containers are kept have their own microclimate, perfect for curing.

The resulting pure white *lardo* is a fragrant, creamy block of sweet, porcine flavour, covered with a crust of spices and coarse salt. Obviously, something special happens in those marble troughs, which makes this a unique product, with an incredible texture and flavour that most people find irresistible.

Lardo di Colonnata production is thought to go back to Roman times, but during the 1990s it famously became victim to EU health regulations, when there were

objections to the marble containers. Thankfully, that threat passed and it now has IGP status, and is listed in Slow Food's *Ark of Taste* catalogue.

Another fine product, lard d'Arnad, is made in the Val d'Aosta. This has PDO status and is also very popular over the border in France. It differs from lardo di Colonnata in several ways: the seasoning is different, the maturation is traditionally done in wooden tubs, and it also goes through a process of brining. Sometimes retailers and restaurants refer simply to 'Italian lardo', so it is worth finding out which of the two types is being offered.

Lardo is also made outside the IGP-designated area in Tuscany, and can be very good, but it does not hit the notes achieved by lardo di Colonnata. Currently, no lardo is actually made in the UK, but the USA has a number of local producers.

Lardo di Colonnata is exported all over Europe and to parts of Asia, and can normally be found in high-end food retailers and online. It is usually cut into very thin, almost transparent slices and served on its own or with other salumi, or on slices of bread or crostini. Once started, it should be kept in the fridge and eaten within a few days.

Parma Ham
Prosciutto di Parma

There is no doubt that Parma ham is one of the most famous air-dried meats in the world, but that can be a double-edged sword, particularly for the purchaser. The name suggests quality, but, as with everything, this is variable. Unfortunately, there are many volume-produced hams and/or 'young' hams on the market to satisfy the very large global demand. Generally speaking, there is nothing actually wrong with them, as Parma ham is one of the most controlled and protected cured meats in the world. However, when you do taste a really good one, you quickly realize why many people consider it the very best air-dried ham.

The word *prosciutto* comes from the Latin and describes the ham at the beginning of the drying process: *pro* means 'before', while *sciutto* comes from *exsuctus*, meaning 'sucked out', or in other words 'dried'.

Production of this exceptional ham centres around the town of Langhirano, located within the area defined by the Parma Ham Consortium (CPP), which includes 33 municipalities south of the via Emilia. It is often said that the ham needs four ingredients: pork, salt, air and time.

The consortium now requires that pigs used in the production of Parma ham must be bred in one of 11 northern and central Italian regions. Only three breeds can be used — Large White, Landrace and Duroc — and they must be fed on cereals and whey from the production of Parmigiano Reggiano cheese. These breeds help to

produce a consistent product, but they have, in fact, replaced the traditional local black pigs, which are now being used by some producers to make other types of 'premium' salumi.

Nowadays, only sea salt is used for curing, though some of the best artisan producers use sale di Cervia (see page 447). The *maestro salatore* (salt master) is responsible for gauging the amount and overseeing the whole curing process.

The Parma region has a microclimate that is ideal for dry-curing. Sea breezes from Liguria cross the Apennines, losing their humidity and some of their saltiness in the process. Now temperate, they are perfect for the maturing process, blowing through the long, narrow windows of the curing rooms and helping to dry the neatly positioned hams. The ham is first cleaned and salted, then left to rest for up to three months. After that it is washed several times to remove the salt, and hung in a dark, well-ventilated environment. After about seven months, the ham is smeared with *sugna*, a mixture of rice flour, salt and pork fat, to stop it drying too quickly for the remainder of its maturation. This final period is one of the key variables in producing the ham. At 12 months, when *pàr sut* in local dialect, *asciutto* in Italian, and 'dry' in English, it is tested with a horse-bone needle for quality and maturity, and if it passes, it will receive the Ducal Crown firebrand. Producers can then sell the hams for slicing and packaging, or mature them for up to another 24 months.

Typically, whole hams are sold at 18, 24, 32 and 36 months. (I consider 24 months to be the minimum for producing outstanding prosciutto di Parma.) The hams may be on the bone or deboned. The latter tend to be slightly more expensive and incur less waste.

It is impossible to pinpoint when prosciutto di Parma originated, but it is known that Hannibal stopped in the Parma area to eat local bread and meats in the 3rd century BC. During Roman times, ham from Parma was certainly one of the delicacies that featured on banquet tables. Indeed, the practice of pairing melon or figs with the ham may have roots in the Roman custom of starting meals with fruit.

One of the earliest references to ham production in Parma appeared about 100 BC in the writings of Cato, who described the practice of burying pork legs in barrels filled with salt. The meat was then dried and smoked. Evidently, the process of making air-cured prosciutto was refined over time, so the smoking step was discontinued.

As evidenced by the calendar carvings on the main door of Parma's 13th-century cathedral, November was the month for killing pigs, and it is also known that the curing of Parma ham historically started at this time of year because a cool temperature plays such an important role in the process. Firm evidence also exists that pork meat was cured in the area during the 14th century, using salt from the wells of Salsomaggiore. After that time, still-life paintings testify to the fact that cured hams were a regular part of household provisions, and probably not considered a luxury product.

Until the 19th century, curing was done in a variety of buildings, and even private homes were pressed into service during the curing season. With hams suspended from the ceiling of every room, the inhabitants of ham-producing towns were said to literally eat, sleep and breathe ham! Eventually, drying was transferred to purpose-built 'apartment houses' with long, narrow windows that opened to allow fresh air to circulate around the hams. Artisan producers use much the same method today, while many of the large producers have modern, temperature-controlled facilities that aim to mimic the classic conditions for every stage of production and maturation.

When buying prosciutto di Parma, the consumer is getting a fully traceable product. Within 30 days of birth, young piglets have both rear legs stamped with an indelible mark that indicates their birthplace, the breeder's code and the month of birth. After the pigs are slaughtered and jointed, a special code identifying the slaughterhouse is fire-branded on to the skin of each freshly trimmed leg.

During the salting stage, a metal seal bearing the consortium's acronym (CPP) and the date at which processing began is attached to each ham.

Finally, the five-point Ducal Crown brand — the CPP's guarantee — is added, along with the identification code of the producer responsible for the curing.

Prosciutto di Parma is certified PDO (Protected Designation of Origin) by the European Union, so you might find the PDO seal on the product label.

If, like most people, you do not purchase a whole ham, the best way to buy prosciutto di Parma is from someone who will slice it for you. Ideally, it should be cut thinly and eaten within 4–5 hours, but certainly on the same day. A good shop or market stall will interleave greaseproof paper between the slices and wrap the whole package in greaseproof. The ham should then be sealed in a paper bag, ideally one lined with foil on the inside.

Packed and deboned hams can be kept for up to six months, provided they are refrigerated at 4–8°C. Hams on the bone can be hung and kept for 12 months in a place with a steady temperature of 17–20°C. The environmental health authorities in many countries advise refrigerating whole hams once have they been started.

The quality of a ham depends on the producer, and the best way to source one to your liking is to do multiple tastings. However, if you don't have the time or confidence to undertake this research, it's best to put your trust in the retailer or restaurateur.

When I was sourcing for the delicatessen I co-founded in London, I visited many producers and restaurants around Parma, and also checked what both Peck in Milan and Volpetti in Rome were currently offering in their wonderful emporiums.

In Parma I always eat at Ristorante Cocchi, where they have some of the very best salumi on offer. This restaurant, incidentally, is where the great epicurean and AC Milan coach Carlo Ancelotti took his player David Beckham to be educated about tortelli and salumi. In his autobiography,

Preferisco la Coppa (I Prefer the Cup), Ancelotti made a word-play in the title, cleverly uniting his two passions, football and food. *Coppa* stands for 'cup' (as in trophy), but also alludes to coppa Piacentina, one of the great local salumi. In fact, shadow Ancelotti closely and you will always find the best Italian restaurants and salumi — either in London, where he managed Chelsea between 2009 and 2011, or in Italy.

Italian restaurants tend to source from one or two local producers, and in Parma itself one of the best selections can be found at Ai Due Platini. However, if salumi is your main focus, visit the Spigaroli brothers' Al Cavallino Bianco restaurant in Polesine Parmense, the PDO-producing area for culatello (see page 248). The food is superb and the salumi they make (especially their superlative culatello di Zibello) is, in my opinion, the apotheosis. Being outside the designated area, the Spigarolis do not produce prosciutto di Parma, but they do produce some of the best hams I have tasted.

In terms of prosciutto crudo (raw ham), of which both prosciutto di Parma and prosciutto di San Daniele are the most famous and widely available, I must note that it is possible to find hams in other parts of Italy that are just as good as these iconic products. Although made with a larger variety of pigs reared on different terroirs, they are nonetheless excellent products. A few of the best are listed overleaf, but can be hard to obtain outside Italy as they tend to be produced in small volumes.

Prosciutto Toscano PDO — from Tuscany
Jambon de Bosses — from the Val d'Aosta
Crudo di Cuneo PDO — from Piedmont
Prosciutto di Carpegna PDO — from Le Marche
Prosciutto di Norcia PGI — from Umbria
Prosciutto di Modena PDO — from Emilia-Romagna
Prosciutto Veneto Berico-Euganeo PDO — from the Veneto

Some of the best Parma ham is made by the artisan producer Piero Montali and his two sons, Raphaele and Stefano, in Langhirano. It is produced only from pigs slaughtered between May and December, as they believe that meat produced in the early months of the year is more likely to have problems during the maturation period.

Montali hams are matured in big brick drying rooms, where wooden hanging rails, the current of sweet mountain breezes and temperatures of up to 18°C encourage enzymes and thus flavour development. This approach is very different from that of some very large producers, who use steel drying racks and concrete cold rooms in order to meet UK and US standards required for export products.

Volpetti Salumeria in Rome, where I first tasted the superb Montali ham, sells it in a category of its own — Prosciutto Piero Montali. In the UK the excellent Ham & Cheese Company wholesales and retails Montali's Sant Ilario Prosciutto di Parma, supplying some of the better restaurants in London. The ham is also available through their retail outlets in Borough Market and Spa Terminus in south London.

Despite being very traditional in his approach, Piero Montali is considered a maverick for making limited quantities and adopting a very strict selection policy when it comes to pigs. He is, in fact, just one of many food-producers and wine-makers going their own way to produce exceptional products.

Now we come to the question of how to eat top-quality prosciutto crudo. I recommend that you have it thinly sliced with some good bread. Alternatively, when melon or figs are in season, it is wonderful as an antipasto (see Essential Ingredients, page 53). I remember being lucky enough to have tickets for the 1990 West Germany v England World Cup semi-final in the Stadio delle Alpi in Turin, and having a wonderful panino made with freshly sliced prosciutto di Parma in a rosetta roll and a decent glass of red wine. This snack was a world away from the appalling and expensive food served in football stadiums in the UK.

Although there are a number of recipes that use prosciutto crudo wrapped around fish or meat, I generally find that the ham loses its subtle flavour and moisture when cooked. However, if you have a whole ham on the bone and the last bits can't be cut with a slicer, don't waste them. Remove them with a knife and use them in soups and pasta dishes.

In most parts of Italy prosciutto is often used as part of a panino (sandwich), either on its own in a crusty rosetta roll or ciabatta, or combined with cheese, such as mozzarella. Panini are often toasted, especially if cheese is one of the ingredients, and have become an integral (and ubiquitous) part of Italian 'fast food'.

Cooked Salumi

Unlike the salumi discussed above, those listed below are cooked or need to be cooked before eating. They can also be added as an ingredient to other dishes.

Cotechino

Cotechino is a sausage consisting of minced lean pork, fat and rind seasoned with mace, pepper, cloves, cinnamon, nutmeg and aromatic herbs. This mixture is stuffed into a natural casing made from cotica (pork rind), which gives the sausage its name. As part of Emilia-Romagna's rich cuisine, it is traditionally eaten with lentils around the start of the New Year as both are symbols of good luck.

These days in Italy cotechino is rarely made at home. Instead, fresh ones are bought from good butchers, or pre-cooked ones are bought in food shops and supermarkets. Mass-produced ones tend to be in a synthetic casing. Cotechino is thought to date from the 16th-century siege of Mirandola city fortress, when a local chef came up with the idea of preserving the remaining livestock by mincing the meat and stuffing it into its rind.

Nowadays, cotechino is produced in nearly all the provinces on the Paduan plain. However, there are some variations to the meat mixture. The Modena PGI version, which is my favourite, uses the lean parts of streaky pork, to which fat (mostly from the jowl and belly) is added. Another version of the same mixture is stuffed into a rind that includes the pig's trotter, so it is called *zampone*, which means 'trotter'.

You are most likely to find uncooked cotechino during the months of December and January, while pre-cooked cotechino is available at any time. Some of the latter (those made by the Spigaroli brothers, for instance) are excellent, but only a limited number is produced. I recently tried the pre-cooked cotechino and zampone from Salumificio Ferrari Erio & Co in Modena, and both were very good indeed.

Fresh cotechino should be treated like raw meat, and stored in the fridge for a few days at most before cooking. The pre-cooked varieties normally have a 'best by' date on the wrapping, and this ranges from three months to a year, depending on the type of packaging.

How to Cook Cotechino

To cook a fresh cotechino, pierce it in several places, then put into a large saucepan of water and boil for 20 minutes. After that, simmer it for 3 hours, occasionally skimming off the fatty film that rises to the surface. A pre-cooked cotechino is simply pierced and simmered (no boiling) for 1 hour. The traditional way of serving cotechino is sliced and placed on a bed of lentils.

Cotechino and/or zampone usually feature in Bollito Misto (see page 206), but two of my aunts — one from Modena and the other from Bologna — always disagreed about the inclusion of cotechino. The only way to stop them arguing was to move the conversation on to discussing whether capon or hen should be included. My aunts' dispute was not unusual because bollito misto is a dish that arouses strong feelings among many people. In fact, all the households along the 30-kilometre route that separated their houses probably had their own variation of the dish, along with their own family dispute.

Guanciale

Made mainly in central Italy from pigs' jowls (or cheeks and part of the neck), guanciale is a salumi that can be sliced and eaten with bread, but is more commonly used as an ingredient in other dishes. Many people who live outside the areas where it is produced have an unfortunate tendency to replace guanciale with the ubiquitous pancetta (salt-cured pork belly) or various forms of bacon. Apart from the fact that most pancetta and bacon are industrially produced and therefore contain a number of undesirable preservatives, they are not really an appropriate substitute at all. This is largely because the flavour of guanciale, driven by the type of fat and the ratio of fat to lean, makes it totally different. The point of using guanciale in other dishes is to use the fat rendered from it as the main cooking fat in the dish.

Most producers of guanciale tend simply to cure the jowls with salt and add only black pepper as seasoning, but some add herbs, such as rosemary, and maybe garlic and ground fennel seeds. In southern Italy, guanciale Calabrese includes red chilli. After salting and seasoning, the guanciale is normally left to cure for 5–7 days, then washed and air-dried. Some producers lightly score the fatty side of the jowl and make a hole in the top so that string can be threaded through for hanging. The guanciale is then hung in cool cellar conditions for 30–60 days.

There is very little historical material on the origins of cured guanciale, but in most parts of the world where some form of bacon has been produced, the jowl was one of the cuts used. In Italy today it is associated mainly with Lazio, Abruzzo and Umbria, parts of Tuscany and, of course, Calabria, where the spicy version is produced. However, there is also a version made in the Gennargentu mountains of Sardinia. Large salumi producers in northern Italy tend to make guanciale alongside other products. Carlo Pieri, whose memorable finocchiona is discussed on page 257, makes an excellent guanciale, but my favourite comes from the Lazio area, where it is made by a very small number of producers.

The best versions of guanciale tend to be made in small batches by butchers and small artisan *salumificios*, and some of their products do find their way into the UK and other European countries. I have tasted artisan versions produced locally in both the USA and the UK and found them to be superior to many of the industrially produced versions made in Italy.

Once started, guanciale will keep for several weeks in the fridge provided it is well wrapped in cling film. This means you can always have it handy to knock up what food historian and writer Katie Parla says are three of the most important pasta dishes in Rome – namely, all' amatriciana, alla griscia and alla carbonara. Recipes for all these dishes are provided in Pasta & Gnocchi (page 62). For those interested in curing, guanciale is one of the easier products to make at home, and Ruhlman and Polcyn provide a very good method in their book on salumi (see page 469).

'Nduja

From Calabria, 'nduja is a spreadable pork salumi with a distinctive scarlet colour as it contains plenty of the local fiery chilli. Like all the salumi mentioned in this chapter, it has become popular and 'crossed over' into other regions and international markets, so the quality tends to range from superb to virtually inedible. It can be spread on bread or crostini for an excellent antipasto, or added to sauces, pizza or pasta dishes to provide a shot of concentrated, spicy porcine flavour.

The very best 'nduja is prepared with nothing but pork, salt and chilli, and it is a wonderful expression of some of the best produce in its home region – the rare breed black Calabrian pig and a blend of the local chillies, usually peperoncino dolce and piccante.

Cuts of belly, jowl and sometimes back fat are minced together with the local chillies, which make up about 30 per cent of this salumi. It is then seasoned with sea salt, encased in a pig's intestine and tied with string. The resulting fat sausage is smoked for 2–10 days, then hung for 30–70 days, depending on size. The smaller ones weigh about 400 g, while big ones can be several kilos.

Most locals suggest that 'nduja is a local dialect word derived from the French *andouille* (a type of smoked sausage), and it was introduced to Calabria during the Napoleonic period

(1806–15). Others suggest that the Spanish were the main influence, having introduced chillies to the area some 300 years earlier, and that there may be a link to chorizo.

'Nduja is available whole, in vacuum-packed portions and in jars. As ever with salumi, buying it whole or in portions and slicing it at home offers by far the best taste experience. But irrespective of form, it is probably more important to find a good producer who has made the 'nduja in the traditional way with just the three basic ingredients. Many of the best producers are in Spilinga, Province of Vibo Valentia, thought to be 'nduja's true place of origin. However, it is still made by many people in Calabria, who raise their own pigs and use the prolific amounts of chillies that grow there. Members of the consortium of 'nduja producers seem to produce a good standard of this distinctive salumi, so check out the names listed by the Consorzio 'Nduja di Spilinga.

'Nduja is exported to most European countries, and is particularly popular in Germany and Austria, whilst in the USA it is made locally by a number of producers. In the UK I'm fairly sure my Calabrian friend Francesco Mazzei, now chef-patron of the London restaurant L'Anima, was the first to feature it on his menus. Early on in his career he used 'nduja in many dishes, ranging from seafood to pasta, and has certainly been instrumental in popularizing it, to the extent that it now appears even on non-Italian restaurant menus. Francesco's creation of an 'nduja pizza for a high street pizza chain has now propelled the product into many supermarkets.

Federico Sali, the former head chef at Locanda Locatelli (consistently one of London's best Italian restaurants) now has his own restaurant, Tinello, and a pasta dish using 'nduja is a fixture on the menu. Despite being a Tuscan, he is happy to showcase its three superb ingredients from southern Italy, namely, Gragnano pasta from Naples, burrata cheese from Apulia and 'nduja from Calabria. The recipe for this dish is on page 106.

Vegetables & Pulses

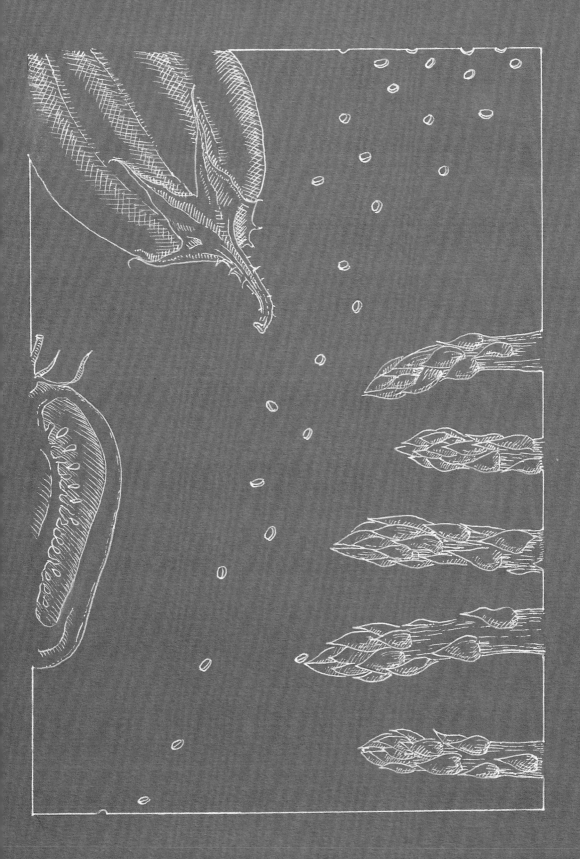

Vegetables & Pulses

I remember as a child passing through Rome on the way back to the UK after living for two years in Brazil, where my father had been posted. I had not eaten fresh peas for some time, and they were then available in most restaurants as a side dish, usually braised with lettuce and small onions. They were so delicious that I ate a portion at nearly every meal for the two-week period we were there. When a vegetable or legume is in season, you should try to take advantage of this gift from nature. Today I look forward to new-season asparagus or broad beans with glorious anticipation.

The abundance and variety of vegetables and pulses that Italians enjoy on a daily basis is quite remarkable. These ingredients provide a great range of nutrients, and have the added advantage of needing very little work to turn them into simple, healthy and superb dishes.

Difficult economic conditions in Italy have recently led to a slight fall in sales of fresh and frozen fruit and vegetables, but consumption of them is still the third highest in Europe (after Poland and Germany). Every Italian consumes an average of 219 g of fruit per day, and 228 g of vegetables, which takes them well over the 400 g recommended by the World Health Organization for a healthy diet. (By comparison, the UK daily per capita average is about 340 g – one of the lowest figures.)

Italian consumers have some enviable choices for sourcing vegetables and pulses, including fantastic markets and grocers, but many grow their own, and foraging is a popular option. Whatever the source, vegetables and pulses can feature in antipasti, first courses and main courses, and it is not unusual to have them in all three. With a main course, however, vegetables are usually served as a side dish, and typically there will be only one.

Italian vegetables and pulses are cooked in a variety of ways – boiled, baked, braised, sautéed or pan-fried – but some are also eaten raw. Generally speaking, consumers focus on eating seasonally, but preserved vegetables (pickled or in oil) and dried pulses supplement the diet when fresh produce is harder to come by.

Most of the vegetables and pulses that were being eaten during Roman times did not change much over the thousand or so years that followed. As Capatti and Montanari observe in their cultural history of Italian cuisine (see page 465), those changes that did occur centred around how specific classes consumed vegetables, and where they would rank in a hierarchy of foods in specific parts of the country. Between the 14th and 15th centuries a number of important vegetables, including spinach, artichokes and aubergines, arrived in Italy from the Middle East and started to spread around the country and across the social strata. Tomatoes, potatoes and a variety of pulses came from the Americas during the 16th century, but their widespread adoption was slow – for example, it took nearly 200 years for the potato to catch on. However, it is believed that Italy was responsible for diffusing its exotic imports into the rest of Europe. The great recipe collections of the 15th and 16th centuries reveal that significant use was made of vegetables, a relatively unusual practice in Europe at the time.

There is a vast array of Italian dishes made with vegetables and pulses, and the recipes given in the following pages have been chosen partly for their simplicity, and because they should be possible to reproduce in most parts of the world.

Artichoke
Carciofo

The globe artichoke (*Cynara cardunculus* var. *scolymus*) is one of the oldest cultivated vegetables in the world. Scholars generally agree it originated in North Africa and Sicily, eventually spreading to other European countries, such as Spain, Portugal and France.

Italy is the largest producer of artichokes in the world, and the main areas of cultivation are Sicily, Apulia, Lazio and Sardinia. It is certainly a staple vegetable in Italy, and may be eaten raw, boiled, braised or fried. A bitter aperitif called Cynar is also made with it, and this is often used instead of Campari in various cocktails.

The English word 'artichoke' originated from the 16th-century Italian dialect word *articiocco*, which in turn derived from the Arabic *al-kharshufa*. The modern Italian word is *carciofo*, but you may still find variations on *articiocco* in some of the northern dialects.

Well over 50 types of artichoke are grown in Italy, from spiny Ligurian ones to small, purplish Tuscan ones. The early-season varieties are harvested in Ladispoli and Cerveteri, while the later ones come from the Agro Pontino plain that extends to Sezze in the province of Latina. The Roman artichoke (*Carciofo romanesco*), from the plains of the Lazio region, is one of the most appreciated. Around April there are numerous artichoke festivals, and the Sagra del Carciofo Romanesco of Ladispoli is one of the most famous.

The European Union has granted the Romanesco artichoke PGI status. The only other variety to have gained that designation in Italy is the carciofo di Paestum, from Campania. However, other excellent varieties are grown elsewhere. Marche, for example, grows the carciofo Monteluponese and the carciofo violetto precoce di Jesi, which is perfect for consuming raw. The Slow Food Foundation also lists some rarer varieties, such as the carciofo bianco di Pertosa and the carciofo violetto di Castellammare (both from Campania), the carciofo di Perinaldo (Liguria), the carciofo spinoso di Menfi (Sicily) and the carciofo violetto di Sant'Erasmo (Veneto). All are well worth trying if you come across them.

Jewish-style Fried Artichokes

Carciofi alla Giudia

My first experience of eating this dish was at Piperno's in the old Roman ghetto. Here they serve crisply fried artichokes, which look like delicate bronze chrysanthemums with curly petals, and are able to offer them all year round as they store them partially cooked in the freezer to serve when artichokes are not in season. While Piperno's are very good, there are better versions to be found in Rome, especially when artichokes are in season. Nonna Betta, also in the ghetto, is a particularly good place to have this dish, as well as other artichoke and Roman-Jewish specialities.

Frying artichokes works well only with carciofo Romanesco (also known as Mammola) or similar varieties that you can eat whole, leaves and all, when they are young and tender. The recipe on page 286 is based on one by Claudia Roden, the acknowledged expert on Middle Eastern and Jewish cooking.

Serves 4 as a first course

- 2 Amalfi lemons
- 8 Romanesco or Mammola artichokes
- 3 teaspoons sea salt
- freshly ground black pepper
- olive oil or sunflower oil, for frying

Method

Squeeze the juice of the lemons into a bowl of cold water, saving some of the juice to rub on your hands so they do not turn black during the next step.

To prepare the artichokes, remove the small outer leaves, and peel and trim the stem. Then, with a sharp knife, cut off the tough tip of each remaining leaf, leaving more and more of the leaf as you near the centre. Using a knife with a rounded end, bend the leaves back over it like the petals of a flower. Finally, cut away and discard the tiny inner spiky leaves and scrape out the hairy choke, without breaking through the base of the artichoke. As each artichoke is pared, place it in the bowl of acidulated water to prevent the cut parts discolouring. Leave to soak for 10 minutes.

Dry the artichokes with a clean tea towel or kitchen paper. Transfer them to a plate, bottoms up and leaves opened out, then press down to flatten them as much as you can without breaking them. Sprinkle with the salt and some pepper.

Heat a 2 cm depth of oil in a frying pan. When hot, add the artichokes, bottoms up to begin with, and fry over a low heat for about 15 minutes, turning them over once. Give them a final turn, so they are leaves down, and raise the heat to very high. When the oil is bubbling, sprinkle cold water over it with your fingers three or four times. This makes the leaves curl up and become crisp and brown. Quickly lift out the artichokes and drain them on kitchen paper. Serve at once with a pinch of sea salt.

Asparagus
Asparagi

Asparagus (*Asparagus officinalis*) arrives during the spring and for 8–10 weeks seems to be overflowing in shops and markets. In Italy, the spears are eaten in many ways – boiled, steamed, grilled or even fried – and they are excellent in risottos and pasta dishes.

The vegetable has been popular since ancient times, as evidenced by images on an Egyptian frieze dating back to 3000 BC, and numerous mentions in texts, ranging from *Apicius* in the 3rd century AD to Artusi in the 19th century. While asparagus is thought to have been introduced to Italy by the Arabs either via Sicily or indirectly through southern Spain, the name itself can be traced back through ancient Greek (*asparagos*) to the Persian *asparag*, which perhaps hints at the geographic origin of the vegetable.

In Italy today green, white and purple asparagus are cultivated, mainly in the north of the country, and wild asparagus is foraged and much sought after. The purple violetto d'Albenga asparagus from Liguria almost became extinct but has been revived, largely thanks to being listed by the Slow Food Foundation. Several other types have badges of excellence. These include white asparagus from Bassano del Grappa in the Veneto, which has PDO status, while Altedo, Badoere and Cimadolmo asparagus all have PGI status. The last two, along with Bassano, are widely exported and command a premium price.

The majority of asparagus grown in Italy is of the green variety. Most of it comes from the Veneto, but Campania, Apulia and Emilia-Romagna all have large tracts of land devoted to it. Smaller areas of cultivation can be found in Lazio, Piedmont and Tuscany.

Asparagus is best eaten as soon as possible after it has been picked, and in my experience, this applies more to the white variety than the green. The result is that unless you have a very short supply chain, it is unlikely you will be able to enjoy white asparagus at its best. This might explain my preference for green asparagus, which I grow on my allotment and can pick at its peak. However, if you buy in season from a trusted greengrocer who can vouch that it was picked a day or two before, you will still have something very special. To this end, it is best to consume it on the day of purchase, especially if the plan is to eat it warm. Otherwise, cook it as soon as possible and eat within a day.

When selecting a bunch, ensure the tips are tightly furled and perky rather than limp, and that the shoots are straight and firm. Keep the preparation minimal: very fresh asparagus simply requires washing, but thick spears might need to have the shoots peeled. If using large asparagus, bend each spear until it snaps and throw the woody end away. If the ends still feel tough, you can pare away the exterior to reveal the more tender flesh beneath.

Asparagus with Butter and Parmesan

Asparagi alla Parmigiana

During the asparagus season, this is one of the main recipes I use for very fresh spears, as an alternative to serving it with plain butter or hollandaise sauce. I first had it when visiting friends near Parma, but I struggled to reproduce it satisfactorily in the UK. The problem turned out to be the butter. Once I started using butter produced by a Parmigiano Reggiano producer, it made all the difference.

Serves 4–6

- 1 kg fresh green asparagus, trimmed as necessary
- 100 g unsalted or slightly salted butter
- 180 g Parmigiano Reggiano PDO cheese, aged at least 24 months

Method

Place the asparagus in a pan of boiling salted water and cook for 5–10 minutes, until the spears are al dente.

Melt the butter in a frying pan over a very low heat. Take off the heat and finely grate in half the Parmigiano. Using tongs, add the asparagus, then move the pan back and forth to coat the spears in the butter mixture.

Divide the asparagus between individual plates and shave the rest of the cheese over each portion.

Asparagus with Parma Ham

Asparagi con Prosciutto Crudo

I have had versions of this dish in homes and restaurants around Italy, most commonly where top-notch asparagus and good local prosciutto crudo are produced. In Tuscany, I have had it with wild boar and with prosciutto crudo from the ancient breed of pig called Cinta Senese, while in Emilia-Romagna I have eaten it with Modena and Parma ham, as well as Culatello di Zibello. All were absolutely delicious. This is a cold dish and a good way to use any asparagus you might have cooked the day before. It is an excellent first course or can be one of several offerings on an antipasti platter.

Serves 4

- 800 g fresh green asparagus
- 250 g Prosciutto di Parma PDO or Culatello di Zibello PDO, aged at least 24 months (you will need 1 slice per asparagus spear)

Method

Place the asparagus in a pan of boiling salted water and cook for 5–10 minutes, until al dente. Drain, then set aside to cool. Cover and keep in the fridge overnight if using the next day.

Lay out your slices of ham lengthways. Place an asparagus spear near the top edge of each slice, then roll the asparagus and ham towards you. The idea is to have the ends of the asparagus sticking out of the ham at either end.

Pasta with Asparagus and Guanciale

Rigatoni con Asparagi e Guanciale

I first had this wonderful combination of ingredients when staying with some friends in Lazio. The dish can be made with a variety of dried pasta shapes, but fresh pasta does not work because it cooks too quickly. The asparagus should be cut in a way that reflects the pasta shape being used. My own preferred shape is rigatoni, so I cut the asparagus to roughly the same length. However, if using wild asparagus, spaghettoni is a better choice because it has a similar long, thin shape. You can use a very aged Parmigiano Reggiano for this dish, but I prefer pecorino Romano.

Serves 4

- 80 g guanciale, cut into lardons
- freshly ground black pepper
- 400 g rigatoni di Gragnano
- 300 g fresh or wild green asparagus, cut into 4 cm lengths
- pecorino Romano, freshly grated, to serve

Method

Place the guanciale in a frying pan over a high heat and cook until it starts to crisp and most of the fat has rendered. Take off the heat and grind some black pepper into the pan.

Meanwhile, cook the rigatoni in a pan of boiling salted water, adding the cut asparagus 5–8 minutes before the pasta is al dente. Drain well, reserving a cupful of the pasta water.

Set aside at least 12 asparagus tips, then return the pasta, the reserved water and the remaining asparagus to the frying pan. Mix in the guanciale by moving the pan back and forth.

Serve each portion with grated pecorino Romano and 3 or 4 of the reserved asparagus tips on top.

Aubergine
Melanzana

Also known as eggplant, the aubergine (*Solanum melongena*) is a member of the nightshade family. First cultivated on the Indian subcontinent, it reached Italy when the Arabs introduced it to Sicily, then gradually spread to the mainland and further north by the 15th century. The Arabic name for it was *al-badinjan*, but the Italians opted for a name based on its unusual shape. They called it *mela insana* (mad apple), which eventually became *melanzana*. Certain dialect forms of this name are still used in some parts of the country: *mulinciani* in Sicily, for example, and *milangiane* in Calabria. Today aubergines are eaten all over Italy and are the key to a number of iconic dishes.

The original wild aubergines were tiny and extremely bitter. Like their fellow nightshades, they stored up bitter alkaloids to deter animals from eating them and digesting the life out of their seeds. At one time it was common to salt aubergines before cooking them in order to draw out the bitterness, but that practice has been discredited. Rather than drawing out bitter moisture, the salt simply reduces the perception of bitterness. In any case, many present-day aubergines have been bred to be larger and less bitter, though it must be said this is sometimes at the expense of flavour.

Due to its subtropical origins, the aubergine (like many fruits and vegetables) is better stored in a cool place well away from the fridge and eaten within a few days of purchase.

When sourcing aubergines, try to find seasonal varieties that have actually been grown in soil and exposed to sunshine, such as those from Turkey, Greece and Egypt. On the whole, these are vastly superior to the almost tasteless ones cultivated in polytunnels or greenhouses and that predominate in cooler European countries. The Italian varieties most commonly exported to other European countries and worth getting hold of are the round Violetta di Firenze and the Rosa Bianca.

If you have an allotment or smallholding, you can always try to grow your own aubergines. I have had superb home-grown Italian varieties in the USA and Australia, as well as some pretty good ones from a friend who lives in Exeter, where there is a slightly warmer microclimate than the rest of England.

Fried Aubergine

Melanzana Fritti

The chef I observed making pasta alla Norma also let me watch him make this simple dish. The aubergines were grown just a few metres from the kitchen and formed a wonderful part of the antipasti we were served — simply fried and served lukewarm with raw chopped garlic, parsley and a little seasoning.

Serves 4

- 2 medium-large aubergines
- 4 tablespoons extra virgin olive oil
- 2 teaspoons sea salt
- 2 garlic cloves, roughly chopped
- handful of flat leaf parsley, freshly chopped
- freshly ground black pepper (optional)

Method

Cut the aubergines into round slices about 2 cm thick. Wash them in a colander, then dry on a clean tea towel or kitchen paper and set aside.

Heat the oil in a large shallow pan and fry the aubergines (in batches if necessary) until they are brown and almost caramelized. Transfer them to a plate covered with kitchen paper, sprinkle with salt and drain.

To serve the aubergines, arrange them on a serving plate and sprinkle with the garlic, parsley and some black pepper (if using).

Grilled Vegetable and Parsley Salad

Insalata di Prezzemolo e Verdure Grigliata

This salad, which I normally serve as a side dish, is a wonderful example of how recipes can travel to the other side of the world and come back again in slightly different forms.

Irrespective of who invented it, this dish is one of the most delicious and refreshing vegetable-centric first courses or side dishes I have ever eaten.

I first had it in an agriturismo in Umbria. The cook was the widow of an Italian diplomat, who had travelled to most parts of the world for both work and pleasure. It was a simple dish and she had shaved some local pecorino on top, but what struck me was how the big leaves of parsley were the true star of the show.

A few years later, I was pleasantly surprised to see an almost identical dish, without cheese, served with sea bass at Alastair Little's eponymous restaurant in Soho. In the mid-1990s, a similar recipe, but without the grilled vegetables, appeared in Simon Hopkinson's book Roast Chicken and Other Stories. Both Little and Hopkinson credit Gay Bilson and her restaurant Berowra Waters in Sydney, Australia, as the source of the dish.

I wonder to this day if the widow had ever eaten at Berowra Waters, or if the salad is more common in Italy than I realized, and was just part of the local repertoire. I am sure Simon Hopkinson must have served it at Hilaire or maybe at Bibendum in London, but I never had the pleasure of eating the dish in either.

Serves 4–6

- 1 aubergine, sliced
- 2 courgettes, sliced diagonally
  to roughly the same size as the
  aubergine slices
- 120 g Tropea onions, sliced
- rapeseed oil, for grilling
- 60 g sun-dried tomatoes
- 100 g Cuor di Bue tomatoes, sliced
  to match the size of the sun-dried
  tomatoes
- 120 g Taggiasca olives, stoned and
  cut in half
- 60 g capers
- 1 large bunch of flat leaf parsley,
  stalks discarded
- 2 teaspoons sea salt
- freshly ground black pepper
- 5 tablespoons extra virgin olive oil
- 2 tablespoons red wine vinegar
- 40 g pecorino Toscano, shaved
  (optional)

Method

Preheat a griddle pan until very hot.

Brush the aubergine, courgette and onion slices with a little rapeseed oil,
then griddle until striped on both sides. Set aside to cool.

Cut the aubergine and courgettes into strips roughly two fingers wide and
long, and place in a large salad bowl. Separate the onion into rings and
add to the bowl.

Add both lots of tomatoes to the bowl along with the olives and capers.
Now add the parsley leaves, making sure they constitute about one-third
of the total ingredients.

Just before serving, add the salt, pepper to taste, olive oil and vinegar and
mix thoroughly. Serve as a starter with shaved pecorino Toscano (if you
wish), or as a side dish with Oven-roasted Red Mullet or Sea Bass (see
page 168 or 183), or Roasted or Grilled Chicken (see page 234 or 236).

Basil
Basilico

Not exactly a vegetable, basil (*Ocimum basilicum*) deserves a mention as the herb most people associate with Italian food. Sadly, that association sometimes leads to overuse, and it makes me cringe when I see certain TV chefs adding it to 'Italian' dishes in conjunction with myriad other herbs, creating a culinary abomination.

Like many herbs, basil is a member of the mint family, so has the characteristic four-sided stems and whorled flowers. The genus name of sweet basil, *Ocimum*, is from a Greek verb that means 'to be fragrant', and the herb is certainly that. The species name, *basilicum*, comes from the Greek *basileus*, which means 'kingly or royal'.

Basil is strongly associated with Christian celebrations of the Holy Cross, and reputedly linked to St Helena, mother of the Roman emperor Constantine the Great. She is said to have discovered the Cross in Jerusalem – on the site of the Church of the Holy Sepulchre. Other theories suggest that the royal link has more to do with India, where basil is sacred and thought to have first been cultivated some 5000 years ago. Even today, holy basil (O. *sanctum*, also known as O. *tenuiflorum*) is planted around Hindu temples, where its pink and purple leaves create a highly ornamental display.

The ancient Egyptians used basil for embalming purposes, but the herb did not enjoy a positive reputation in ancient Greece and Rome. The prevailing belief was that basil would only prosper where there was abuse, so it was associated with poverty, hate and misfortune. In medieval times it was thought that scorpions came from basil, and folk wisdom advised placing a few basil leaves under a flowerpot in order to catch them. This legend no doubt ties into the Greek lore of the basilisk, the king of serpents, reputed to cause death with a single glance.

Even amongst 16th- and 17th-century herbalists, basil was valued mainly for its medical properties rather than its unique flavour.

In most frost-free climates, sweet basil may grow as a perennial, coming back unaided year after year. In the UK, though, it can only really grow outdoors during the warmest months of the year. I find that growing your own from seed produces something far better than the forced varieties sold in most supermarkets and greengrocers.

If you are lucky enough to source some Ligurian or French Riviera basil, it is best to consume it as soon as possible. Do not keep it in the fridge or it will lose almost all its flavour and pungency. Instead, treat it like cut flowers, and keep it in a tall water-filled vase or jar for a couple of days. (The same applies to parsley.)

The four basic types of garden basil are the familiar sweet green basil, the dwarf green basil, the purple-leaved basil and the scented leaf basil. The most widely grown is sweet basil, which reaches about 60 cm in height, has comparatively large leaves, 5–7.5 cm long, and produces white flower spikes. Its cousins include lettuce-leaf basil and Genovese basil, which have even larger leaves, spicy Thai basil, and the tropical variety Siam Queen, which has an intense fragrance and flavour. There are over 222 cultivars of basil and the number keeps growing.

Basil is grown all over the world these days, and in UK supermarkets it is not uncommon to see it imported from such diverse places as France, Israel, Spain, Jordan, Egypt and East Africa. It is possible to get very good Italian basil from high-quality greengrocers too.

In Italian cooking, basil is typically used raw, chopped or torn, and added to dishes just before serving. However, it can also be a main ingredient when pounded into a paste, as in pesto alla Genovese, for example. There is some debate about the merits of torn versus chopped, but I have not noticed any difference in terms of taste. However, tearing is recommended when you wish the basil to look more decorative or rustic.

Don't be tempted to use any old basil. Specific cultivars and provenance do make a difference to the taste profile of your dish. As a child I spent many summers in and around the French Riviera and Liguria, and I remember vividly how good the basil always was. But it was not until the age of 19 that I came to understand why.

During the long summer break from university, I got a job as a guide escorting British tourists by coach to the resort of Alassio in the Ligurian province of Savona. En route, my job was to pay the motorway tolls and provide a commentary on some of the towns, cities and countryside we drove past. I also had to encourage them to drink plenty of mineral water to avoid dehydration. Of course some, especially those on their first foreign trip, found the idea of paying for water an anathema, so I became an expert in spotting the signs of dehydration.

Once in the resort, I stayed in one of the hotels that provided full board, and generally ate with the tourists. Pesto featured at nearly every meal, served in little glass bowls as a condiment or with a pasta dish that was always one of the choices for a first course. I was amazed that over the three-month period I worked as a guide, I never had one single complaint about the pesto, whilst many other dishes, including fried red mullet for instance, caused rumblings of discontent. I like to think that these trailblazers from every corner of Britain contributed to the popularity of pesto in the UK and beyond!

Those three months as a guide also served as an opportunity to immerse myself in the local basil and the dish most closely associated with it – pesto alla Genovese (see page 279) – which today has crossed over to become popular throughout Italy and around the world.

The terroir where Ligurian basil is grown gives it a sweet aroma that makes it impossible to confuse with others. The tender leaves, harvested in their infancy, are combined with fresh garlic, pine nuts from Tuscan forests, grains of sea salt, a generous grating of Sardinian raw sheep's milk pecorino (aged but not bitter), and a healthy glug or two of the sweetest Ligurian extra virgin olive oil. This represents the pesto that one finds on most Ligurian tables.

Beans and Chickpeas
Fagioli e Ceci

Pelligrino Artusi, author of one of Italy's most famous cookbooks (see page 465), claimed that beans are the meat of the poor. While that might have been true in the past, the fact is that today all Italians, irrespective of social class, consume beans with great gusto.

The Italian philosopher and novelist Umberto Eco, in an article for the *New York Times*, argued that the cultivation of beans and pulses in Europe after AD 1000 was of enormous importance, saving Europeans from the tragic fate of malnutrition and possible extinction. As most beans came originally from the New World, I would argue that their contribution is as important as the USA's role in the Second World War.

The 17th-century author Giovanni Battista Barpo produced a number of agricultural and gastronomical texts in which he wrote about the health and nutritional benefits of bean consumption. In fact, he created a bit of a stir when he suggested that beans were not only beneficial to the kidneys and spleen, but would enhance male sexual performance too.

Beans were also popularized by the Renaissance chef Bartolomeo Scappi, who in his cookbooks described dishes of beans, eggs, cinnamon, walnuts, sugar, onions and butter. The story goes that Catherine de' Medici of Florence was supposedly so enamoured of the beans that grew in her native land that she smuggled some to France when she married Henry, Duke of Orleans, later to become Henry II of France. If we are to believe this story, we have Catherine to thank for the invention of cassoulet, amongst other great French bean-centric dishes.

There are many exceptional bean varieties that can be found only in Italy, and, despite having visited most parts of the country, I still discover new ones. Among the rarer beans I came across recently is the Pigna from Liguria, introduced to me by Enzo Cassini, whom I like to consider Liguria's unofficial gastronomic ambassador to London. Other rare Ligurian beans that I had already heard of were the Badalucco, a large kidney-shaped bean, and the Conio, an oval-shaped and much smaller bean. I have since tasted all these beans (cooked from dried) and they were truly exceptional, but I agree with Enzo that the Pigna has a slight edge over the others. I look forward to tasting them fresh when I visit Liguria during the harvest in mid to late September.

If you are not fortunate enough to be able to source some of the rarer beans found in Italy today, you should at least be able to find one of the most beautiful beans bar none, namely, the borlotti. When in season and brightening up markets with their pods, the beautifully coloured beans look (to paraphrase Steve Parle, chef-patron of Dock Kitchen in London) as if they have been clad by Missoni, an Italian fashion house originally known for its colourful knitwear.

In my opinion the most interesting and noteworthy variety of chickpea (*Cicer arietinum*) is the black one from Murgia Carsica in Apulia. Until recently it had almost disappeared from cultivation because farmers switched to growing more profitable crops, and consumers were sold on other varieties of chickpea that required less soaking time. Being listed by the Slow Food Foundation has helped to revive the black chickpea, and in the UK the artisan food importer Claudio Gallucci has brought it to the attention of consumers and chefs.

The Ceci Neri di Murgia is small, very dark and wrinkled, with a hooked shape. During the 19th century it was consumed especially by rural families, serving as an excellent supplement to what was a low-protein diet. The chickpeas were particularly recommended for women who were about to give birth, and the iron-rich water in which the chickpeas were soaked was given to them as a tonic.

Black chickpeas can be used in the same way as other varieties, but require at least 48 hours of soaking before they are cooked. When dried, they can be kept for up to a year and do not seem to lose any flavour over time.

Pasta and Bean Soup

Pasta Fagioli

Most Italian families have a recipe for this staple dish, and the recipe overleaf is from mine. Some people use more than one type of bean, but I prefer to use just borlotti, and I always add plenty of guanciale and Parmigiano Reggiano rinds to intensify the flavour.

Italian-Americans refer to this dish as pasta fazool (a corruption of fasuli, the Neapolitan word for chickpeas) and it is fair to say it has crossed over from its ethnic roots in the same way as chicken soup and, to a lesser extent, avgolemono soup.

This dish is often served as a first course, in the same way as pasta or soup would be, but I prefer to eat a hearty portion of it for a one-course meal. I would not use fresh borlotti for this recipe as they are best enjoyed in a salad, so use either dried ones that have been soaked overnight, or some ready-to-use ones sold in jars. If using the latter, reduce the cooking time by 30 minutes or so.

This recipe makes enough for six servings, but if you are not going to eat it all at one sitting, add only as much cooked pasta as you need for the number of servings you want. You should not store soup with pasta in it because the pasta will expand and become an overcooked mush when reheated.

Serves 6

- 80 g guanciale, roughly chopped
- 2 Tropea onions, roughly chopped
- 3 carrots, roughly chopped
- I celery heart, roughly chopped
- I litre veal or chicken stock
- 2 Parmigiano Reggiano cheese rinds
- I sprig of rosemary
- I bay leaf
- 3 teaspoons sea salt
- freshly ground black pepper
- 500 g borlotti beans, soaked
  overnight
- 300 g fresh or canned San Marzano
  PDO tomatoes, chopped
- I teaspoon double-concentrated
  tomato purée
- 450 g small dried soup pasta, such
  as ditali or ditalini (allow 75 g per
  serving and cook only as much as
  you need for the quantity of soup
  you plan to eat straight away)
- 2 tablespoons extra virgin olive oil
- 50 g Parmigiano Reggiano PDO,
  freshly grated

Method

Place the guanciale in a large, flameproof casserole dish and cook over a high heat until the fat runs and the pieces are crisp on the outside. Transfer to a plate and set aside.

Add the chopped vegetables to the fat remaining in the casserole dish and fry until the onion is soft but not brown. Now add the stock, cheese rinds, herbs, salt and pepper, and cook on a high heat for 10 minutes, until virtually boiling.

Meanwhile, drain the borlotti beans and mash half of them. Lower the heat under the stock, then add the tomatoes, the tomato purée and all the beans. Cover and simmer for I hour on a low heat.

Add the cooked guanciale to the dish and simmer for another 30 minutes. Remove the cheese rinds, bay leaf and rosemary, then check and adjust the seasoning. Leave the soup to rest off the heat.

Cook the pasta in boiling salted water until al dente. Drain and return
it to the empty saucepan, then add just as much soup to it as you need at
that time, keeping any extra for another day.

Serve the pasta fagioli in soup plates, with a drizzle of extra virgin olive
oil and some grated Parmigiano.

Pasta with Black Chickpeas and Raw Tomatoes

Pasta e Ceci Neri di Murgia al Crudo

I had this dish in Apulia with freshly made orecchiette (little ears) pasta, which is traditional to the area. Most dried versions of this pasta are not very good, with the exception of Pastificio dei Campi, which manages to hold its shape. That said, this dish works well with lots of short pasta shapes, but the one I prefer is paccheri, as pieces of tomato, chickpea and garlic seem to get caught in it, giving you a wonderful mouthful every time.

Serves 4

- 400 g spaghetti
- 600 g top-class fresh tomatoes, such as Cuor di Bue (do not use canned)
- 4 tablespoons top-quality extra virgin olive oil
- 4 garlic cloves, chopped (may be left whole if you want to remove them from the finished sauce)
- 1 teaspoon tomato purée plus a pinch of sugar (unnecessary if you have really good tomatoes)

- 4 teaspoons sea salt
- freshly ground black pepper
- 6–8 basil leaves, torn just before use
- 24-month-old Parmigiano Reggiano cheese (optional)

For the chickpeas
- 200 g Ceci Neri di Murgia (black chickpeas), soaked in water for 48 hours
- 3 teaspoons sea salt
- 2 tablespoons extra virgin olive oil

Method

First prepare the chickpeas. Drain off the soaking water, then put the chickpeas into a large pan with plenty of cold water: there should be a good 10 cm above them. Bring to the boil, then cover and simmer for 1½ hours. Add the salt and simmer, still covered, for another 10 minutes. Drain the chickpeas and let them cool to room temperature. Add the oil and mix well, then set aside.

Cook the spaghetti in boiling salted water until al dente.

Meanwhile, put all the remaining ingredients, apart from the Parmigiano, into a large bowl and mix in the chickpeas.

Drain the pasta, then stir it into the chickpea mixture. Grate or shave some Parmigiano over the salad if you wish, and serve straight away.

Broad Beans

Fava

The broad bean (*Vicia faba*) is a very ancient foodstuff, thought to have originated in the Middle East and North Africa. There is certainly evidence of it being cultivated over 4500 years ago, and it is mentioned often in both ancient Greek and Roman writings. Cato, for example, suggests eating cooked broad beans with vinegar, while Pliny the Elder wrote about a popular dish called *puls fabata*, the predecessor of *maccu di fave*, a dried broad bean purée that is eaten in Sicily.

Broad beans can be eaten raw when picked young, in springtime, whilst more mature beans are delicious simply boiled or combined with other vegetables and cured meat. Interestingly, many ancient and modern recipes for broad beans can also be successfully made with peas (*Pisum sativum*), but not with other beans.

In Italy, broad beans are traditionally sown on 2 November – *il Giorno dei Morti*, or what English speakers call All Souls Day. Also, small cakes are made in the shape of broad beans; these are known as *fave dei morti* (beans of the dead). The association with death stems from a time when, according to tradition, Sicily experienced a failure of all its crops apart from broad beans. The population prayed to their patron saint, Joseph, and believed it was his help and the beans that kept them from starvation. Thereafter, it became traditional to place broad beans on church altars on 19 March, St Joseph's feast day. Some people still carry a broad bean for good luck, and believe it means they will never be without the essentials of life. Perhaps in a nod to this belief, Roman families traditionally make an excursion into the countryside on 1 May and eat fresh broad beans with pecorino Romano cheese. Northern Italy, on the other hand, has no such practices because broad beans were traditionally fed to animals. However, the beans are widely eaten there now, partly because migrants from the south have popularized them, and partly because northerners increasingly holiday in parts of Italy where the beans have long been popular.

Broad beans are available fresh, frozen, dried or preserved in jars and cans. Fresh young broad beans eaten shortly after picking are wonderful raw, whilst all other forms are better cooked. The young ones need to be removed from their pods, blanched for a minute in boiling water, then peeled. This last stage is very important no matter what form of beans you use, or their age. Some argue that peeling is hard work and only really worthwhile with young beans, but I don't agree. We tend to get a very good crop from our allotment in late May and early June, most of which are eaten on the day they are picked, whilst the rest are frozen. Both frozen and dried varieties can be kept for 6–12 months, but fresh ones are best eaten within 24 hours of picking or purchase.

Broad Bean and Pecorino Salad

Insalata di Fave con Pecorino

My family and I always look forward to eating this dish when the first of the season's broad beans arrive. It is a simple salad, eaten in most parts of central and southern Italy, with local extra virgin olive oil and a sharp, hard sheep's milk cheese. In London we tend to use a pecorino Toscana and the sublime extra virgin olive oil from Capezzana (see page 436).

Serves 4

- 300–400 g small young broad beans, blanched
- 5 tablespoons extra virgin olive oil
- 1½ teaspoons sea salt
- 80 g pecorino Romano cheese

Method

Peel the broad beans and separate them into halves. Place in a bowl with a drizzle of the oil, mix lightly and leave for about 30 minutes.

Divide the beans between 4 soup plates. Stir some of the salt into each separate portion, then drizzle about a tablespoon of the oil over each plate. Shave some pecorino on top and serve as is, or with some grilled sourdough bread.

Rigatoni with Broad Beans, Guanciale, Porcini and Pecorino Romano

Rigatoni con Fave, Guanciale, Porcini e Pecorino Romano

I first had this dish in Viterbo whilst staying with some friends, and it has become one of my favourite store-cupboard standbys. The dried porcini were my contribution, as I had recently picked them up in Borgotaro, Emilia-Romagna, an area well known for its excellent fungi.

At home I normally make this dish with some home-frozen or freshly picked broad beans and high-quality dried porcini mushrooms if fresh ones are not in season. It is never possible to make this dish with both fresh broad beans and fresh porcini because their seasons do not overlap.

Serves 4

- 80 g dried porcini mushrooms
- 200 g small young broad beans, defrosted if frozen
- extra virgin olive oil, for drizzling
- 80 g guanciale, cut into lardons
- 1 teaspoon sea salt
- freshly ground black pepper
- 400 g rigatoni di Gragnano
- 80 g pecorino Romano cheese, freshly grated

Method

Soak the porcini mushrooms in hot (not boiling) water for 20–30 minutes, stirring occasionally, until fully rehydrated. Drain and return the porcini to the bowl.

Blanch the beans in boiling water for about 1 minute, remembering that very small, freshly picked beans may not need that long, but defrosted ones and those bought from a greengrocer or market almost certainly will. Peel the beans and separate them into halves. Place them in a bowl with a drizzle of the oil, mix lightly and set aside for 20–30 minutes.

Heat a large, heavy-based frying pan. When hot, fry the guanciale until it is crisp on the outside but still soft in the centre. Add the mushrooms and fry until they start to brown, then add the broad beans and cook for 2 minutes, stirring carefully. Add the salt and some freshly ground black pepper to taste.

In the meantime, cook the rigatoni in a pan of boiling salted water until al dente. Drain, reserving 2 ladlesful of the pasta water. Add the pasta to the guanciale pan, then mix together by moving the pan back and forth. Finally, mix in the reserved pasta water and most of the cheese. This will create a creamy emulsion that coats the pasta. Serve each portion with more pecorino grated on top.

Fennel

Finocchio

In Italy it is still possible to find wild fennel, which is used mostly as a herb, but there are also uses for its pollen. Carlo Pieri, for example, uses both wild fennel seeds and pollen in his finocchiona (see page 257).

Fennel (*Foeniculum vulgare*) is a hardy perennial that is indigenous to most Mediterranean countries, but has become widely grown in many parts of the world, especially on dry soils near coasts and riverbanks. There are several types of fennel, which are grown for different reasons. Sweet and bronze fennel are cultivated for their leaves, which are used as a herb. They look similar to dill, but are much coarser in texture. Florence fennel, the most widely available, is cultivated for its bulb, which is harvested before the flowers form and eaten as a vegetable.

The ancient Greeks knew fennel as *marathon* because it grew around the battleground of that name. It was revered by the ancients for its medicinal properties (an amazing 22 remedies were made from it) and it was also highly valued for culinary purposes. Small wonder, then, that fennel made its way into myths and legends. The Greeks held that the gods at Olympus delivered knowledge to man in a fennel stalk filled with coal. More prosaically, the vegetable was awarded to Pheidippides, the runner who delivered the news of the Persian invasion to Sparta. (At that time a gift of fennel was apparently quite an honour.)

The use of fennel has continued over the centuries, but more for cooking than anything else. It features in the medieval recipes of Maestro Martino and in those of Artusi during the 19th century.

Fennel has three distinct parts — base, stalks and leaves — all of which can be used in cooking. Most commonly, you simply cut the stalks away from the bulb at the place where they meet. They can be used for soups, broths and stews, while the leaves can be used as a herb, though they are not as aromatic as those of wild fennel. If you are not going to be using the intact bulb in a specific recipe, first cut it in half, remove the base, and then rinse it with water before proceeding to cut it further. After that it is best to slice it vertically through the bulb, but if your recipe requires it chopped, diced or julienned, first remove the hard central core. (This might be easier if you quarter the bulb first.)

Good-quality Florence fennel should be whitish or pale green and have bulbs that are clean, firm and solid, with no signs of splitting, bruising or spotting. The stalks should be relatively straight and closely superimposed around the bulb, not splaying out too much around the sides. Both stalks and leaves should be green. There should be no signs of flowering buds as this indicates that the vegetable is past maturity. Fresh fennel should have a fragrant aroma, smelling subtly of liquorice or anise. It is usually available from the autumn right through to the early spring.

Fresh fennel can be stored in the refrigerator, where it will keep fresh for about four days. However, as with most vegetables, it will lose both aroma and flavour if left that long, so try to consume it soon after purchase. Dried fennel seeds should be stored in an airtight container in a cool, dry place, where they will keep for about six months.

Fennel and Blood Orange Salad

Insalata di Finocchie e Arance

I first had the combination of blood oranges and fennel when visiting Sicily in early February 2000. It is a truly wonderful 'marriage', though sometimes other ingredients may be added, such as sultanas and toasted pine nuts. I can do without those extras. For me, the oranges, fennel, sea salt, olive oil and vinegar provide a perfect balance of textures and flavours.

The choice of vinegar is very important. Over the years I tried a wide variety, eventually settling for a 25-year-old Spanish Pedro Ximenez, but a few years ago I think I found the perfect match: a 12-year-old black vinegar made from Zibibbo grapes grown on the island of Pantelleria (between Sicily and Tunisia), which is also famous for one of the world's great dessert wines, Passito di Pantelleria.

The vinegar in question is made by Pietro Gaetano Catalano and is called *Suavis Neropantelleria l'Altra* ('the other face of balsamic') because some aspects of its production resemble the method for producing Traditional Balsamic Vinegar PDO (see page 439). Pietro is a well-known cook and artisan producer and, it seems, an excellent vinegar-maker too. A friend of mine picked up the vinegar for me from his shop in Trapani, but at the time of writing I have not personally been there or spoken to him. Both tasks are on my gastronomic to-do list for the future.

Serves 4

- 3–4 Sicilian blood oranges
- 2 Florence fennel bulbs
- 2 teaspoons sea salt, preferably from Trapani
- 5 tablespoons extra virgin olive oil
- 2 tablespoons sherry vinegar or 12–15 drops black Sicilian vinegar

Method

Peel the oranges. Trim the fennel bulbs, discarding the stems but reserving some of the fronds. Chop the fronds finely and set aside.

Using a very sharp knife, cut the oranges and fennel into slices about 1.5 cm thick. Don't worry if they are not perfectly even. Divide the slices between 4 serving plates, sitting the fennel beside the orange. Sprinkle the salt and some of the chopped fennel fronds over each serving.

Drizzle the oil on the fennel and the vinegar on the oranges. Serve as a first course, especially if the courses to follow are going to be on the heavy side.

Roast Fennel and Onions

Finocchi e Cipolle Arrosto

I had this dish in Calabria, where it was cooked on an open fire and simply served with a slice of local chestnut flour bread. What a wonderful combination! It can be served cold on bruschette as an antipasto for 8 people, or as a first course with a slice of sourdough bread either fresh or grilled and rubbed with a little extra virgin olive oil. There is also no reason why it cannot be served as a side dish with baked fish, roast pork or veal. (Also see the recipe on page 230.)

Serves 4

- 4 Florence fennel bulbs
- 6–8 Tropea onions, or enough to match the quantity of fennel
- 2 tablespoons extra virgin olive oil
- 2 teaspoons sea salt

Method

Preheat the oven to 180°C/gas mark 4.

Chop the fennel and onions into pieces of roughly similar size. Place them in a baking dish, sprinkle with the oil and salt, then bake for 20–25 minutes, until caramelized.

Onions
Cipolle

The onion plant (*Allium cepa*) is not known in the wild, but is thought to have been grown and selectively bred for at least 7000 years. In Italy it is a very important vegetable, and may be eaten raw or cooked, as well as being preserved.

I am often amazed at the blasé attitude that many home cooks and, sadly, some professional chefs have towards the onion. It was interesting to see the reaction a few years ago in London, when Mikael Jonsson, chef-patron of Hedone, probably the most important restaurant to open in the UK in the last 10 years, featured a dish involving the sublime doux de Cévennes onion as the star ingredient. Many restaurant critics, professional and amateur, were, to put it mildly, incredulous. It was clear that they did not know their onions.

In Italy there are a number of truly wonderful onions, many of which are exported both fresh and preserved. The following have their own Slow Food Foundation listing and are at various stages of revival, but well worth sampling if you happen to come across them:

Acquaviva Red – from Apulia
Cavasso and Valcosa – both from Venezia Friuli Giulia
Curreggio and Fontaneto Blond – both from Piedmont
Giarratana – Sicily
Statina and Vernina Certaldo – both from Tuscany

Other notable onions include the Patanna from Trapani in Sicily, the Montoro Bronze from Campania, and the Tropea from Calabria. The last of these is a particular favourite of mine and, thank goodness, exported all over Europe. I am always delighted when I receive a text message from my friend Andreas Georghiou, London's finest greengrocer, informing me that he has just received some Tropea onions. Sweet and red, they are wonderful either raw or cooked. The main growing area for them is south of Tropea, around Ricardi and Capo Vaticano, but they are actually cultivated all over Calabria. Those grown close to the sea are extremely sweet because of the sandy soil and the milder climate the area enjoys throughout the year. They come in two shapes, torpedo or flat and round, and for export are normally strung in *ristras*, a traditional style of bunching. Depending on what country you live in, you might also be able to grow them yourself from seed. I have heard of some being grown successfully in south-west England, but I have not yet tried any.

Tomato and Tropea
Onion Salad

Insalata di Pomodori e Cipolle di Tropea

In the early part of summer, when the Tropea onions are at their best, there is probably no better way to eat them than in a simple tomato salad sprinkled with local olive oil and wild oregano.

To turn the basic salad into a wonderful one-plate meal, add about 200 g borlotti or cannellini beans and 300 g good-quality canned tuna — perfect for a quick summer lunch.

Serves 4

- 5 Cuor di Bue tomatoes
- 2 Tropea onions
- 2 teaspoons sea salt
- freshly ground black pepper (optional)

- 3 teaspoons wild oregano
- 6 tablespoons extra virgin olive oil

Method

Slice the tomatoes and put them into a salad bowl. Slice the onions into rings as thinly as possible. Separate the rings and scatter them over the tomatoes. Add the salt, and some pepper if you wish, then the oregano and mix well. Set aside to rest for 5–10 minutes.

When you are ready to serve, drizzle the olive oil over the salad, mix again and serve as an antipasti or first course.

Puntarelle

Puntarelle (literally 'little tips') is a late autumn/early winter chicory that originated on the Catalonia coastline of Lazio Gaeta. It has a frizzy head of dandelion-like leaves attached to an oval base of white stems, and it is the white parts that the Italian name 'little tips' refers to. Normally sown in the summer, the plants are harvested from November right up to mid-February. The shoots have a pleasantly bitter taste while the texture is both tender and crisp.

A wild form of chicory is believed to have grown in the ancient Middle East, and spread outwards from there. It was certainly known in Roman times, as Pliny the Elder wrote about it.

Puntarelle is strongly associated with Lazio, especially Rome, where it is prepared in homes and local restaurants throughout the season. The leaves are served on their own as a dressed salad, the idea being that their bitterness will wake up your taste buds for the meal ahead.

Nowadays, puntarelle has spread far and wide outside Rome. Indeed, such is the demand that it is now cultivated in many other places and shipped to the rest of Italy and Europe. It has become very popular in high-end Italian restaurants on both the east and west coasts of the USA, and is now cultivated in California.

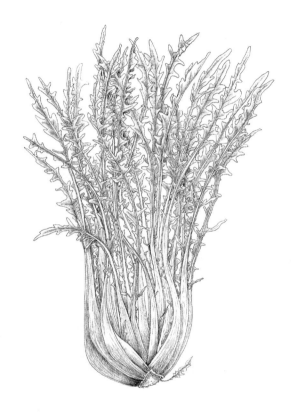

Puntarelle with Anchovy Sauce

Puntarelle in Salsa di Alici

This dish is also known as puntarelle al Romana, and you may come across a variation that uses lemon juice instead of vinegar.

The preparation that puntarelle requires means that making a salad for a large group of people can take quite a bit of time, so in Rome it is possible to buy the shoots ready-prepared, though at 20 times the price of the untouched heads. My advice is to take your time and regard it as a peaceful, if repetitive, activity.

The dressing for this salad is great with any type of bitter green because the anchovies are subtle (not too salty) and provide an added dimension of flavour to what otherwise would be a simple vinaigrette. (This recipe, incidentally, is one of the rare occasions in Italian cooking where you will find oil and vinegar actually combined like French vinaigrette.)

Variation using colatura di alice

Use colatura di alice (see page 152) and a little extra virgin olive oil instead of the anchovy dressing.

Serves 4

- 400 g puntarelle

- 4 anchovy fillets, rinsed and drained
- 1 garlic clove, crushed

- 3 tablespoons red wine vinegar
- 6 tablespoons extra virgin olive oil
- sea salt and freshly ground black pepper

Method

Separate the puntarelle leaves, then cut off and discard the green bits leaving only the white parts – the shoots. Using a sharp knife, make 4–6 lengthways incisions from the base of each shoot almost all the way to the tip. Place them in a bowl of cold water for about 30 minutes, and the previously straight stems will curl up.

For the anchovy dressing, put the anchovies and garlic into a mortar and mash to a paste using the pestle. Whisk in the olive oil and vinegar, then add salt and pepper to taste.

Drain and dry the puntarelle, then transfer to a salad bowl. Pour the dressing over and mix thoroughly to ensure everything is fully coated.

Radicchio

Produced mainly in the Veneto, radicchio is a wonderful ingredient that can be eaten raw in salads or cooked in sauces to go with pasta and risotto.

Modern cultivation of radicchio began in the 15th century in the Veneto and Trentino, but the deep red varieties known today were actually developed by a Belgian agronomist, Francesco Van den Borre, in 1860.

The three most sought-after varieties are radicchio di Treviso, which has two forms: the Precoce, with a conical shape and tight, predominantly red leaves, and the Tardivo, which has splayed red and white leaves with much more pronounced ribs. Both forms have a crunchy texture and a pleasantly bitter taste. The third variety is Castelfranco, which is a cross between Trevisano and escarole, and looks like a little lettuce with specks of red. All three have PGI status and are exported throughout Europe.

The most common variety and, in my view, the least interesting in terms of texture and flavour, is radicchio di Chioggia, which looks like a small, round, red cabbage head. Other varieties include the Rosa di Gorizia from Friuli-Venezia Giulia, which really does look rose-like, and the green Grumolo variety from Lombardy.

I find all three of the PGI varieties are excellent in a salad with a little Gorgonzola, salt and pepper, and a simple dressing of olive oil and red wine vinegar. Cooked versions appear in risotto around the Veneto region, and I particularly like a dish I had when I first visited La Bottega del Vino in Verona. The dish was basically bigoli (the thick and long local pasta, which is a bit like bucatini but without the hole through it) with a ragú of sausagemeat that included radicchio di Treviso and Amarone wine.

Mixed Radicchio and Orange Salad

Insalata di Radicchio e Arance

The combination of radicchio and oranges, especially blood oranges, works very well, providing a fresh sour/sweet contrast. A third dimension can be added by including some Gorgonzola piccante. I like to mix two radicchios — Treviso and Castelfranco — for this salad, but it is still delicious with just one of them. I also like to use a Corvina grape variety wine vinegar from Verona. Guerrieri Rizzardi makes wonderful aged Amarone vinegar, as well as Bardolino, Valpolicella, Soave and Amarone wines for which the company is better known.

I find that this particular salad works wonders if you have overindulged in wine the night before, or at least it did so when I last had it in Verona, following a couple of days of wine tasting.

Serves 4

- 1 medium head radicchio di Treviso, leaves separated and torn in half
- 2 small heads radicchio di Castelfranco, leaves separated and left whole
- 2 blood oranges, peeled and sliced about 2 cm thick
- 1 teaspoon sea salt
- 4 tablespoons extra virgin olive oil
- 2 tablespoons Amarone wine vinegar
- 80 g Gorgonzola piccante (optional)

Method

Put all the radicchio leaves in a salad bowl. Cut the blood orange slices into quarters, then mix with the radicchio. Add the salt and mix again.

Drizzle the salad first with the olive oil, then with the vinegar and mix again. Crumble the Gorgonzola (if using) over the salad and give it one final mix. Serve as a refreshing first course at lunchtime.

Romanesco Broccoli
Broccolo Romanesco

Here we have a beautiful vegetable that looks like a cross between broccoli and cauliflower. In Italy, where it was first described in the 16th century, it is sometimes called *cavolo* (cabbage) *Romanesco*, though it doesn't much resemble any cabbage I've ever seen. Perhaps the German name *Pyramidenblumenkohl* (pyramid cauliflower) best describes it, but in English it is known as either Romanesco broccoli or Romanesco cauliflower. Anyway, it is truly delicious and, in my opinion, often far better tasting than either of the vegetables it resembles.

Romanesco broccoli is cultivated in many countries, including the UK and USA. Look for heads that are firm to the touch and a vivid light green colour. They should be cooked as soon as purchased. Any leftovers can be stored in an airtight container in the fridge for 2–3 days.

Steamed Romanesco Broccoli with Olive Oil and Lemon

Broccolo Romanesco a Vapore con Olio di Oliva e Limone

This is a very simple dish and works just as well with ordinary broccoli or cauliflower. It can be eaten hot, or served cold as an antipasto or first course, or as an accompaniment to cold meats and fish.

Serves 4

- 500 g Romanesco broccoli
- 4 tablespoons extra virgin olive oil
- 1 Amalfi lemon

Method

Remove all the leaves from the broccoli and break the head into pieces. Cook in a steamer or shallow-boil in salted water until al dente. Drain and set aside to cool to room temperature.

Divide the broccoli between 4 deep plates and dress each serving with the olive oil and a squeeze of lemon juice.

Romanesco Broccoli with Garlic, Olive Oil and Chilli

Broccolo Romanesco Aglio, Olio e Peperoncino

Unlike the previous recipe, the broccoli in this dish should be boiled rather than steamed, and served hot.

Serves 4

- 500 g Romanesco broccoli
- 6 tablespoons extra virgin olive oil
- 3 garlic cloves, finely chopped
- ½ green chilli, seeded and chopped, or 1½ teaspoons dried red chilli flakes
- freshly ground black pepper

Method

Remove all the leaves from the broccoli and break the head into pieces. Cook in a large pan of boiling salted water until al dente, then drain and set aside.

Heat the oil in a frying pan, add the garlic and chilli, and cook over a high heat until just before the garlic starts to brown. Add the broccoli and move the pan back and forth for a few minutes to ensure everything is coated in the oil and garlic. Season with pepper. Serve as a side dish.

Pasta with Romanesco Broccoli with Garlic Olive Oil and Chilli

To convert the recipe into a first course or one-plate meal, boil some pasta, such as penne or spaghetti, in the cooking water while the broccoli is cooling. Shortly before it is ready, fry the garlic and chilli as described, then add the broccoli and heat through. (If using a small pasta shape, break the broccoli into pieces of a similar size beforehand.) Drain the pasta, add it to the frying pan and mix well.

Tomatoes

Pomodori

Perhaps no fruit or vegetable is more strongly associated with Italian food culture than the tomato or *pomodoro*. But, as noted by David Gentilcore in his very thorough history of it in Italy (see page 466), the arrival of the tomato in present-day Italy and its diffusion into mainstream cooking is more recent than most people imagine.

The tomato plant (*Solanum lycopersicum*) originated in the Andes of South America and was introduced to Europe by the Spanish in the 16th century. In Italy it is thought to have emerged in and around Naples and Sicily. Initially, it was not treated seriously as a foodstsuff, so the oldest Italian recipe that is known to incorporate it — salsa di pomodoro alla Spagnola (Spanish tomato sauce) did not appear in print until 1692, in Antonio Latini's *Lo Scalco alla Moderna* (The Modern Steward). The recipe did not suggest combining it with any form of pasta.

According to Food and Agriculture Organization (FAO) statistics, Italy is the seventh biggest producer of tomatoes in the world, but exports more than it produces. This is due mainly to the fact that it was very early in developing a substantial industry for canning, distribution and export. Like many other foods produced in Italy, the country's tomatoes have a higher perceived value than those produced elsewhere, and can command a premium price around the world.

The main areas for tomato cultivation are Campania, Calabria, Apulia, Sardinia, Sicily and Emilia-Romagna. Well over 300 varieties are grown, but not all are destined to be canned. Some are cultivated for the production of tomato purée, while others are used for passata and juice. Fresh tomatoes fall into two categories: those destined mainly for supermarkets, so they are bred for fast ripening and long shelf life, and those grown more for flavour, which are often protected varieties. Some of the latter — the San Marzano variety, for example — are exceptionally good, and are exported all over the world, either fresh or preserved in tins or jars.

San Marzano tomatoes

Compared to the elongated oval shape of the Roma tomato, with which most people are familiar, Marzano tomatoes are thinner and pointier in shape. The flesh is much thicker with fewer seeds, and the taste is stronger, sweeter and less acidic. Some describe the taste as bitter sweet, like high-quality chocolate. Because of their excellence, and the fact that they originated near Naples, San Marzano tomatoes (which take their name from their home town) have been designated as the only ones that can be used for True Neapolitan Pizza (see page 409).

Only San Marzanos grown in the Valle del Sarno can be classified as Pomodoro S. Marzano dell'Agro Sarnese-Nocerino and have the DOP emblem on the label. However, they are grown worldwide in fairly large quantities, often labelled as an heirloom variety, and sold at a premium over more common varieties. As is typical of heirloom plants, the San Marzano is an open-pollinated variety that breeds true from generation to generation, so the home gardener can always save some seeds and grow it successfully, provided there is lots of sun.

Brands available in supermarkets in Europe and North America include Cento, Nina, Annalisa, La Bella, Solinia, Vantia, La Valle and Strianese. However, because of San Marzano's premium pricing, there is an ongoing battle against fraudulent produce. In November 2010 the Italian police confiscated 1470 tonnes of improperly labelled canned tomatoes worth €1.2 million, and in 2012 a well-known brand was investigated for misleading labelling on its cans. The current popularity of San Marzano tomatoes is a far cry from the situation in the 1970s and 1980s, when they almost died out in the hands of big industrial producers. Thanks to regulation and their PDO status, both fresh and canned San Marzano products with assured provenance and quality can now be readily sourced.

I recommend those produced by I Sapori di Corbara. I came across this company, better known for its pomodorini di Corbara (a variety of small tomato) when I met the wonderful chef Gennaro Esposito, holder of two Michelin stars. Gennaro made his version of paccheri al pomodoro e basilico using the Corbara product (we were outside the season for fresh tomatoes) and Pastificio dei Campi pasta. This simple dish, made with ingredients originating within 20 square kilometres of the restaurant, was pure joy. The key point about I Sapori di Corbara is that they harvest the tomatoes and preserve them in cans or jars with only water and salt added, and actually run out of stock every year, unlike some other producers, who seem to have unlimited 'reserves'. Inevitably, I Sapori di Corbara products are more expensive and exclusive. In the UK they are available in a few shops and online, but top-class fresh San Marzano tomatoes are available in season from a number of greengrocers and online suppliers.

Pomodorino del Piennolo del Vesuvio PDO

The main competitor in terms of fame to the San Marzano in Campania is the Pomodorino del Piennolo del Vesuvio PDO, a cherry tomato that is grown in the rich volcanic soils around Mount Vesuvius. This variety is often just called 'Piennolo' because the traditional preservation technique involves the formation of *piennoli* (pendulums). Whole bunches of tomatoes are collected between July and August, then placed on a hemp thread that is tied in a circle to create a single large cluster. These clusters are kept suspended in a dry and well-ventilated environment, and left to mature slowly over several months. During this time they lose their firmness but take on a unique and delicious flavour, becoming an essential ingredient of many typical Neapolitan dishes. They are ready for consumption in the spring following the year of cultivation, and can be used straight from the pendulum or bought in jars called *pacchetelle*. Piennolo tomatoes can be eaten fresh, but are hard to obtain outside Italy. If you come across them in jars, they are certainly worth the price.

In Apulia, with the help of their own Slow Food Foundation listing, the Torre Guaceto Fiaschetto and the Canne Regina tomatoes are being preserved, the latter using a similar method to that of the Piennolo.

Probably the best tomato for eating raw is the Cuor di Bue (oxheart, also known as beefsteak). This variety is cultivated in many parts of Italy and exported all over Europe and beyond. I have also had superb locally grown ones in France, Spain and Greece.

Sicily and Sardinia have a longer season for fresh tomatoes, so outside the summer months fresh tomatoes exported via Milan tend to come from these two islands. Sicily produces wonderful small cherry tomatoes called Datterini, as well as the more famous Pachino PGI. In fact, tomatoes with the Pachino classification include four varieties, namely Ciliegino (cherry), Costoluto (similar to Cuor di Bue), Tondo Liscio and the Grappolo (grape). The Sardinian green Camone tomato is one of the best winter tomatoes you can obtain in Europe.

Fresh seasonal tomatoes are, with a few exceptions, a summer crop, so out of season the best alternatives are high-quality canned or bottled tomatoes. Fresh ripe tomatoes should be kept in a cool, dark place (never the fridge) and eaten or cooked within a day or two of purchase. Refrigeration leads to a decline in taste.

Nowadays, we find tomatoes in supermarkets all year round, but generally those available outside the summer months are grown in very advanced greenhouses or polytunnels. In the UK these tend to come from the Isle of Wight, but they are also produced this way in Spain, Portugal, Italy and The Netherlands. On the whole despite significant investment in research and development, these all-year varieties are fairly bland, especially when eaten raw.

Spaghetti with Tomato and Basil

Spaghetti al Pomodoro e Basilico

This is a simple dish but it is amazing how many people overcomplicate it or make a total hash of it. As with any recipe, success lies 75 per cent in good-quality ingredients, and 25 per cent in execution. Therefore, if you are making this dish during the winter, or live in a country where good sun-ripened tomatoes are not easy to find, use a reliable brand of canned San Marzano tomatoes. Avoid the brands that ruin the tomatoes by pasteurizing them or adding preservatives (look at the label to see who these are). Similarly, choose a top Italian extra virgin olive oil (Capezzana, for example), good fresh garlic (my preference is for an Italian purple variety) and fresh basil, again with a provenance from a hot sunny country rather than northern European greenhouse varieties (I like Ligurian).

Finally, do choose a good brand of pasta. I recommend spaghetti or spaghettini from Pastificio dei Campi or Pastificio Masciarelli (see page 75 and 76).

Serves 4

- 600 g San Marzano tomatoes, preferably ripe and fresh (if unavailable, use canned ones)
- 4 tablespoons top-quality extra virgin olive oil
- 4 garlic cloves, chopped (may be left whole if you want to remove them from the finished sauce)
- 1 teaspoon tomato purée plus a pinch of sugar (unnecessary if you have really good tomatoes)
- 4 teaspoons sea salt
- freshly ground black pepper
- 400 g spaghetti
- 6–8 basil leaves, torn just before use
- 24-month-old Parmigiano Reggiano cheese (optional)

Method

If using fresh tomatoes, place them in boiling water for 15 seconds, then peel, deseed and chop each half into 7–8 pieces.

Heat the oil in a large frying pan and fry the garlic without browning. Add the tomatoes, plus the tomato purée and sugar (if using), then stir in the salt and add pepper to taste. Cook over a high heat for 2–3 minutes, breaking up the tomatoes with a wooden spoon so you have a coarse sauce. Simmer, uncovered, for 5 minutes.

Cook the spaghetti in a large pan of boiling salted water until al dente. Drain, reserving a cupful of the cooking water. Add the pasta to the sauce along with half the basil and 2–3 tablespoons of the reserved water. Stir well.

Serve the pasta in deep dishes, sprinkling the remaining basil over the top and adding some freshly grated Parmigiano if you wish.

Both variations below take 10–12 minutes to prepare from scratch, and even when using the very best ingredients, the cost is comparable to the vastly inferior ready-made sauces that fill the shelves of shops and supermarkets.

Spaghetti with Raw Tomatoes (Spaghetti al Crudo)

For this you need some top-class fresh tomatoes, such as Cuor di Bue (do not attempt this dish with canned tomatoes). Simply follow the steps on page 353, but put all the sauce ingredients into a large bowl rather than a pan. Stir in the pasta and it will warm the tomatoes and create a wonderful dish for a hot day.

Spaghetti with Raw Puttanesca Sauce

Follow the previous variation, but replace the basil with flat leaf parsley and add 2 tablespoons capers, 10 chopped black olives, 8 chopped anchovy fillets and plenty of freshly ground black pepper.

Tomato and Mozzarella Salad

Insalata Caprese

This is a simple refreshing salad, but will stand or fall depending on the quality of each ingredient. If you cannot get beautiful sun-ripened tomatoes, outdoor-grown basil, very fresh mozzarella and top-notch olive oil, it is better not to attempt it. If you can, I think you will agree with those who say that there is no finer way to enjoy these ingredients. The dish is the perfect antipasto, and a slightly larger portion works well as a generous first course.

Serves 4–6

- 5 Cuor di Bue tomatoes
- 250–300 g Mozzarella di Bufala Campana PDO
- 2 teaspoons sea salt
- freshly ground black pepper (optional)
- 6 tablespoons extra virgin olive oil
- 12 basil leaves

Method

Slice the tomatoes to the thickness you prefer, then slice the mozzarella slightly thicker. Arrange both on a large serving platter or individual plates, with the mozzarella overlapping the tomatoes. Add the salt, then some pepper if you wish, and drizzle the olive oil all over. Tear the basil leaves and sprinkle them on top of the salad.

Serve with the bread of your choice and use it to mop up the delicious juices that will be left on your plate.

Tomato and Burrata Salad

Insalata di Pomodoro e Burrata

In the summer, burrata is a lovely change from mozzarella, and its 'messy' nature makes a more rustic-looking salad too.

Serves 4

- 5 Cuor di Bue tomatoes or 400 g Datterini or cherry tomatoes
- 250 g burrata or burratina
- 2 teaspoons sea salt

- freshly ground black pepper (optional)
- 6 tablespoons extra virgin olive oil
- 12 basil leaves

Method

If using Cuor di Bue tomatoes, cut them in half and remove the central membrane, then roughly chop each tomato half into 4 or 5 pieces. If using smaller tomatoes, simply cut them in half. Place the tomatoes on a serving platter or individual plates.

Tear the burrata into strands over the tomatoes. Add the salt, then some pepper if you wish, and drizzle the olive oil all over. Tear the basil leaves and sprinkle them on top of the salad.

Serve with the bread of your choice to mop up the delicious juices that will be left on your plate.

Bread and Tomato Salad

Panzanella

This salad is common in Tuscany, where stale bread is usually mixed with tomatoes and dressed with extra virgin oil and red wine vinegar. However, different versions do exist, and it is also found in other parts of central Italy. In Tuscany, it is often made with the local unsalted breads when they are partly or even fully stale. The moisture from the tomatoes and oil and vinegar gives the bread a new life, and provides a wonderful texture contrast to the tomatoes.

Panzanella is a delicious first course, especially during the summer, when tomatoes are at their best, but it also works well as a side dish with grilled fish, roast chicken or guinea fowl.

Serves 4

- 400 g full-flavoured, sun-ripened tomatoes, each cut into 4 or 5 pieces
- 150 g cucumber, unpeeled and cut into pieces about half the size of the tomato pieces
- 150 g good-quality, almost-stale bread, such as sourdough, cut into pieces roughly the same size as the cucumber
- 100 g red onion, chopped
- 2 teaspoons sea salt
- freshly ground black pepper
- I heaped tablespoon small capers, such as those from Pantelleria (optional)
- 4 tablespoons extra virgin olive oil
- 2 tablespoons good-quality red wine vinegar
- 40 g fresh basil or parsley, but not both, torn

Method

Place the tomatoes, cucumber, bread and onion in a salad bowl and mix thoroughly. Cover with a plate and leave in a cool place or the fridge for 30 minutes.

Just before serving, add the salt, pepper, capers (if using), oil and vinegar and mix thoroughly. Add half the torn basil and mix again. Divide between individual plates and sprinkle the remaining basil on each portion.

Tomato and Bread Soup

Pappa al Pomodoro

There are many versions of this dish, but — as ever — my advice is to keep it simple and not add too many ingredients. It can be made with fresh or canned tomatoes, and as long as they are top notch, the dish will be a winner.

I remember making this dish for my first-born son when he was four years old, and him asking me why I was giving him baby food, which is interesting because pappa roughly translates as 'mush' or 'baby food'. The dish is really much nicer than that sounds!

If you live in a part of the world where good sun-ripened tomatoes are not easy to find, try to source some jars or cans of San Marzano tomatoes.

Serves 4

- 500 g full-flavoured, sun-ripened tomatoes, or the same weight of canned tomatoes, including juice
- 6 tablespoons extra virgin olive oil
- 3 garlic cloves, finely chopped
- 3 teaspoons sea salt
- freshly ground black pepper
- 150 g good quality, almost-stale bread, such as sourdough, torn or cut into chunks
- 40 g fresh basil or parsley, but not both, torn

continues over >

Method

If using fresh tomatoes, place them in a large pan of boiling water for 3 minutes. Using a slotted spoon, scoop them out and transfer to a bowl of iced water. Retain the cooking water for later use. Peel the tomatoes and discard the seeds. When the flesh is cool enough to handle, chop roughly (no particular size is required). If using canned tomatoes, strain off and reserve the juice, then chop the flesh in the same way as fresh tomatoes. The reserved juice can be used instead of pasta water later in the recipe.

Put 4 tablespoons of the oil into a large pan and fry the garlic without browning until soft. Using a fork or the back of a wooden spoon, crush the garlic into a paste. Add the tomato flesh, salt and a generous seasoning of pepper. Bring to the boil, then simmer for 15 minutes, stirring occasionally to prevent sticking. Add a touch of the reserved water or tomato juice if the mixture does begin to stick.

Cover the mixture with the bread, then pour over 150 ml of the reserved cooking water. (If using canned tomatoes, measure the reserved juice and top it up to 150 ml with hot water.) Take the pan off the heat and leave to rest for 45 minutes so that the bread absorbs the tomatoes and liquid.

Before serving, warm up the soup, then add the basil or parsley. Serve in soup plates, drizzling the remaining olive oil on each portion.

Truffles and Porcini Mushrooms
Tartufi e Porcini

Arguably, the two greatest wild ingredients available in Italy are truffles and porcini mushrooms. Both are expensive, and demand exceeds supply, so it will not be a surprise to learn that true provenance is an issue.

Over the space of a few weeks I happened to be in Hong Kong, London, New York and Dubai and in each country I happened to eat in Italian restaurants. It was during the white truffle season, and in each restaurant I witnessed waiters holding truffle shavers. Apart from thinking that these shavers have replaced the clichéd giant pepper mills of the past, I also wondered about the freshness of the truffles and whether they could really all be from Alba, as promised on the menus.

The white truffle or tartufo d'Alba *(Tuber magnatum)* comes from the Langhe and Montferrat areas of Piedmont, around the cities of Alba and Asti. They can also be found in Molise, Abruzzo, Umbria and Tuscany, as well as in Croatia and France. With the possible exception of some I have had in Tuscany, Umbria and Croatia, none seem to match the intense aroma and umami concentration of the ones from Piedmont.

In terms of black truffles, Italy's best is the Norcia black truffle from Umbria. Good as it is, though, I don't think it reaches the heights of the best from the Périgord in France.

My advice regarding truffles, Italian or otherwise, is to understand the supply chain and know your source, personally if possible. The alternative is to put yourself in the hands of a trusted restaurateur or dealer. In London, for instance, one of my contacts is Meera Cortesi, who has a very short supply chain operating via her husband's family in Umbria. She supplies some of the best restaurants in the UK, plus a few retailers and private customers.

If you do purchase truffles, be they white or black, eat them as soon as possible because they really do start to lose their flavour and aroma within hours of being dug up. I have been lucky enough to have eaten both white Alba truffles and black Norcia ones literally minutes after they have been found. On both occasions they were simply shaved over fried eggs, which many would agree make one of the finest accompaniments for this luxury product. Both are also wonderful shaved over a Risotto Bianco (see page 124) or fresh tagliatelle dressed in butter. My friend Roberto Pisano, whom I mention in the context of bottarga, his other true love (see page 153), shaved some on a zabaglione made with Moscato d'Asti and it was truly sensational.

PORCINI

The porcino mushroom (*Boletus edulis*) is widely known by its Italian name, but you may also know it by the French name *cep,* and the English name penny bun. *Porcino* comes from the Latin, meaning 'piglet', and is thought to be linked to the Roman *suilli* (hog mushroom), a word still present in both Neapolitan and Calabrian dialects.

Porcini grow in many parts of the world, but you should not think about foraging for them unless you have some expertise in mushroom identification. Most of those sold in the UK come from the New Forest in Hampshire, south Wales and Scotland, but those in the know are aware of good spots elsewhere, even in London. I have seen many French and Italian chefs surreptitiously heading to Wimbledon Common, for instance.

Like most fresh vegetables, porcini need to be eaten as soon as possible, and you are most likely to get good fresh ones if they grow in the country where you live. The alternative is to use dried ones, or those preserved in jars. In both cases, if you want to be sure they come from Borgotaro, make sure they bear the PGI label.

The best porcini in Italy are from Borgotaro and have PGI status. There is even a festival that celebrates them every September — one of the great food festivals in Italy.

Porcini are delicious in risottos and with fresh pasta, but also complement veal and beef stews as a side dish. My favourite way of eating them is to have them simply fried in olive oil with a touch of garlic and a pinch of sea salt, then pop them on grilled sourdough bread with a sprinkling of freshly chopped parsley. If you add a poached or fried egg on top you have a superb one-plate meal that can be prepared in less than 10 minutes.

FOR RECIPES USING TRUFFLES AND/OR PORCINI, SEE:

- *Vincisgrassi (page 77)*
- *Mushroom Risotto and White or Black Truffle Risotto (page 126)*
- *Truffled Anchovies (page 149)*
- *Chopped Raw Meat (page 210)*

Fruit &
Nuts

Fruit & Nuts

I am fairly sure that if I had not been in Italy as a very young child, my love of both fruit and nuts would not be so strong. I was given seasonal fruit and nuts as a snack in between meals, and fruit was nearly always served at the end of a meal.

Fruit

Fruit remains a very important food in Italy today, and can be incorporated into every stage of a meal. There is a long tradition of using fruit, such as figs and melon, with prosciutto as part of an antipasti or first course. In addition, fruit is used in salads, such as the simple orange salad made in Sicily and the northern seasonal salad made with pears. In terms of meat dishes, it is may be combined, fresh or dried, in certain main courses, such as rabbit or kid cooked with sultanas. It's probably true to say, though, that fruit is most often eaten instead of, or as well as, dessert at lunch or dinner, or as a snack during the day. When not eaten fresh, fruit — especially oranges and lemons — is often eaten candied.

The term 'fruit' applies to the usually fleshy product of a plant that contains its seeds. In fact, many things we think of as vegetables — for instance, green beans, tomatoes and cucumbers — are actually fruit. In this chapter, I deal just with those fruits for which Italy and its islands are most renowned — namely, citrus fruit, peaches and pears.

I always looked forward to the arrival of the first figs and blood oranges, and it was as a child that I first tried the combination of pears and cheese, something I still love.

The traditional meal in Roman antiquity generally started with eggs and ended with fruit. However, fruits were also used in main courses, combined, for example, with garum (see page 150) and vinegar. Romans were fond of sweet and sour dishes, and there are numerous dishes today, especially in southern Italy, that continue that *agro e dolce* tradition. Romans ate watermelon, wild strawberries, melon, blackberries and medlars, and also many Asian introductions, including peaches, apricots and cherries.

In Pliny the Elder's *Naturalis Historia* (written about AD 79) he listed the fruits that grew in Italy. There were 15 varieties of olive, pine cones (for their pine nuts), quinces, pomegranates, peaches, grapes, 12 kinds of plum, 30 types of apple, 41 kinds of pear, 29 varieties of fig, nuts (including walnuts, hazelnuts and almonds), chestnuts, cherries and a few now-forgotten fruits, such as sorb (from the service tree) and carob (from the European cornel, a type of dogwood). Crops of all these things were carefully tended and harvested, as the Romans were familiar with the techniques of grafting trees and plants.

The Roman diet also included dates imported from North Africa or Syria, and it is known that these were used in cookery. Of the citrus fruits, however, the Romans knew only citron (*Citrus medica*), a very bitter form of lemon. It was not until the Renaissance that lemon (*C. limonicum*) and bitter orange (*C. aurantium*), for which Italy is now so famous, were introduced from the Arab world.

Bitter orange is true to its name and must be cooked or candied to be edible. The sweet orange (*C. sinensis*) that we know today appeared only in the 15th century, and it was not used in cookery before the 16th century. In fact, when the word 'orange' is mentioned in a medieval text, it always refers to the bitter orange. The first documents that record the use of candied fruit in Europe date back to 16th-century Italy, where they became a key ingredient in some of the most famous sweets, including the Milanese panettone and cassata Siciliana.

Like most Mediterranean countries, Italy produces a wide variety of wonderful fruit, much of which commands a premium when exported. Fruit farming is therefore a fairly sophisticated business these days, in terms of both production and distribution. Among the surprising facts noted by the FAO is that Italy is the world's largest producer of kiwi fruit, outstripping both New Zealand and Chile, the other principal producers.

Citrus fruit

Italy grows truly outstanding citrus fruits, ranging from Sicilian blood oranges and Ciaculli mandarins to Amalfi and Sorrento lemons. The last two have IGP status and therefore grow only in officially designated areas, which include the towns of Atrani, Ravello and Positano. Amalfi lemons have rough unwaxed skin and a prominent 'nipple', whilst the Sorrento is smoother and more oval in shape.

The production of Amalfi lemons (*Sfusato amalfitano*) is limited to 25 tonnes per hectare, which are harvested by hand from February to October. The fruit yields no less than 25 per cent of its volume in juice, and has a higher vitamin C content than most other lemons. I have never found a better lemon for enhancing a dish with juice or zest. When purchasing them or their by-products, look out for the IGP logo, which proves you are getting the real thing.

The Sorrento lemon (also known as the Femminiello Sorrentino or St Teresa) is a little more acidic than the Amalfi type, and in my view better for making home-made lemonade or the local liqueur called limoncello.

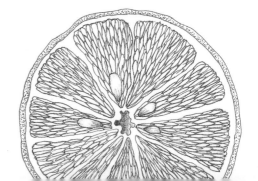

Peaches

The peach (*Prunus persica*), which now grows so abundantly in Italy, originated in China and travelled west along the Silk Road, eventually being adopted by the Romans, who began cultivating it around the 1st century AD. Italy is now the biggest European producer of peaches and their cousin nectarines (*P. p. nectarina*), ahead of Spain, France and Greece. The south, especially Sicily, is renowned for peaches, whilst the north, particularly Emilia-Romagna, tends to produce more nectarines. My friend Francesco Cucurullo, whom I originally met by discovering the excellent wines produced on his estate in Caltanissetta, Calabria, has 20 hectares devoted to the cultivation of eight different varieties of peach and five varieties of late-ripening yellow nectarines. These southern fruits, picked between late August and October, are truly wonderful — some of the best I have had anywhere. The 600 tonnes of hand-picked peaches and nectarines from Francesco's estate, Masseria del Feudo, are distributed throughout Italy and Europe. (The estate also happens to be relatively close to Sicily, where Pino Cuttaia, one of the country's finest chefs, has his restaurant La Madia. Situated between Ragusa and Agrigento on the south coast of the island, it's a long detour, but definitely worth it.)

Pears

The centre and north of the country grows some wonderful pears, such as the Lessina Misso in the Veneto and the Cocomerina from Emilia-Romagna. Both are very rare but undergoing a revival thanks to being listed by the Slow Food Foundation. Among more 'everyday' pears, the Coscia, originally grown in Tuscany, now thrives in Emilia-Romagna, along with other crossbreeds of the common European pear (*Pyrus communis*), such as Abate Fetel, Passa Crassana, and Santa Maria. Generally, Italy is blessed with a wide variety of pears that appear first in midsummer, and then continue in a steady stream through the autumn and winter months.

There is a proverb in Italy: *Al contadino non far sapere quanto è buono il formaggio con le pere* (Do not let the farmer know how good a pear is with cheese), the thinking being that if the farmer ever cottoned on to the combination, the supply of pears and cheese would be scarce. However, as Massimo Montanari explains in his book about this marvellous combination (see page 468), the proverb is much more complex than its superficial meaning. Suffice to say, the combination of ripe pear and cheese, such as mature pecorino from Tuscany or Sardinia, is truly delicious and a wonderful way to end a meal or transition from savoury to sweet if you are having a dessert. Both Gorgonzola dolce and piccante work well too. The beauty of pears is that hard ones ripen well in the bowl at home, but if you are impatient, they can also be poached or baked in wine.

Nuts

Let's start with a definition: a nut is an edible kernel containing usually one seed surrounded by a hard or tough outer case. The generic Italian word for 'nut' is *noce*, but — as in English — every type of nut has a specific name. In this chapter we are concerned mainly with two outstanding types of nut grown in Italy today — namely, *nocciole* (hazelnuts) and *pistacchi* (pistachios).

After Turkey, Italy is the largest producer of hazelnuts, one of the key ingredients in the chocolate spread Nutella and also in the sublime Gianduia sweet chocolate, which contains about 30 per cent hazelnut paste. Both products originate in Piedmont, which is the centre of hazelnut production in Italy, despite Lazio producing greater volumes. The province of Cueno alone has 7000 hectares dedicated to hazelnut cultivation, and that represents around 85 per cent of Piedmont's total production.

Featuring in both savoury and sweet dishes, nuts are important in Italian food culture. Of course, they may also be eaten simply roasted, with or without the addition of sugar and salt.

The finest hazelnuts in Europe are grown in Cortemilia, global capital of the most renowned hazelnut, *Tonda Gentile delle Langhe* ('sweet, round and refined from the Langhe'). The rich taste, superb quality and long shelf life of this variety are what sets it apart from others. Limited production makes it a premium product, with prices well over double that of Turkish and other Italian hazelnuts. The Tonda Gentile, along with the Giffoni hazelnut from the province of Avellino, both have IGP status, whilst the so-called Roman hazelnut grown in Lazio has PDO.

If you are in Turin, a visit to one of the two Guido Gobino shops is a must. Leaving aside that he is a world-class chocolatier, his Giandujotti (small Gianduia chocolates) are among the finest pieces of confectionery I have ever tasted. He also has a shop in Milan, and exports to many countries.

The Scyavuru company makes outstanding crema di pistacchi, which is delicious just eaten by the teaspoon or as a base for desserts and ice cream. It also makes a pesto di pistacchi, which can be added to pasta with a touch of garlic and chopped flat leaf parsley to make a quick but very tasty first course or one-plate meal.

Given its location, only a kilometre north-east of Mount Etna, the town of Bronte (which means 'thunder') is well named. The Arabs, who once controlled the region, are responsible for introducing pistachio trees from what is now Lebanon and Syria. In fact, the Sicilian word for pistachio is *frastuca*, which comes from the Arab *fustuq*, and *frastucara* is the local word for a forest of pistachio trees. Pliny the Elder is fairly specific in suggesting that the Roman consul in Syria introduced the pistachio to Sicily.

Bronte pistachio production is fairly limited, and the cultivation and harvest is laborious work: the trees bear fruit only every two years, and are planted in areas that do not allow for the use of harvesting machines. The cultivation area is around 3000 hectares, and the output is about 1 per cent of the total world production.

Sicilian pistachios are more elongated than those from elsewhere, and a more intense and brilliant green. The flavour, however, is more delicate and aromatic. All these qualities are probably due to the lava terrain on which they are grown, and the benign Mediterranean climate. The Bronte pistachio commands a premium and is sought after by top chefs and confectioners around the world. The better gelaterias often use Bronte pistachio paste for their ice cream, and sprinkle roasted pistachios on top.

Pear, Radicchio, Gorgonzola and Hazelnut Salad

Insalata di Pera, Radicchio, Gorgonzola e Nocciole

Whilst visiting a friend in Verona for a long weekend in the mid-1990s, I had various salads that combined cheese, pears, nuts and radicchio. The nuts tended to be walnuts and the cheese, more often than not, a mature Monte Veronese, but I found the combination worked well even when different nuts and cheese were used. Anyway, my favourite combination, using Gorgonzola dolce and hazelnuts, is given below.

Serves 4

- 2 large medium-ripe pears
- 300 g radicchio di Treviso or tardivo
- 2 tablespoons red wine vinegar
- 4 tablespoons olive oil
- 200 g Gorgonzola dolce PDO
- 15 Tonda Gentile delle Langhe hazelnuts, roasted and crushed

Method

Cut the pears in half lengthways and scoop out the cores with a teaspoon. Cut the halves into about 6 long, thin wedges.

Cut the radicchio leaves into strips or, if using tardivo, into short medium-sized pieces.

Arrange the radicchio and pear on a platter and dress with the vinegar and oil. Crumble the cheese over the top, then sprinkle with the nuts.

Genovese Pesto

Pesto alla Genovese

The word pesto comes from *pestare*, which means 'to pound or crush', and gives a big hint as to how the sauce should be prepared.

As for the derivation of the dish, ancient Romans ate a paste of crushed garlic, cheese and herbs called *moretum*, and one variant included pine nuts, but the proportion of cheese seems to have been much higher than that of the herbs, so it was rather less of a herb sauce than pesto proper.

The first mention of a recipe for pesto as it is known today was in the book *La Cuciniera Genovese (The Cooking of Genoa)*, written in 1863 by Giovanni Battista Ratto. A little over a decade later the definition of 'pesto' in the Genoese Italian dictionary by Giovanni Cassacia said it was autochthonous with the city (i.e. originated in Genoa).

There is also a possible link between pesto and *agliata*, a paste made from walnuts and garlic, which was very popular with Ligurian seafarers. This would also link it with one version of the French garlic sauce *aillade* (the other being closer to *aïoli*) and perhaps even to the Greek *skordalia*.

Making pesto properly is another good case for slow food because it should ideally be made shortly before it is eaten. It is also one of the many recipes where you need to be very flexible in terms of quantities; tasting and adjusting them during preparation is a must. The quantities in the recipe are just a guideline, and you will have to adjust them based on how the ingredients interact during the pounding process.

To my mind there is no substitute for pounding by hand, and I recommend using a marble pestle and mortar, though some prefer to use a wooden pestle and marble mortar. Pesto made in a food processor tends to require *extra olive oil and in my view, the machine is too harsh on the ingredients, making both the texture and flavour somewhat insipid.*

The recipe given here is not the only way to make pesto. In fact, around Genoa and all over Liguria each person has a secret recipe: you will never find two versions of pesto that are exactly the same. The main variables tend to be the choice of oil and pecorino, and whether or not to include Parmigiano Reggiano.

Pesto is normally served with pasta, to which some people add a few cooked green beans (boiled with the pasta) and/or potatoes. I must admit, I have never liked the combination of pasta and potatoes — I find it too heavy. The most common way to eat pesto alla Genovese is with trenette or trofie as a first course. It is also delicious with gnocchi, and I remember having gnocchi with pistou (the French version of pesto) served as a side dish with a Provençal beef daube (stew) in La Merenda, one of my favourite restaurants in Nice. Run by Dominique Le Stanc, who abandoned his Michelin-starred restaurant at the Negresco hotel to cook simple regional food, this small restaurant has no telephone but is always busy. A lot of the dishes are typical of what one finds on both sides of the border between France and Italy.

Finally, pesto can also be served as a condiment with cooked meats and fish, and used on tomatoes instead of fresh basil.

Serves 6–8

- 4 bunches of fresh basil, ideally PDO Genoese, good Provençal or home-grown outdoors
- 1–2 garlic cloves, preferably Imperia from Vessalico, or French pink or violet varieties, such as Ail Rose de Lautrec
- 30 g pine nuts

- 10 g coarse sea salt, ideally Sale di Cervia
- 30–40 g Parmigiano Reggiano cheese (aged 24 months), grated
- 40–50 g Fiore Sardo (pecorino Sardo) cheese, grated
- 50–70 ml PDO extra virgin olive oil from Liguria

Method

Wash the basil leaves in cold water and dry them on a tea towel but without rubbing. The following steps must be done as quickly as possible to avoid oxidation.

Put the garlic and pine nuts in a mortar and pound with the pestle until smooth.

Add a few grains of the salt and some of the basil leaves, then pound the mixture, using a light circular movement of the pestle against the sides of the mortar. Repeat this process until all the basil has been pounded.

When the basil drips bright green liquid, add both cheeses and mix well. Pour a thin layer of the oil over the pesto and mix very lightly.

You can store your pesto in an airtight container in the fridge for a couple of days, but it will never be as good as freshly made.

Pistachio Pesto

Pesto di Pistacchi

I have had many different pistachio-based pestos in Sicily, both in restaurants and in homes. These have varied from a version of the traditional Ligurian pesto, using pistachios instead of pine nuts, to other combinations that included different types of nut, parsley, garlic, various cheeses, and even a pinch of chilli.

However, if using Bronte pistachios, I think few other ingredients are required. The bright green nuts provide the dominant flavour you need, so adding any other nuts and strong flavourings (as some people do) seems superfluous to me. The paste can be made in advance and will keep for up to three days in the fridge.

You can also spread this pesto on crostini to serve as one of several antipasti, or as a canapé with aperitifs. I prefer to eat it with dried spaghetti or penne, but it works equally well with fresh home made tagliatelle, pappardelle and gnocchi (see pages 80 and 116). I do not recommend adding cheese to the pesto, or grating any over the finished dish, because it adds no value — it just distracts from the star of the show: the Bronte pistachios.

FOR MORE RECIPES THAT INCLUDE NUTS, SEE:
- *Pear, Radicchio, Gorgonzola and Hazelnut Salad (page 377)*
- *Mantuan Almond Crumble Torte (page 392)*
- *Hazelnut Ice Cream (page 397)*

Makes about 220 g (enough for 6 x 80–90 g portions of pasta)

- 2 garlic cloves, crushed
- 1 teaspoon Trapani sea salt
- 200 ml extra virgin olive oil, plus extra for drizzling
- 200 g unsalted roasted Bronte pistachios, plus a few extra for garnish

Method

Using a mortar and pestle, crush the garlic and salt into a paste. Add a little olive oil, then half the pistachios and work together with the pestle. Continue adding the oil and pistachios a bit at a time until everything has been used and you have a rough paste.

Serve at room temperature on top of cooked pasta, or mix the pesto through the drained pasta to warm. Garnish with a few crushed pistachios and a drizzle of olive oil.

Desserts & Ice Cream

Desserts & Ice Cream

In general, Italians do not eat many desserts. Meals tend to end with cheese and fruit, and who's to argue with that when both the cheese and fruit are so good? That is not to say Italians don't ever eat sweet things: there are many temptations in the form of pastries, cakes, chocolate and confectionery, lots of them associated with seasonal or religious occasions.

When I am in Italy for an extended period of time, my attitude to desserts and sweets is very similar to what I think about bread and pizza. If you find a shop that sells top-notch products, why bother making them yourself?

I also have to admit that my repertoire of Italian desserts is rather limited, partly because my wife does a much better job with them. But, more contentiously, I do not think they are Italy's strong point. I have consistently upset my Italian relatives over the years by stating that when it comes to desserts, especially those involving pastry, France is on a totally different level.

Having said that, credit needs to be given where it's due, and in terms of chocolate, for instance, Bonajuto in Modica, Sicily, Amedei near Pisa in Tuscany, and Guido Gobino in Turin are truly world class. William Curley, arguably the UK's best chocolatier, uses Amedei products to produce his amazing range of chocolates and patisserie.

Many of the traditional sweets and cakes in Italy, such as *panettone*, *colomba* and *pandoro*, have a long shelf life and are therefore exported to all corners of the globe. If you do your research, you will increasingly find artisan versions of these products, which are a cut above the mass-produced ones that appear at Easter and Christmas in supermarkets and retailers all over the world.

Historically, many cakes and sweets were produced by religious orders in convents and monasteries, who sold their goods as a means of supporting themselves. For example, the wonderful *sfogiatelle* (shell-shaped, cream-filled pastries) from Naples are thought to have been invented by nuns. If you are ever in Erice in Sicily, a visit to Pasticceria Maria Gramitico is a must. Maria worked in the cloistered convent and orphanage of San Carlo in Erice, and most of the wonderful pastries and cakes in her shop today are from recipes she learnt whilst working there after the Second World War. These beautifully handcrafted items were originally sold to customers from behind a grille in the convent wall.

Italy also produces a very wide range of biscuits, from the usual mass-produced packets to really delicious artisan products that are as good as it gets. Take the Savoiardi biscuit, for example: there are versions on the market that are almost inedible, whilst Di Ciaccio, based in Gaeta, Latina, produces its sublime Antico Savoiardo, as well as an extensive range of other fantastic baked goods.

The dessert recipes here have been chosen for their relative simplicity, but some are included because they have either been forgotten or are less known outside their regions, or in Italy itself.

Zabaglione

Zabaione

I adore this dessert and wish it would feature more on Italian restaurant menus all over the world. In the past, it was often made to order at the tableside in restaurants, providing a little theatre whilst you waited for it to be prepared. Now, unfortunately, you are more likely to be offered pre-made tiramisu.

I always have the ingredients necessary to whip up this dessert at home. It is basically egg yolks beaten with caster sugar and a sweet wine. In the south Marsala tends to be used, whilst in Piedmont, from where it originates, Moscato d'Asti or other sweet white wine is more common. Like the choice of alcohol, the name also varies — 'zabaione' in the north, and 'zabaglione' in the south.

The origins of this dessert are contested. It may well have started off as a restorative drink in the 9th century, but it was certainly a dessert by the 16th. In Piedmont the credit for zabaione goes to a Franciscan monk called Brother Pasquale de Baylon (1540–92). While based in Turin, he advised his flock (especially those who complained about a lack of 'sprightliness' in their spouses) to make a recipe he had devised. This, he claimed, would restore strength and vigour.

Nearly a century after his death, Brother Pasquale was sanctified by Pope Alexander VIII, and rapidly became renowned among the women of Turin, who believed his recipe restored the potency of their menfolk. Over time, the name of San Pasquale de Baylon (as he was now known) entered the local Turin dialect as San Bajon, and this gradually became 'zabaione' or 'zabaglione'. In fact, the first written record of the recipe given his name

was in *Cuoco Piedmontese*, a best-selling cookbook printed in 1766, which was inspired by French cooking and practices.

When making this dessert, always use the best free-range eggs and caster sugar you can find. As for the alcohol, my preference is for a Marsala, such as the excellent Curatolo Arini (Fine/Dry).

Serves 4

- 4 egg yolks
- 4 tablespoons caster sugar
- 4 broken eggshell measures of dry Marsala or Moscato d'Asti wine

Method

Put the egg yolks and sugar in a glass bowl and whisk in one direction until a paste forms. Add half the wine and whisk again until you have a smooth, thick custard with just a few bubbles.

Place the bowl over a pan of simmering water (the water must not actually touch the bowl) and carry on whisking while gradually adding the remaining wine. This can take 10 minutes or more, depending on how vigorously you whisk. The idea is to thicken the mixture with air and to warm it, so you might have to take the bowl off the heat every now and then to avoid cooking it through. The result should be a silky cream that is almost as thick as mayonnaise. The test for readiness is that a Savoiardi biscuit will stand upright in the zabaglione once it has been poured into a glass.

Mantuan Almond
Crumble Torte

Sbrisolona

First created during the 16th century, sbrisolona is a delicious hard crumble almond tart that was a popular dessert among poor families around the town of Mantua. The original version was made by mixing cornmeal and hazelnuts or almonds with lard. The present-day version uses butter rather than lard, and can be bought from artisan bakeries and cake shops, especially in Mantua. It will keep for weeks when well packed and sealed.

Serves 4–6

- knob of butter, melted, plus extra for greasing
- 210 g whole almonds, freshly roasted
- 250 g plain flour
- 150 g finely ground cornmeal
- 200 g granulated sugar
- grated zest of 1 small unwaxed lemon
- 1 teaspoon vanilla extract
- 2 egg yolks

Method

Preheat the oven to 180°C/gas mark 4. Butter a cake or tart tin large enough to contain the mixture.

Set aside 10 whole almonds, then grind the rest coarsely. Sift the flour and cornmeal on to your work surface. Make a crater in the centre and add all but 2 tablespoons of the sugar, the ground almonds, the lemon zest, vanilla extract, egg yolks and melted butter. Quickly work the ingredients together with your fingertips to form a crumbly mixture.

Spread the crumble inside the prepared tin, breaking up any large chunks. Sprinkle the whole almonds randomly over the top, pressing them down slightly so just the top surface of the nuts is visible.

Bake the tart for about 1 hour, until it is golden and looks like a big biscuit. After removing it from the oven, give it a good shake to separate it from the tin, then slide it on to a serving plate. Sprinkle with the remaining sugar.

Strawberry and Mascarpone Gratin

Fragole e Mascarpone Gratinate

I first had this dessert at the Walnut Tree Inn. It reminded me of another dish I had once had — a sweet raviolo stuffed with mascarpone and strawberries that had been passed under a grill and served with a strawberry coulis — but Franco Taruschio's dessert is much lighter, and always delights dinner party guests.

Serves 4

- 450 g strawberries, or whatever berries are in season
- 2 tablespoons Maraschino liqueur
- 2 teaspoons caster sugar
- 225 g mascarpone
- about 4 teaspoons muscovado sugar

Method

Preheat the grill on its highest setting.

Cut each strawberry into 3 or 4 equal pieces and arrange them in the bottom of 4 individual gratin dishes. Bathe the strawberries with the Maraschino liqueur, then sprinkle with the caster sugar. Spread the mascarpone over the top and sprinkle with the muscovado sugar.

Place the dishes under the grill until the sugar has caramelized then serve hot.

Ice Cream

Many people have the idea that good *gelato* (ice cream) is ubiquitous in modern Italy, but that's far from true. What I would say is that most decent-sized towns will have a notable gelateria that uses really good ingredients — something that will be evident from the volume of customers it enjoys.

The problem in Italy, and anywhere else for that matter, is that ice cream (rather like pizza) can be a low-cost high-margin licence to print money. Finding the good ones means tasting, which, depending on the quality you encounter, can be lots of fun.

Much of the best equipment for making ice cream is produced in Italy, as are the various industrial pastes used to provide flavour. Although both are widely exported, neither is a guarantee of good ice cream. Like all good food, the quality depends on the maker. I would argue that in London, for instance, where there has been a proliferation of Italian gelaterias over the last 10 years, we have maybe two or three that are actually any good.

If you live in a part of the world where you cannot find really good Italian gelato, then making it at home is your best bet. An ice-cream machine makes the process quicker, but equally good ice cream can be produced by hand with just a fork.

Vanilla Ice Cream

Gelato alla Vaniglia

For many years La Bottega del Gelato in Bayswater and Benigra in Tottenham Court Road provided Londoners with high-quality gelato and sorbets. When those shops disappeared, the saviour of Italian gelato came in the form of Christian Oddono, who, together with some fellow students, opened a gelateria in South Kensington. The recipe here is based on one from Oddono's.

Popular Variations

Follow the basic recipe overleaf, and add other ingredients to flavour it as suggested below. Flavouring pastes can be bought in specialist shops and online, but these are intended for trade use.

Chocolate Ice Cream

Try using Bonajuto or Amedei chocolate, either crumbled or grated.

Hazelnut Ice Cream

Add a handful of Piedmontese hazelnuts, skins removed.

Pistachio Ice Cream

Add a handful of Bronte pistachios, skins removed.

Serves 4

- 500 ml full-fat organic milk
- 250 ml organic double cream
- 140 g white granulated sugar
- 6 egg yolks
- I vanilla pod, split open lengthways
- zest of ½ Amalfi lemon

Method

Pour the milk and cream into a pan and place over a gentle heat. When warm, add the sugar and stir until all the grains have dissolved. Add the egg yolks and whisk until the mixture thickens enough to coat the back of a spoon. This is the custard base, which can be used for any flavour of ice cream.

Scrape the vanilla seeds into the custard. Add the lemon zest and continue to whisk until all the ingredients have blended together.

Slightly increase the heat under the pan until the custard registers 65°C on a thermometer. Cook, stirring, for 3–4 minutes to pasteurize the ingredients. Be careful not to overheat the mixture or the eggs will scramble. Transfer the mixture to a lidded container and, when cool, place in the fridge overnight so that the flavours can infuse.

Pour the vanilla base into an ice-cream machine if you have one, and follow the manufacturer's instructions.

If you do not have a machine, place the container in the freezer for I hour, until ice crystals begin to form. Take it out and whisk it well, then freeze for 30 minutes. Repeat the whisking and freezing process up to 5 times, until the ice cream is smooth. Finally, leave to freeze hard. Allow to soften slightly before serving so that it is easier to scoop.

Other Important Italian Products

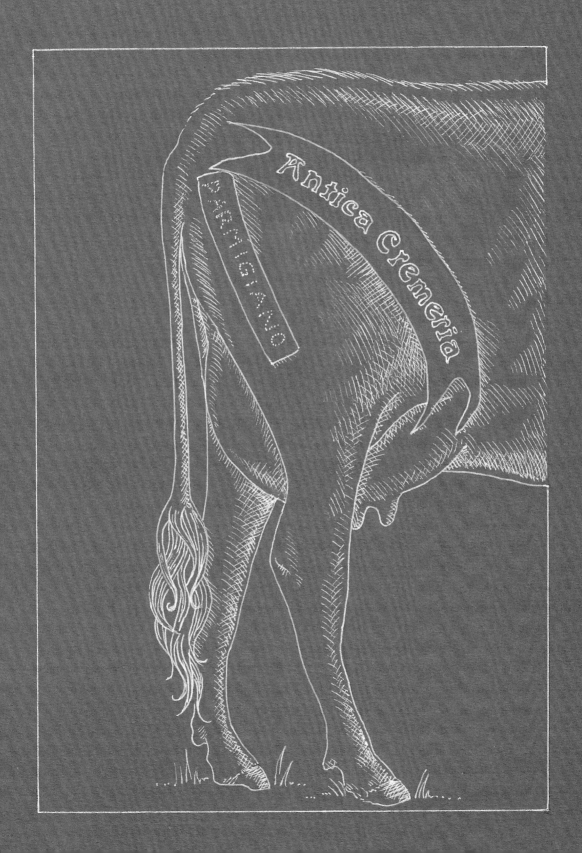

Other Important Italian Products

Bread & Pizza

I have many friends around the world who are wonderful home bakers. They produce bread that is both healthier and more delicious than what is available in the shops, which is a very good thing because, despite pockets of excellence, good bakeries are still rare indeed. However, my views about making Italian bread are similar to those I hold on dentistry — basically, unless there are extenuating circumstances, do not try to do the job yourself. Why? Because for good results you almost always need an oven capable of reaching very high temperatures.

Let's start by looking at the development of bread and trying to discover how we have come to accept the generally poor products being sold to us today.

BREAD

The 'cradle of civilization' — the area of the Middle East that now encompasses Turkey, Syria, Lebanon, Palestine, Israel, Iraq, Kuwait and Iran — was responsible for many cultural advances, from agriculture and art to law and technology. Within that sophisticated society, something similar to what we now call bread emerged, around 6,000 years ago. However, as noted by the historian William Rubel in his book *Bread: A Global History* (see page 468), there is archaeological evidence in the same area that wild grains were being turned into food as far back as 25,000 years ago.

In the territory that now forms the modern Italian state, the Romans played a key role in the development of bread-making. When Hellenized Asia Minor was added to Roman dominion in the 2nd century BC, Greek bakers appeared and were permitted to form a collegium of foreign bakers. It is believed that white wheat-based bread also appeared around this time. For a staple product once made to high standards in virtually every culture of the world, it is very sad to see how the quality of bread has declined.

In the 1970s the baker Carlo Veggetti was a key figure in leading the fight for real bread in Italy, not only helping to preserve traditional bread-making, but also bringing this bread to the people through his il Fornaio chain of bakeries.

Italy has not been immune to the decline in real bread-making. Evidence of this can be seen especially in large urban centres, where bland and highly processed bread is commonly available. However, the battle against 'industrial' bread has been waged by some people ever since its introduction in the 1950s and 1960s, and no doubt accounts for the high number of Italian artisan bakers now at work — some 30,000 at the last count.

Today in Italy, people do not bake bread at home very much: most leave it to tried and trusted third parties. In fact, I can count on one hand the number of times I have had homemade bread in Italy. However, bread is a very important component of meals both at home and in restaurants, where it usually forms a part of the cover charge.

It should be noted that baking bread has been heavily regulated in Italy, and a combination of laws and rules instigated by central government and bakers' guilds has generally served to discourage innovative baking. However, efforts to remove red tape and make it easier for people to set up bakeries have been made, resulting in real progress in recent times.

Historically, especially in rural parts of the country, the baker's oven was regarded as an extremely important communal resource, and used for more than just bread: prepared dishes would also be cooked in it. In fact, the baker's oven still plays an important community role today, not just in Italy, but in many other parts of the Mediterranean, most notably Greece.

There are several wonderful Italian breads you might come across, or at least look out for, when visiting Italy. If you are keen to try making your own, the well-researched work of Carol Field is certainly worth consulting, as are the books by Dan Lepard, whose vast baking repertoire includes numerous Italian breads (see page 467).

You might be surprised to learn that there are more types of bread in Italy than there are days in the year. Some are unique, produced only in certain regions or localities, while others (especially in parts of the country close to a border) can be similar to what you might encounter in neighbouring countries. Bread can, in fact, offer huge insights into the history and culture of each of Italy's 20 regions. For example, the michetta (sometimes called rosetta) of Lombardy is a lighter and softer version of the Austrian Kaisersemmel, whilst the dark rye breads of Alto Adige, such as ur-paarl nach Klosterart, have Germanic origins. See the following pages for a selection of some of the best regional breads.

If I had to pick one bread that has unique characteristics and needs to be sourced only from the area where it originates, it would be pane di Altamura from Apulia. This is a bread that many aficionados would cite as one of the best breads in the world. It was traditionally kneaded at home into very large loaves, then taken to the public ovens to be baked. In order to distinguish each person's loaf, the bakers would stamp it with the initials of the head of the respective family.

Very crisp and fragrant, pane di Altamura has a distinctive straw-coloured crumb that is soft to the touch. Probably its most distinctive characteristic, though, is that it keeps for quite a long time. This would have been an essential quality for the peasants and shepherds who lived in isolated farms in the hilly terrain of Alta Murgia and could not get to the public oven all that often. The fact that it has a long shelf life now means that this bread can be found in speciality shops outside Apulia — sometimes as far away as the UK and other parts of Europe.

Other breads that have travelled well include the Piedmontese grissini (breadsticks) and the Sardinian pane carasau (a crispbread also known as carta di musica — 'music sheets'). Both are often seen in Italian restaurant breadbaskets all over the world.

Typical Italian Breads from The Regions

Abruzzo – pane di mais; pane di senatori; pane di spiga

Apulia – pane di Altamura; rota; sckanata

Basilicata – pane di Matera

Calabria – buccellato; cuddurra; filone; frese; pane di castagne

Campania – pane cafone; pane con i cicoli; pane di Padula; pane del pescatore; pizza; puccetto rustico; tarallo; tòrtano

Friuli Venezia Giulia – biga servolana; cornetto Istriano; grispolenta; pan di Frizze; pane di mais; rosetta

Emilia-Romagna – coppia Ferarese; piadina

Lazio – ciambella sorana; ciriola romana; falia; pane di Lariano; pizza bianca

Lombardy – busella; michetta; pan coi fichi; pane di segale

Marche – crescia maceratese; crostolo; filone casereccio; focaccia farcita; pane di farro

Molise – v'scuott (sometimes called taralli)

Piedmont – blòva; grissini; pane di Carlo Alberto; pane nero di Coimo

Sicily – cuccidati; mafalda; pane di Monreale; pane e birra; pane nero; vastedda

Sardinia – civraxiu; moddizzosu; pane carasau; pane con gerda

Trentino-Alto Adige/Südtirol – ur-paarl nach Klosterart

Tuscany – bozza pratese; ciaccino; ficattola; focaccetta d'Aulla; neccio; pane di Montegemoli; panina gialla aretina; schiaccia; testarolo

Umbria – pan caciato; pane casereccio; pane di strettura; pane di Terni; pan nociato; pizza di Pasqua; porta al testo

Valle d'Aosta – micoula; pane di segale

Veneto – bibanesi; ciabatta Italia; clòpa; montasu; pan biscotto; pane azzimo; plava; puccia

Pizza

My first experience of pizza was in Rome when I was a small child. My parents brought home some *pizza al taglio* (pizza by the slice) that was still warm. It had a simple topping of fior di latte mozzarella, tomatoes, salt and pepper and was delicious. Later that same year I was taken to L'Antica Pizzeria da Michele in Naples, where I had my first pizza Margherita. Topped with mozzarella, tomato and basil, the dough was so light that even at the age of four, I could easily have eaten another.

Neapolitan and Roman pizzas remain my benchmark, and in their various forms are always top in surveys of the world's most popular foods.

Etymologists and historians have sought to link the word 'pizza' to the names of myriad ancient and medieval flatbreads, ranging from Greek pitta bread to the Indian paratha. In reality, a savoury flatbread resembling the present-day Italian pizza is a relatively recent invention. During the 18th century, it was common for the poor around Naples to top their yeast-based flatbread with tomato, and so the pizza began. The dish gained in popularity, and soon pizza became a tourist attraction as visitors to Naples ventured into the poorer areas of the city to try the local speciality. Since then, it has become a global phenomenon that has been both enhanced and bastardized all over the world.

Until about 1830, pizza was sold from open-air stands outside pizza bakeries. This tradition is kept alive today, and a slice of pizza wrapped in paper is still a favourite fast food. It was not until 1889 that restaurateur Raffaele Esposito is alleged to have created pizzas close to those we know today. Wanting to make a good impression when King Umberto and Queen Margherita visited his restaurant, he made three pizzas with different toppings, and the Queen's favourite was based on the colours of the Italian flag: green (basil leaves), white (mozzarella) and red (tomatoes). Legend has it that this combination was named pizza Margherita in her honour.

Pizza purists consider there to be only two true pizzas — the marinara and the Margherita — and those are all they serve. These two 'pure' pizzas tend to be standard on most pizzeria menus today, and I consider the Margherita to be the benchmark when making comparisons between different establishments. The marinara is a slightly older recipe than the Margherita, and is topped with tomato, oregano, garlic and extra virgin olive oil. Its name comes from the seaman's wife (la marinara) who traditionally made it for her husband when he returned home.

The True Neapolitan Pizza Association, which was founded in 1984, has set very specific rules for what constitutes an authentic Neapolitan pizza. These include:

- The pizza must be baked in a wood-fired, domed oven.
- The base must be hand-kneaded, never rolled with a rolling pin or prepared by any mechanical means.
- The pizza must not exceed 35 cm in diameter or be more than 3 mm thick at the centre.

The association also selects pizzerias all around the world to produce and spread its philosophy.

Among the many famous pizzerias in Naples where traditional pizzas can be found are Da Michele, Port'Alba, Brandi, Di Matteo, Sorbillo, Trianon and Umberto. Most of them are in the ancient centre of Naples. At the time of writing, though, the temple of Neapolitan pizza is not in the centre, but in Caiazzo, 50 km outside the city. Here Franco Pepe produces superb pizzas made with carefully sourced local ingredients. His restaurant, Pepe in Grani, opened in late 2012 and is really worth the journey. The restaurant provides another example of culinary excellence in a fairly remote location, which has not only attracted pilgrims from far and wide, but also boosted the economy of this small town.

Even though pizza is eaten all over Italy, it is most strongly associated with Naples and Rome. However, their styles of pizzas are slightly different. In Naples the bases are generally soft and pliable, whilst in Rome they prefer a thin, crispy base. As observed by Daniel Young, what both have in common is a charred, chewy, puffed-up *cornicione* (crust), which is the essential 'frame' for every great pizza. However, other things to look out for include the quality of the key ingredients, such as the flour, yeast, olive oil, cheese and tomatoes. With a little salt and a few basil leaves, this combination can provide a culinary experience to match the best of what Italy has to offer.

Another favourite in Rome is pizza al taglio, which is baked in rectangular trays and sold by weight. The most highly regarded and innovative exponent of this style of pizza is Gabriele Bonci, and if you are in the city, you should try a slice at his restaurant Pizzarium.

It could be argued that Rome is currently displaying more innovation in pizza-making than Naples, and a key figure in that is Stefano Callegari, co-owner of the excellent Sforno. Here he makes marvellous Neapolitan pizza, but has also invented a new category of street food called trapizzino, which is part pizza, part sandwich (tramezzino). Specially designed and baked pizza bianca squares are cut in half to produce triangles, which are then slit at the top to create a leakproof and delicious receptacle that is filled with a traditional stew, such as coda alla vaccinara (oxtail), lingua in salsa verde (tongue) or chicken cacciatore. Trapizzini are great for eating on the move, and have also reintroduced some very traditional dishes to a younger audience in a new format. If you are in Rome, be sure to try them in one of the two branches of Trapizzino.

Callegari, who has always been daring, created a cacio e pepe pizza as a sort of homage to the pasta dish (see page 100), but also a pizza that includes port and Stilton as the main ingredients. I spent a day with him in London and introduced him to Stichelton, an unpasteurized blue cheese, and remember the odd glances we got from passers-by as we ate large pieces outside Neal's Yard Dairy in Covent Garden.

In London Giuseppe Mascoli, a native of the Amalfi coast and founder of Black's private club in Soho, has been the catalyst in improving the quality of Neapolitan-style pizza. He founded the Franco Manca pizza restaurants, which use hand-built, Neapolitan wood-fired ovens and, wherever possible, local ingredients (the exceptions being olive oil and tomatoes). Mascoli and his partner Bridget Hugo have even written a book on making artisan pizza at home without the benefit of those ultra-hot ovens (see page 467). Having tasted some of them, I can say they are certainly better than 90 per cent of what you will find in UK restaurants. However, with two branches of Franco Manca close to where I live, plus some other really good pizzerias nearby (such as Santa Maria and Sacre Cuore), I prefer to leave pizza making to those better qualified and with the right equipment.

Cheese

To say that cheese is very important in Italian food and culture would be an understatement. In 2011, FAO statistics estimated per capita consumption at about 21 kg (the world's sixth largest) and total production at close to 2 million tonnes (the fourth largest after the USA, France and Germany). These figures make Italy a serious player in the world of cheese.

In Italy, cheese can appear at various stages in a meal, perhaps as part of an antipasto, or incorporated into a variety of first courses, and sometimes main courses too. As in other countries, cheese can also be the final course, or the one that precedes dessert or fruit.

I remember when I was sourcing Italian cheeses for Melograno Alimentari, the Italian deli I co-founded in London, there were at least 300 varieties and sub-varieties of cheese on the original list I put together. What I discovered was that many of the hard cheeses travel and keep well, but importing the softer and fresher cheeses presented much more of a challenge in terms of retaining their quality.

Cheese is one of the earliest processed foods. Biochemical analysis of ceramic containers found in Poland suggests that Neolithic peoples were making a form of cheese in Europe as early as 7500 BC. There is certainly evidence that forms of cheese were being made in 7000 BC in what is present-day Turkey, and around 5000 BC in Africa. Almost inevitably, the Romans made a major contribution to formalizing the cheese-making process. Columella,

In my opinion, Italy rivals France in having the greatest variety and selection of cheeses, which may come from artisans or large-scale producers, or even be made at home.

Monte Veronese
d'Allevo PDO

Robiola delle
Langhe

Pammigiano
Reggiano PDO

Caprini Freschi

Pecorino
Sardo PDO

Scimudin

Taleggio PDO

Gorgonzola
Dolce PDO

the most important writer on Roman agriculture, who produced De Re Rustica (literally 'About Rustic Things') around AD 64, described the process of making cheese, including rennet coagulation, pressing the curds, salting and ageing. About 30 years after that, Pliny the Elder mentions the diversity of cheeses enjoyed by Romans during the early period of the empire in his Naturalis Historia (c. AD 77–79).

There is a lot of advice from makers, retailers and public health authorities on how to store cheese. Personally, I tend to consider refrigeration the enemy of cheese, especially soft ones. My advice, once you have found a reliable seller, is to buy just the amount of soft cheese you need for that day or the next and to keep it in a cool place, such as a larder, but not in the fridge. Consume it all on the day you intended, and stock up again as and when you need it. With hard cheeses, such as Parmigiano Reggiano or pecorino, wrap them in cling film, leaving the rind exposed so that it can 'breathe', and store in the least cold part of the fridge for up to two weeks. I tend to go through about 250 g of Parmigiano Reggiano a week, so I stock up with that quantity on most weekends.

One of the Italian words for cheese is formaggio, which comes from the Latin formaticum, by way of caseus formatus (moulded cheese). In large parts of central Italy, though, the Tuscan dialect word cacio is used instead.

There are obviously far too many Italian cheeses to cover in this book, so this chapter focuses on a small but classic selection that I make sure is always available in my deli. These cheeses generally tend to travel well. The one exception is the mozzarella, which can only really be at its best if it reaches your plate within 2–3 days of production. Of course, thanks to air freight, that is now possible.

Burrata

Burrata is a relatively modern cheese made from *ritagli* (scraps) of mozzarella. It was thought to have been invented in Andria, a town in the province of Murgia, Apulia, in the 1920s.

Burrata, which means 'buttery' in Italian, is a hollow ball of buffalo mozzarella filled with cream mixed with leftover scraps from the mozzarella-making process. Cut into the ball and the creamy mixture oozes out. It is the cheese bits that make the cream taste buttery, although not over-rich, since this is still a fresh cheese.

The finished burrata is traditionally wrapped in a green leaf of a flowering plant called asphodel, from the same plant order (but not the same family) as the leek. However, both burrata and its smaller cousin buratina are now more commonly packed in the same way as mozzarella — either in plastic bags or containers filled with the brine they were soaked in.

This cheese should be bought and eaten in the same way as Mozzarella di Bufala Campana PDO (see page 417). Whilst much creamier than mozzarella, it nevertheless works well in simple salads or with spicy pasta dishes, where it has a cooling and balancing effect on chilli, for instance.

Mozzarella di Bufala Campana PDO

Buffalo mozzarella is the most famous of the fresh, stringy cheeses produced in the seven provinces of central-south Italy: Caserta and Salerno, and parts of Benevento, Naples, Frosinone, Latina and Rome. It is richer in protein, fats and calcium than other types of mozzarella, and this is thanks to the buffalo milk, which has a different composition from cows' and sheep's milk. Litre for litre, it also yields double the quantity of cheese.

The process of making mozzarella is surprisingly quick. Fresh milk is delivered to the cheese-makers, where it is curdled, then drained to eliminate the whey. After this, the curd is cut into small pieces and ground into crumb-like pieces in a sort of primitive mill. After that it is put into a mould and immersed in hot water, where it is stirred until it takes on a rubbery texture. The cheese-maker then kneads it by hand, like a baker making dough, until it becomes a smooth, shiny paste. Strands of this are pulled out one at a time, lopped off and shaped into individual mozzarellas. In fact the word mozzare means 'to lop off' and this gives the cheese its name.

The balls of mozzarella are soaked first in cold water, then left to soak in brine. There they absorb as much salt as necessary and take on their characteristic consistency. The end result must be fibrous and elastic, springing back to its original shape when poked. The whole of this process takes less than 24 hours. Mozzarella prepared in the evening is ready the next morning, oozing with freshness and rich flavour. It is best eaten within a few hours, but remains good for a day or two.

The cheese comes in balls of various sizes. So-called pearls, cherries and bocconcini start at 20 g, while knots and plaits can weigh up to 3 kg. The most common sizes are 125, 250 and 500 g.

In 1993 Mozzarella di Bufala Campana was granted DOC status, and in 2008 the European Union awarded it PGI and PDO status too. These are significant honours, and the Consortium for the Protection of the Buffalo Cheese of Campana (an organization of approximately 200 producers) is responsible for the 'protection, surveillance, promotion and marketing' of the product.

There are three main types of mozzarella cheese. The first is made from pasteurized buffalo milk, the second from non-pasteurized buffalo milk, and both can be labelled Mozzarella di Bufala Campana PDO. The third type, which is not a PDO product, uses cows' milk and is normally called fior di latte (flower of milk). This type is made all over Italy and is best for cooking. It has different quality levels, ranging from poor mass-produced stuff that has very little flavour, to very good products made by small cheese-makers. The only way to learn the difference is to taste them side by side. You'll be amazed at just how much they can vary.

There are several theories, all of which are plausible, about how the buffalo came to live in Italy. It is widely thought that the Goths, a Germanic people who played an important part in the fall of the Roman Empire, were responsible for introducing it. However, following an outbreak of malaria, the buffalo area was cleared of people and it was not until the 18th century that they started to move back. In their absence, the buffalo had become wild and multiplied, but once domesticated again, its milk was recognized as a suitable and profitable alternative to cows' milk in the making of dairy products such as cheese and butter. A second theory is that in the year 1000, the Normans brought the buffalo from Sicily into mainland Italy, and that Sicily originally had them from the Arabs. A third theory is that the Arabs introduced the buffalo to Mesopotamia and that pilgrims and Crusaders brought them back to Europe following the Holy Wars.

Finally, and perhaps conclusively, archaeologists point to fossil evidence that, they claim, proves the buffalo originated in Italy.

The majority of Mozzarella di Bufala Campana PDO is packaged for long conservation and sent by road all over Europe. In reality, the only way for most people who live outside the production areas (or within, say, 24 hours of it by road) to receive the product in optimum condition is to get it by air, which makes it fairly expensive.

Fior di latte is ideal for pizza and other dishes where the cheese is cooked and required to melt. The buffalo milk cheese is usually better eaten raw, either with a drizzle of extra virgin olive oil or in a simple tomato and basil salad.

There are many countries in the world that produce buffalo mozzarella, including Bulgaria, Turkey, Egypt, the USA and the UK, to name but a few. I have had some fairly decent versions in Egypt and Turkey, but generally none compares with the very best freshly made Mozzarella di Bufala Campana PDO from a top cheese-maker.

When I am asked what is the very best, I usually say I have not had better than from Tenuta Vannulo in Paestum, just down the coast from Naples. This estate, which practices organic farming, raises a herd of 600 buffalo and has its own dairy in which it produces the cheese. The only way to obtain some is to visit the estate (by appointment) and purchase that day's freshly made mozzarella. Needless to say, they sell out very quickly.

Other top-notch producers include Caseificio Rivabianca, also in Paestum, whilst the best I have tried from outside Campania is Tenuta Giutti in the province of Latina in Lazio. Like Tenuta Vannulo, both use milk from their makers' own herds of buffalo.

Mozzarella di Bufala di Campana should be eaten almost as soon as you get hold of it, and is best at room temperature. I've never seen local buyers of my acquaintance put it anywhere near a fridge.

The production and distribution of buffalo mozzarella is probably worth in excess of half a billion euros, so inevitably (some might say) it attracts fraudsters, who pass off inferior products as the real thing. In most cases, this comes down to the buffalo milk being cut with cows' milk.

Parmigiano Reggiano PDO

What is known in English as Parmesan is a cooked but not pressed cheese, widely considered to be one of the best in Italy and, arguably, the greatest hard cheese in the world. It is a hard matured cheese that, at its very best, has a rich, nutty flavour with a grainy and crumbly texture. It is a highly concentrated cheese, containing 70 per cent nutrients, especially calcium, lipids, protein and phosphorus, and only 30 per cent water.

Parmigiano Reggiano PDO can be produced only in the provinces of Parma, Reggio Emilia and Modena, and on the land enclosed between the rivers Po and Reno in the provinces of Mantua and Bologna. All these places (apart from Mantua in Lombardy) fall within Emilia-Romagna.

The process of making this iconic cheese has remained unchanged for centuries. Every day after the evening milking, the milk is left to rest overnight in large vats, where the fat rises to the surface. This is skimmed off and used to make excellent butter (delicious with sourdough bread, or good for cooking, especially in dishes containing Parmigiano Reggiano). The liquid left behind is fermented and turned into whey.

When the morning's milk arrives from the farm, it is combined with the skimmed milk from the night before in bell-shaped copper cauldrons. Calf rennet and fermented whey, the latter rich in natural lactic acids obtained from the previous day's processing, are added. The milk coagulates in around 10 minutes, and the resulting curd is then broken down into small granules using a traditional tool called a spino. At that point, the mixture is heated at 55°C until the cheesy granules sink to the bottom of the cauldron in a single mass.

After resting for about 30 minutes, the mass is deftly removed by the cheese-maker, then cut in two and wrapped in muslin. The cheese is then placed in a mould that will turn it into a thick 'wheel' about 18–24 cm high, 40–45 cm in diameter and roughly 40 kg in weight. It takes on average about 600 litres of milk from grass-fed cows to produce each wheel of cheese.

Every wheel is branded with a unique number, which remains with it thereafter, just like an identity card.

After a few hours in the mould, a special marking band is wrapped around the wheel to engrave the month and year of production on it, as well as its dairy registration number and the distinctive dotted inscriptions around the circumference. A few days later it is immersed in heavily salted water for 20–25 days. On being removed, it is transferred to an ageing room for 12 months. These rooms have wooden shelves that can be 24 cheeses high by 90 cheeses long – about 2000 wheels per aisle. Each cheese and the shelf underneath it are cleaned manually or robotically every seven days, and the cheese is turned at the same time.

When the cheese has matured for 12 months, the Consorzio Parmigiano Reggiano inspects each wheel. A master grader, whose only instruments are a hammer and his ear, taps the cheese at various points and just by listening can identify undesirable cracks and voids within the wheel. Those cheeses that pass the test are heat-branded on the rind with the Consorzio's logo. At this point they can be sold to *affineurs* (cheese refiners), such as Luigi Guffanti, whose products are widely sold, or to wholesalers who will mature the cheese for another 6, 12 or 18 months. Alternatively, the cheese-makers themselves can continue the ageing process at the dairy.

Since 2007, colour-coded seals have been applied to Parmigiano so buyers can see at a glance how old it is: red for 18 months, silver for 22 months and gold for 30 months. If you do not see one of these seals on the packaging, it is best to avoid the product. Having said that, the general standard of the product is fairly high, so my advice is to taste as many varieties as you can. Parmigiano Reggiano PDO is exported all over the world and probably travels better than any other cheese, so there is no reason why it should not be in optimum condition wherever you come across it.

Parmigiano Reggiano is a variety of grana (grainy) cheese, the other main ones being Grana Padano and Grana Trentino. All these cheeses have a flaky and granular texture. Their common origins are thought to date back to the mid-12th century in Lombardy, when they were first created by Cistercian monks at the Abbey of Chiaravalle, near Milan. From there, the production of grana spread throughout the region now known as Emilia-Romagna, and then into many areas of northern Italy, including the fertile plains of the Po valley. Parmigiano is mentioned specifically in Boccaccio's *Decameron* (completed in 1353), where it is mentioned in the context of pasta in the mythical land of Bengodi (see page 68).

The production methods for making the three varieties of grana are similar, but each follows its own strict set of guidelines and laws. These specify not only how the cheese should be produced, including the type of rennet to be used, but also the farming and cattle-feeding practices, as these affect the quality of the milk. All three grana carry the label DOP (Denomination of Protected Origin), a prestigious EU designation guaranteeing the origin and authenticity of the cheese.

In my opinion Parmigiano Reggiano PDO is at its best for grating over food or eating on its own from 24 months, whilst some of the more mature cheeses (30–36 months plus) are best for eating as they are, or with a few drops of traditional balsamic vinegar (see page 439).

It is best to buy Parmigiano Reggiano from a retailer who has a fairly constant turnover of whole wheels, as the cheese from a freshly cut wheel generally tends to be superior.

Many milk-producing areas of the world, including Emilia-Romagna and Lombardy, have tended over the years to use the high-yielding Holstein breed of cow at the expense of traditional breeds. Over the last 15 years, though, Italy has seen a revival in the use of a local red cow known as the Reggiana, and a white cow called the Bianca Modenese or Bianca Valpadana. These breeds produce less milk, but it is usually higher in protein and produces a richer, fuller and often softer cheese. Some of the best cheese makers focus on these breeds, or sometimes combine their milk with that of Holsteins. Single-breed products command a premium, so tend to cost more.

Despite the rigorous standards and markings applied to the Parmigiano Reggiano, there are certain other factors that determine its quality — namely, the input of the cheese-maker, the terroir the milk comes from and the breed of cow that produces it.

To store Parmigiano Reggiano, wrap it in cling film, leaving the rind exposed to 'breathe', and keep in a cool place at 4–7°C. If that has to be a fridge, it's likely to be the least cold part of it. When using the cheese for cooking and eating, keep a whole piece at room temperature and grate it over the food just before serving: this will ensure the cheese is at its best. If you grate cheese in advance and keep it in a bowl or even a sealed plastic container, it will become dry and some of the flavour will be lost.

Parmigiano Reggiano PDO is often called the 'king of cheese' and is certainly noble enough to be served on its own in a cheese course. With a few drops of traditional balsamic vinegar from Modena or Reggio Emilia it is a pure delight. It is also one of the cheeses used to grate on to pasta dishes or shave over a variety of vegetables and even meat-based dishes. Take care not to overdo the use of grated cheese. It is not required on every pasta dish and should not be used as a substitute for, say, pecorino Romano, which is made with ewes' milk and has a totally different taste profile.

Pecorino

Italy has a 2000-year tradition of making pecorino, a hard ewes' milk cheese that is common in central and southern Italy, including the islands of Sicily and Sardinia. Four varieties of it have PDO status, namely, pecorino Romano, pecorino Toscano, pecorino Sardo and pecorino Siciliano.

Each variety has a different style, usually based on how long it has been matured and if anything extra has been added to the cheese. (In Sicily, for example, pecorino pepato, also known as tumazzu di piecura ccu pepi, contains peppercorns.) Mature cheeses are called *stagionato* (seasoned), whilst *semi stagionato* and *fresco* refer to younger cheeses.

Pecorino is made by stirring rennet or a vegetable enzyme into warmed sheep's milk to start coagulation and the formation of curds. Excess whey and lactose are then pressed out. The cheese is then shaped into large wheels and allowed to rest and season naturally in cool temperatures with very low light and only a certain amount of humidity. Fresh pecorino matures for just a few weeks, but stagionato takes up to a year. Even among cheeses of the same age, the taste will vary, depending on the quality of the sheep's milk, but also according to the way they have been preserved and aged.

Romano is the saltiest type of pecorino, and therefore most commonly used for grating on various pasta dishes, particularly in and around Rome, though it is not necessarily made there, or even in Lazio (see page 61).

Other types of pecorino cheese can be used for grating, but are more commonly eaten with bread or as part of a cheese course.

The best pecorino tends to be made by small producers and artisan cheese-makers, and good cheese shops in the UK, USA and Australia, will normally have a decent selection of Tuscan, Sicilian and Sardinian varieties. However, in my experience, good pecorino Romano is much harder to source outside Italy. One particularly consistent producer of pecorino Romano PDO who does export to the rest of Europe and beyond is Brunelli, whilst the Locatelli brand is the most well distributed in the USA.

To buy and store pecorino, follow the advice given for Parmigiano Reggiano PDO (see page 421).

Italian Cheeseboard

When asked by a London restaurateur to put together a well-balanced cheeseboard of great Italian cheeses that travelled well and were readily available, I drew up the list below.

Caprini Freschi – from Piedmont, this is a simple fresh goats' milk cheese; some versions are coated in herbs or ash.

Gorgonzola Dolce PDO – aged just 3 months, this is a younger and therefore milder version of aged gorgonzola. The shorter ageing time means it is wetter and whiter then gorgonzola piccante, which tends to have bluer streaks.

Monte Veronese d'Allevo PDO – made from cows' milk and full of small holes inside, this hard cheese stands in contrast to the Parmigiano Reggiano because it is aged less and has a wonderful sharp taste.

Parmigiano Reggiano PDO – Piedmont's finest, at least 30 months old.

Pecorino Fiori Sardo PDO – matured for at least a year, this contrasts beautifully with the two other hard cheeses in the selection.

Robiola delle Langhe – this delicious fresh cheese with a soft rind is made in the Cueno province of Piedmont from a blend of milk from cows, goats and sheep.

Scimudin – similar to Brie, this soft, triple cream cheese made from cows' milk comes from the Alpine province of Sondrio in Lombardy. Its snow-white rind encases a deliciously silky, smooth cheese with a light nutty taste and a gentle wild mushroom aroma. The unpasteurized version is far superior to the pasteurized one.

Taleggio PDO – a washed-rind cows' milk cheese, this is yellowish in colour, springy to the touch rather than runny, and velvety in texture. It has a strong, pungent aroma of dried fruits, citrus fruits, straw and roasted nuts. I tend to seek out a cave-aged version from Lombardy.

Olive Oil & Balsamic Vinegar

Mediterranean food has certain iconic ingredients, two of which are olive oil and wine vinegar. According to the UN Food and Agriculture Organization, Italy is the second biggest producer of olive oil, and the third largest consumer, coming just behind Spain in production and Greece in consumption. As the second biggest wine producer in the world, the country also produces wine vinegar. In this chapter we are concerned mainly with balsamic.

Whilst some of the very best olive oil and vinegars come out of Italy, no two ingredients better illustrate the wide variability in quality, and the fraud and confusion associated with them.

Olive Oil

In simple terms, olive oil is a fat obtained by pressing the fruit of the olive tree (*Olea europaea*). Traditionally, this was done with stone or wooden equipment.

Studies suggest that wild olives were first collected during the Neolithic period some 8000 years BC, and that the wild olive tree itself originated around the Mediterranean, from Asia Minor down to North and East Africa. It is also thought that olive cultivation started in Asia Minor some 6000 years BC and spread east, west and south. After that, the Egyptians, Phoenicians, Romans and Arabs all helped to spread the olive to areas where we see significant cultivation and consumption today.

Many myths and legends surround what Homer called 'liquid gold'. The ancient Greeks believed the olive tree was a gift from the goddess Athena, and used olive oil in their religious rituals. Later, during the 6th and 7th centuries BC, it had become so important that the Laws of Solon outlawed the cutting down of olive trees on pain of death.

Over time, olive oil (from the Latin *oleum*, by way of the Greek *elaion*) became ingrained in these cultures, not just for rituals, but for food and to promote health and beauty. The Romans rubbed it on their bodies to moisturize after bathing.

With the fall of the Roman Empire in the 5th century AD, olive cultivation declined for a thousand years. But olive oil steadily regained its role in the Middle Ages, driven, to a certain extent, by the Roman Catholic church, which used it for anointing the recipients of various sacraments, such as baptism, confirmation and the last rites. (It should not be forgotten that the name 'Christ' originates from the Greek *khristos*, meaning 'anointed one'.) The olive tree and the oil from its fruit are, in fact, important in all the Abrahamic religions, and are mentioned in the holy texts of Judaism, Christianity and Islam. Today olive oil still plays an important part in Italy's dominant religion.

By the 16th century, olives were being cultivated in the Americas, and in more recent times have been introduced to countries with suitable climates, such as South Africa and Australia, which are now producing olives and olive oil commercially.

Grades of Olive Oil

The International Olive Council (IOC) has determined that there are five grades of oil. The US Department of Agriculture has its own classifications, which differ in some respect from the IOC's, but the one for extra virgin olive oil is almost identical. From a culinary point of view, we are concerned mainly with the first two categories below.

Extra Virgin — this term relates to oil produced from the first pressing of olives using just mechanical means — no chemical treatment. It accounts for about 65 per cent of the total production in Italy, as compared to Greece at 80 per cent and Spain at 30 per cent. It is the highest quality of oil and should contain no more than 0.8 per cent fatty acids. It is generally judged to have a superior taste with an element of fruitiness.

Virgin — this name is given to oil produced in the same way as extra virgin, but it has a higher fatty acid content (up to 1.5 per cent) and is of slightly lower quality. Nonetheless, it is still judged to have a good taste.

Lampante — literally 'lamp' oil, this is a virgin product because it is extracted by mechanical methods, but it is made from bad or poorly processed olives, so needs refining to make it edible. It was, in the past, used for burning in lamps, and may be used for industrial purposes today.

Refined – applies to oil that has been chemically treated to neutralize defects (strong tastes) and reduce its high fatty acid content. By definition, therefore, virgin and extra virgin oil cannot contain any refined oil.

Olive pomace – refers to oil made from the olive pulp (pomace) left after previous pressings. Its extraction involves solvents, some of which remain in the oil and can be health hazards. This, combined with the fact that the final product contains only 5–8 per cent olive oil, means it's really not a good buy.

Despite the definitions and protected designations (PDO and IGP), it is very difficult for the majority of consumers (especially outside Italy) to source really good Italian extra virgin olive oil. There are a number of reasons for this difficulty, and I will attempt to explain why below.

Olive oil is produced in 18 of the 20 regions of Italy, and, as of 2011, there were 39 products with protected status, the most of any European country. While this is an impressive number, it still represents only about 1 per cent of Italy's entire extra virgin olive oil production.

First, it should be noted that demand exceeds supply. Italy produces barely enough oil made with home-grown olives to meet even internal demand, so it therefore imports olive oil. Despite this, exports of Italian oil far exceed what the country is capable of producing, which means that most of what passes for Italian olive oil is actually blended. In fact, Italy probably produces only around a third of the olive oil that will be sold as Italian for both internal and export markets.

Nonetheless, Italian olive oil has long had a certain cachet in export markets, much as French perfume does. The difference is that no one expects perfume to be made with products grown entirely in the country of origin, but with olive oil they absolutely do. Given the profits to be made by producing Italian olive oil, perhaps we shouldn't be surprised that so much of what's available in the shops is far from being the genuine article.

Adulteration of olive oil covers a multitude of sins. In simple terms, it involves passing off something that is not what is specified on the label – perhaps refined oil being sold as extra virgin. In that scenario the best you can hope for is that the product is safe. At worst, the oil can be unfit for human consumption and lead to poisoning and even death. Fraud investigations involving olive oil have certainly kept national police forces and the EU's antifraud office pretty busy. You can find out more about this, and about olive oil in general, in Tom Mueller's excellent book *Extra Virginity* (see page 468).

Another factor complicating things for consumers, especially those who do not live in oil-producing countries, is that they may not really have a benchmark for what constitutes good or bad olive oil. In this case, they need to buy and taste until they learn what to look for. Generic signs of quality include a degree of bitterness, a hint of pepper and a certain amount of pungency. Sweetness, smoothness or butteriness are more likely to indicate that the oil is old, or possibly that it has been treated in some way to remove 'defects'.

Olive oil is essentially a fresh product that starts to deteriorate just a few months after harvest, especially in bottles and when subjected to light and fluctuations in temperature. In that sense, it is rather like a fruit juice — a perishable product. In my experience, extra virgin olive oil tastes best soon after it is made, but if you buy a well-made oil and keep it sealed in a cool, dark place, it will probably remain a decent product until the next harvest comes around.

With freshness being all important, it's essential to note the harvest date when buying olive oil. A sell-by date on its own provides no useful information. If you take my advice, you'll buy oils only from the most recent harvest.

Like wine, olive oil varies in flavour, depending on where the olives were grown and how it was produced. There are over 700 types of olive and they are used for making thousands of different olive oils. Some are single cultivar, some are multiple, and some oils are blended after pressing. Just as with wine, you need to know as much as possible about the terroir, fruit, producer and specific harvests. What you like is subjective, but your oil should be chosen on more than taste alone – it also depends what you are planning to eat with it.

Some of the best olive oils I have tasted have been in Italy, France, Greece and Spain, and from non-commercial producers – usually a family or village that produces purely for local needs, with any surplus going to cooperatives or local restaurants. Of course, sourcing in this way is not practical for most people, but if you get the opportunity, it's well worth it.

You can find outstanding extra virgin olive oil in most of the producing regions of Italy, some of which are known for a particular style of olive oil. Liguria, for example, producers like Cassini Vittoria uses the late-harvested taggiasca olive to produce an oil that is very light and fruity, perhaps specially created to go with the local vegetables, pulses and seafood. In Tuscany, on the other hand, is generally known for producing more pungent, fruity and grassy, bright green blends from Frantoio and Leccino olives, especially around Florence. This is rated one of the very best. Around Lucca the more Leccino-centric olive oil is less intense in taste and colour. Some of the highly rated producers worth looking out for are Fattoria di Monti, Felsina and Frantoio Franci.

I discovered two of my favourite olive oils while tracking down Tuscan wines. The Tenuta di Capezzana estate in

Carmignano, owned by the Contini Bonacossi family, and the Fontodi estate in Panzano in Chianti, owned by the Manetti family, have renowned vineyards: olive oil is not their primary business, but they apply the same care and attention to producing fine oil as they do to their superb wines.

In Sardinia, where strong, crisp, clean and fruity olive oil is produced with the Bosana olive, producers such as Giuliana Puligheddu and Sandro Pisu achieve stunning results. Sicily, the most southern area for producing olive oil, tends to be known for making oil of medium-ripe fruitiness, plus a little bitterness and pungency, but often with great complexity. The island produces both single-variety oil, and blends of Biancolilla, Nocellara de Belice and Cerasuola olives. Producers such as Frantoi Cutrera and Olio Talbi are regarded as some of the best in Italy.

Ca'Rainene near Lake Garda, and Tenuta Pennita in Emilia-Romagna show that very good extra virgin olive oil is also produced north of Tuscany and east of Liguria.

I tend to treat great Italian extra virgin olive oil like fine wine — in other words, with great respect. I never cook with it, and certainly do not mix it with any type of vinegar, no matter how good. Like any other ingredient, it should add flavour to enhance or complement, so I drizzle it sparingly on other food or dishes. Inevitably, the best extra virgin olive oil, especially that from Italy, will be expensive, unless you have access to a mill or producer and therefore a very short supply chain.

Remember that Italian extra virgin olive oil of all qualities is widely available around the world, and in many countries specialist retailers will offer tastings and events involving the producers.

Some people advise using lesser quality olive oil for cooking, but I really cannot understand why you would want to do that unless you do not care about the end result. The question to ask is whether the dish is going to be enhanced by using olive oil of a particular grade or origin at that stage in the cooking process. For me the answer is generally no. I find a neutral-tasting oil, such as rapeseed, works well for cooking. After that I might finish a dish with a drizzle of the very best. Also, given the difficulty of finding top-notch Italian oil, when I do use very good oil for cooking, it is quite likely to be from Greece, France or even a New World producer who has an acceptable price-to-quality ratio.

It is very interesting that today, following the pattern of the wine industry, some of the most interesting premium olive oils are emerging from countries such as Australia, Chile and South Africa. In Greece and Spain too, where volume rather than quality has historically been the order of the day, outstanding 'boutique' extra virgin olive oils are now being produced.

Traditional Balsamic Vinegar

There are many parallels between traditional balsamic vinegar and proper Italian extra virgin olive oil. However, it is very likely that even fewer people around the world have experienced the former.

There are only two consortia producing true PDO traditional balsamic vinegar – Modena and neighbouring Reggio Emilia. The true balsamic vinegar is made from a reduction of pressed Trebbiano, Lambrusco, Spergola and other grapes. The resulting thick syrup, called *mosto cotto*, is subsequently aged for a minimum of 12 years using a version of the solera system common in making fortified wines. This involves mosto cotto being placed in a series of 5–10 progressively smaller barrels, from around 60 litres down to 10 litres, because the liquid evaporates as it gets older. Three of these barrels are normally used for condimento (balsamic vinegar that is aged for less than 12 years). However, all the casks are made of only permitted woods – chestnut, walnut, cherry, oak, mulberry, ash, acacia and juniper – which impart a subtle flavour to the vinegar.

True balsamic vinegar is a deep, glossy brown and has a complex flavour that balances the natural sweet and sour elements of the cooked grape juice with hints of wood from the casks. The genuine article is a product made by artisans and has PDO status. Unfortunately, there are many inferior balsamic products on the market, and deliberate confusion is caused by labels that include a place name, such as Modena. However, there are ways of distinguishing the good from the bad.

The PDO authority in Reggio Emilia indicates the different ages of its balsamic vinegar by the colour of the label. A red label means the vinegar has been aged for at least 12 years, a silver label means at least 18 years, and a gold label indicates 25 years or more.

The PDO authority in Modena uses a different system to indicate the age of its balsamic vinegars. A white coloured cap means the vinegar has aged for at least 12 years, and a gold cap bearing the word extravecchio (extra old) indicates that the vinegar has aged for 25 years or more.

In addition, the bottle shape is an indicator of PDO vinegar's provenance. The 100 ml regulation bottle shape for Reggio Emilia is short and fat, while the Modena bottle is taller and thinner.

Anything other than the traditional products described above, with the exception of some condimenti produced by artisan producers, is really not worth considering. However, when buying condimenti, going by the place name alone is not reliable. I have come across some products made within Reggio Emilia and Modena that are very poor, but I have also found some perfectly reasonable ones made outside those places. In my experience, the best are made by the traditional producers, and vastly superior to most of the Aceto Balsamico di Modena IGP that came into being in 2011. The IGP (protected geographical) status permits no chemicals, colourants or artificial ingredients to be included in the balsamic, but does allow it to be blended with up to 10 per cent red wine vinegar. For me, this is something completely different and does not deserve to be known as balsamic vinegar.

Anything else you come across is likely to be an industrially produced blend of vinegar, caramel, cornflour, gum and myriad additives. The bottle may be labelled Aceto Balsamico di Modena (minus the IGP designation) but is a world away from the traditional product. Often it is cheap — usually less than a couple of pounds, dollars or euros for 100 ml — but, as with olive oil, there have been cases of fraud. Sometimes a poor product is put in fancy bottles with red or gold seals and sold at an inflated price.

The tradition of making condiments and/or vinegars using grape must and similar methods to those described above has been going on in parts of Emilia-Romagna since the Middle Ages, and some people think there may even be a link back to Roman times. However, the word 'balsamic' in relation to a product close to what we have today is a 19th-century occurrence. (The term 'balsamic', incidentally, is related to 'balsam', a healing ointment or balm, and probably arose because of the therapeutic value attributed to vinegars in general.) The commercialization of the traditional product is actually very recent in both Italy and beyond. Elizabeth David made no mention of it in her book *Italian Food*, first published in 1954. Certainly, its availability throughout Italy can be dated to the late 1970s, whilst it was only in the 1980s that I can first remember seeing it in European capitals and New York, for instance. Prior to the 1970s a great proportion of balsamic was produced at home for family use only. Barrels passed, and still do, from one generation to the next, and may be up to 200 years old.

Making traditional balsamic in both Reggio Emilia and Modena at household or extended household level still goes on, and some of the well-known producers have only recently moved into larger premises, often nearer to the vineyards that provide the grapes. Andrea Bezzecchi of the excellent Acetaia San Giacomo in Reggio Emilia recalls that before moving to his current premises, visitors had to walk through his bedroom to see the barrels.

Once opened, a bottle of Aceto Balsamico Tradizionale can keep until used up, as long as it is recorked tightly after each use. Given that only a couple of drops are needed at a time, a 100 ml bottle will normally last me 3–6 months. I tend to keep it in a cool, dark larder, along with my extra virgin olive oil and wines that will be consumed within a month.

I do not think many people drink Aceto Balsamico Tradizionale these days as they did in the past. Try it instead on seared scallops and poached or pan-fried turbot and brill. Do not cook it – simply sprinkle a few drops over the food before serving. For me, however, it is best consumed by adding a few drops to a really good Parmigiano Reggiano, which is also a perfect transition from savoury to sweet, so try it before dessert or as a finale to a meal; a few drops on wild or seasonal strawberries makes for an exceptional ending.

A good condimento also works well with a tomato and buffalo mozzarella salad. I avoid mixing olive oil and balsamic as you end up muddying the water, so to speak. Instead I drizzle the olive oil on just the tomatoes, then add a few drops of condimento on the mozzarella, or vice versa. Either way, it can be a delight. Another suggestion is to sprinkle a few drops on grilled radicchio di Treviso.

Whilst sourcing for the Italian deli I co-opened in London during the summer of 2011, I must have tasted over 30 top balsamic vinegars from both Modena and Reggio Emilia. I discovered that, as with wine, the terroir and skill of the producer are paramount. Even when the same basic grape varieties and production process are being used, different makers create very distinct products with their own individual character. The vinegars I selected are, in my opinion, the best. Both are available throughout Europe and North America.

- Acetaia San Giacomo Aceto Balsamico Tradizionale di Reggio Emilia PDO, whose makers also produce an excellent condimento.
- Acetaia Pedroni Aceto Balsamico Tradizionale di Modena PDO.

Salt

Salt (sale in Italian, from the Latin sal and the Greek hals) is a mineral substance composed mainly of sodium chloride. In its natural form as a crystalline mineral, it is known as rock salt or halite. Salt is also present in vast quantities in the sea, where it is the main mineral constituent: the open ocean has about 35 g per litre (a salinity of 3.5 per cent).

Salt as a flavour enhancer or preservative for food has been known on the Italian peninsula and islands since prehistoric times. It came either from rock salt deposits, or from estuaries and bays where the salt was obtained from evaporated sea water. The Etruscans, a pre-Roman tribe, sourced rock salt from Viterbo and sea salt from the Tiber estuary. Although the Romans valued salt — in fact, they gave their troops an allowance to buy it — they also used garum fish sauce as a salty flavour enhancer.

It can be argued that salt is the most important ingredient in cooking and preserving food. In view of that, it continues to amaze me that it is so often treated with a lack of respect and seriousness by both home cooks and sometimes even professional chefs. In my experience, your first bite of poorly seasoned food is an indication that what will follow is likely to be flawed or disappointing.

In this book I mention generic sea salt as an ingredient in most savoury recipes because specific Italian sea salts are generally hard to obtain outside Italy. However, there are two that are worth sourcing if you can, and these are described on pages 446 and 447. I do not recommend using what is commonly known as 'table salt' because it generally contains a range of additives and anti-caking agents, which, far from enhancing food, often ruins it.

Understanding how to use salt in both cooking and preserving food is very important, and often the sign of a good cook. Quantities given in recipes should be viewed just as a guideline because it is essential to taste food as it cooks and to adjust the seasoning as you go along. The reason for this is that other ingredients, such as cheese, cured meat or fish, may already have salt in them. When using pecorino Romano in a pasta dish, for example, it is important to slightly reduce the amount of salt added to the cooking water to compensate for the saltiness of the cheese. Achieving the right balance is the key to successful seasoning, and over time becomes intuitive.

The writer Mark Kurlansky covers the socio-economic, historical, cultural, religious and culinary importance of salt in great detail in his excellent book on the subject *Salt: A World History* (see page 467). He takes the reader on a 5000-year journey through China, India, Egypt and Japan, as well as most of Europe, North Africa and the Americas, highlighting how profoundly salt has influenced people's lives. Salt emerges as a pivotal player in the history of nations and their populations, be they kings, popes or lowest of the low.

There are a number of outstanding sea salts produced around the world and each has its devotees. Among UK products, I rate Maldon and my personal favourite Halen Môn, which have both established an international reputation for excellence. In the USA high-quality sea salt is produced in Hawaii, Maine and parts of the Pacific north-west. Jacobsen sea salt, produced in Oregon, is also top notch. Other superior salts include Fleur de Sel de Guérande, from Brittany in south-west France, and the various Flor de Sal products from Spain, Portugal, Mexico and Brazil. In my opinion, Italy produces two outstanding sea salts that are as good as, if not better than, any in the world.

Trapani Sea Salt

Sale di Trapani

The town of Trapani is situated on perhaps the most western point of Sicily. The coastline from Trapani to Marsala, a distance of 30 km, is lined with saltpans. These large pools of salt water, divided by narrow strips of land, form irregular and multicoloured flats, where for centuries salt has been produced. The route along this stretch of coast is called la Via del Sale (the Salt Road) and is remarkable for its numerous Dutch-style windmills, which are used for pumping sea water and also grinding salt. Here too you will see mountains of salt covered with terracotta tiles, the traditional way of storing it until packed. The saltpans are thought to have been established by the Phoenicians over 2000 years ago and have had their vicissitudes since then. Today, however, the Saline di Trapani e Paceco wetlands are a major nature reserve, managed by the World Wide Fund for Nature since 1995.

Trapani sea salt is one of the Slow Food presidia and has a mild salinity, whilst also being rich in potassium and magnesium. It is a wonderful hand-processed, chemical free sea salt with a high moisture content, not dissimilar to Sel de Guérande in terms of feel, but with a milder taste. (Note that neither of these salts is damp to the touch. They merely contain more moisture than processed rock salt.)

Cervia Sea Salt

Sale di Cervia

The second excellent Italian salt is Sale di Cervia from Emilia-Romagna. It too is one of the Slow Food presidia, but is not well known outside its place of origin. For me it has to rank as one of the very best sea salts in the world, perfect for cooking and finishing food. I'm not alone in holding this opinion, as the makers of the very best Parmigiano Reggiano cheese and salumi also consider it an essential ingredient in their products.

Sale di Cervia is pure sea salt with 2–4 per cent natural humidity. Like Trapani salt, it is never artificially dried or blended with anti-caking additives. All the minor elements found in sea water – iodine, zinc, copper, manganese, iron, magnesium and potassium – are present, which makes it a useful source of the body's recommended daily intake of these minerals. The salt workers closely monitor the entrance of concentrated salt water into the saltpans, and as soon as sodium chloride has formed by evaporation, they run off the remaining brine, which contains the bitter chlorides. The resulting product is therefore referred to as *sale dolce* (sweet salt). Salifiore (the equivalent of fleur de sel), which collects on the surface of the water, is of higher quality than salt taken from other parts of the pan, so it commands a premium price. Cervia sea salt is sometimes called sale di papa (the pope's salt) as it is traditionally sent as a gift to the head of the Catholic Church. Pope Francis received his jar of Cervia salt on 27 November 2013.

Cervia is a small town between Ravenna and Cesenatico on Italy's Adriatic coast, where salt production dates back more than 2000 years. The name comes from the Latin acervus, meaning 'a mound of white salt'. Cervia salt, like that from Trapani, is harvested from saltpans by hand with large wooden rakes in precisely the same way it was originally done by the Etruscans.

Wine

For me it is difficult to contemplate Italian food without thinking of wine — specifically Italian wine. Naturally, in a country where regional and local food are so important there also tend to be wonderful wines to go with them.

I would argue that, with the possible exception of France, Italy provides the biggest choice in terms of wine-making styles using indigenous and international grape varieties. These wines not only match regional and local cuisines, but can also complement more exotic flavours, such as those in Chinese, Thai, Persian and Indian food.

I am often asked to recommend Italian wines, and have even helped restaurateurs with their wine lists. In 2010 I put together a list of over 300 wines from around 100 wine-makers for a food and wine shop that I co-founded in London. We ran many wine events featuring the wine-makers themselves, whom we either specifically invited, or who happened to be passing through London at the time.

The general feedback was very positive: many customers were not aware of the variety of truly excellent Italian wines available, ranging in price from £8 to £900-plus per bottle. The quality of Italian wines has improved to such an extent over the last 40 years that it is now true to say that Italy produces some of the best wines in the world.

The map opposite shows some of my personal favourites in terms of wine makers or estates in Italy. The vast majority of the wines are available all over the world, and certainly in the UK, most of Europe and the USA.

Italy has been one of the top two wine producers by volume for many years, and within that volume there is both exceptional quality and value to suit all budgets and tastes.

VALLE D'AOSTA
La Cave de Morgex, Les Crêtes

LOMBARDY
Bellavista, Ca' del Bosco, Nino Negri

TRENTINO–ALTO ADIGE/SÜDTIROL
Cantina Terlano, Elena Walch, Mezzacorona,
Tenuta J. Hofstätter, Tenuta San Leonardo

FRIULI VENEZIA GIULIA
Le Vigne di Zamò, Livio Felluga, Miani, Princic Dario

VENETO
Allegrini, Giuseppe Quintarelli, Inama,
Pieropan, Romano dal Forno

PIEDMONT
Angelo Gaja, Bruno Giacosa,
Bruno Rocca, Castello di Nievi,
Ceretto, Damilano, G.D.
Vajra, La Spinetta, Poderi Aldo
Conterno

EMILIA–ROMAGNA
Fattoria Zerbina, La Stoppa, Podere La Berta

MARCHE
Andrea Felici, Fattoria San Lorenzo, Fulvia
Tombolini , Umani Ronchi

LIGURIA
Azienda Agricola Maria Donata
Bianchi, Lunae, Terre Bianche

TUSCANY
Biondi Santi, Cabreo, Casanova di Neri,
Castello di Bolgheri, Castello del Terriccio,
Fattoria di Magliano, Fèlsina, Fontodi, Isole
e Olena, Le Macchiole, Le Pupille, Tenuta
Capezzana, Tenuta dell'Ornellaia, Tenuta
Guado al Tasso (Antinori), Tenuta San
Guido, Tua Rita Suvereto, Valdicava

ABRUZZO
Cantina Frentana, Gran
Sasso, Masciarelli

MOLISE
Di Majo Lorante

UMBRIA
Arnaldo Caprai, Castello
della Sala (Antinori),
Falesco, Paolo Bea

APULIA
Alberto Longo, A Mano,
Gianfranco Fino, Tormaresca

LAZIO
Coletti Conti, Falesco, Marco
Carpineti, Trappolini

CAMPANIA
Benito Ferrara, Cantine Lonardo,
Fattoria Galardi, Mastroberardino

CALABRIA
Librandi, Odoardi,
Statti, Terre di Balbia

BASILICATA
Cantine del Notaio, Elena
Fucci, Tenuta del Portale

SARDINIA
AA Panevino, Alberto Loi,
Agricola Punica, Argiolas,
Cantina Mesa, Tenuta
Masone Mannu

SICILY
Arianna Occhipinti, COS,
Donnafugata, Fazio,
Masseria del Feudo

Milan

Bologna

Florence

Rome

Where to Buy Italian Food

Italian food is exported all over the world, and a really wide range of products is available in supermarkets and delicatessens, as well as online. The mass-produced commodity products are fairly ubiquitous, but finding artisan and premium ones might take a little more effort.

If you are looking for a specific product, sometimes the best way to find out if it is available is to contact the producer directly. Look for a website, which will often indicate where you can buy their products, or send an email enquiry. In my experience, they're usually happy to help.

In countries where large numbers of the Italian diaspora settled, especially in North and South America, you will often find local producers of fresh pasta, salumi, cheese and bread.

Overleaf is a short list of suppliers that I am happy to recommend, but, as with any such list, be aware that sometimes a change of ownership or philosophy may affect both the product ranges and/or quality.

UK

Andreas Fine Fruit and Vegetables Ltd

4 Cale Street
London SW3 3QU
Tel: +44 20 7589 5775
www.andreasveg.co.uk

Bread Bread

Unit 37, Mahatma Gandhi Estate
Milkwood Road
London SE24 0JF
Tel: +44 20 7733 7675
www.breadbread.co.uk

The Chelsea Fishmonger

10 Cale Street
London SW3 3QU
Tel: +44 20 7589 9432
www.thechelseafishmonger.co.uk

La Credenza Ltd (wholesale only)

Unit 9, College Fields Business Centre
Prince George's Road
London SW19 2PT
Tel: + 44 20 7070 5070
www.lacredenza.co.uk

L'Emporio Fine Foods Ltd
134 Druid Street
London SE1 2HH
Tel: +44 20 7232 2188
www.lemporiofinefoods.com

The Ham and Cheese Company
Arch 10, Dockley Road Industrial Estate
Dockley Road
London SE16 3SF
Tel + 44 7970 532485
www.thehamandcheeseco.com

Olivino Delicatessen
12 Lower Belgrave Street
London SW1W OLJ
Tel: +44 20 7730 9042
www.olivorestaurants.com

Pescheria Mattiucci
8 Blenheim Crescent
London
W11 1NN
Tel: +44 20 7229 3400
www.pescheriamattiucci.com

Vallebona

59 Weir Rd
London SW19 8UG
Tel: +44 20 8944 5665
www.vallebona.co.uk

Valvona & Crolla

9 Elm Row
Edinburgh EH7 4AA
Tel: +44 131 556 6066
www.valvonacrolla.co.uk

USA

Creminelli Fine Meats
310 Wright Brothers Drive
Salt Lake City
UT 84116
Tel: +1 801 428 1820
www.creminelli.com

Eataly Chicago
43 East Ohio Street
Chicago
IL 60611
Tel: +1 312 521 8700
www.eataly.com/chicago

Eataly NYC
200 Fifth Avenue
New York
NY 10010
Tel: +1 212 229 2560
www.eataly.com/nyc

Fra' Mani Handcrafted Foods

1311 Eighth Street
Berkeley
CA 94710
Tel: +1 510 526 7000
www.framani.com

Salumeria Biellese

378 8th Avenue (corner of 29th Street)
New York
NY 10023
Tel: +1 212 736 7376
www.salumeriabiellese.com

Salumeria Rosi

283 Amsterdam Avenue
New York
NY 10023
Tel: +1 212 877 4081
www.salumeriarossi.com

Australia

Simon Johnson
181 Harris Street
Pyrmont
NSW 2009
Tel: +612 8244 8240

Simon Johnson
24A Ralph Street
Alexandria
NSW 2015
Tel: +61282448220
www.simonjohnson.com

Bibliography

There is a wealth of literature on all aspects of Italian food, and even a quick look through a library catalogue will show that the subject has attracted writers of every stripe: historians, anthropologists, etymologists, food writers, cooks and chefs. If you are interested in further reading, you will not be short of sources, whether in Italian, English or many other languages.

To follow is a short selected bibliography of books that I think are pertinent specifically to *Semplice*. I have spent many happy hours reading them and discussing the subject of Italian food with numerous other people, but responsibility for any errors of fact or interpretation in this book remain entirely mine.

Pellegrino Artusi, *La Scienza in Cucina e l'Arte di Mangiare Bene* (self-published, 1891); reprinted as *Science in the Kitchen and the Art of Eating Well* (University of Toronto Press, 3rd edition, 2003)

Edward Behr, *50 Foods: The Essentials of Good Taste* (Penguin Press, New York, 2013)

Ada Boni, *Il Talismano della Felicità* (The Talisman of Happiness, 1929; 7th edition, Preziosa, Rome, 1941)

Alberto Capatti and Massimo Montanari, *Italian Cuisine: A Cultural History* (Columbia University Press, New York, 2003)

Alfredo Carannante, Claudio Giardino and Umberto Savarese, *In Search of Garum: The 'Colatura d'Alici' from the Amalfitan Coast* (Proceedings of the 4th Italian Congress of Ethnoarchaeology, Rome, 17-19 May 2006, ed. Francesca Lugli et al, BAR International Series 2235, 2011)

Elizabeth David, *Italian Food* (Penguin, London, 1989)

Alan Davidson, *Mediterranean Seafood*, 2nd edition (Penguin Books, London, 1981)

John Dickie, *Delizia: The Epic History of Italians and Their Food* (Sceptre, London, 2008)

Carol Field, *The Italian Baker: The Classic Tastes of the Italian Countryside — Its Breads, Pizza, Focaccia, Cakes, Pastries, and Cookies* (10 Speed Press, Berkeley, California, 2005)

Fool Magazine, No. 4, Italian issue (Malmo, Sweden, 2014)

David Gentilcore, *Pomodoro! The History of the Tomato in Italy* (Columbia University Press, New York, 2010)

Olindo Guerrini, *L'Arte di Utilizzare gli Avanzi della Mensa* (The Art of Using Leftovers), (Formigini, Rome, 1918)

Ancel and Margaret Keys, *Eat Well and Stay Well* (Doubleday, New York, 1959)

Ancel and Margaret Keys, *The Benevolent Bean* (Farrar, Strauss & Giroux, New York, 1972)

Ancel and Margaret Keys, *How to Eat Well and Stay Well the Mediterranean Way* (Doubleday, New York, 1975)

Kenneth F. Kiple and Kriemhild Coneè Ornelas (eds), *The Cambridge World History of Food, vols 1 and 2* (Cambridge University Press, New York, 2000)

Mark Kurlansky, *Cod: A Biography of the Fish That Changed the World* (Vintage, London, 1999)

Mark Kurlansky, *Salt: A World History* (Vintage Books, London, 2003)

Dan Lepard, *The Handmade Loaf: Contemporary European Recipes for the Home Baker* (Mitchell Beazley, London, 2004)

Giuseppe Mascoli and Bridget Hugo, *Franco Manca: Artisan Pizza to Make Perfectly at Home* (Kyle Books, London, 2013)

J.F. Mariani, *How Italian Food Conquered the World* (Palgrave Macmillan, New York, 2011)

Jeannie Marshall, *The Lost Art of Feeding Kids: What Italy Taught Me About Why Kids Need Real Food* (Beacon Press, Boston, 2014)

Jane Mason, *All You Knead Is Bread: 50 Recipes from Around the World to Bake and Share* (Ryland Peters & Small, London, 2012)

Tony May, *Italian Cuisine* (St Martin's Press, New York, 2005)

Harold McGee, *On Food and Cooking: The Science and Lore of the Kitchen* (Unwin Paperbacks, London, 1988)

Massimo Montanari, trans. Beth Archer Brombert, *Cheese, Pears and History in a Proverb* (Columbia University Press, New York, 2012)

Tom Mueller, *Extra Virginity: The Sublime and Scandalous World of Olive Oil* (Atlantic Books, London, 2013)

Charles Perry, *The Oldest Mediterranean Noodle: A Cautionary Tale*, (Petits Propos Culinaire, 9 October 1981)

Hans-Peter von Peschke and Werner Feldmann, *La Cucina Dell'Antica Roma* (Guido Tommasi, Milan, 2001)

Carlo Petrini, *Slow Food: Le Ragioni del Gusto* (Laterza & Figli, Rome, 2001), published as *Slow Food: The Case for Taste*, trans. William McCuaig (Columbia University Press, New York, 2003)

Michael Pollan, *The Omnivore's Dilemma: The Search for a Perfect Meal in a Fast Food World* (Bloomsbury, London, 2011)

Gillian Riley, *The Oxford Companion to Italian Food* (Oxford University Press, New York, 2007)

Waverly Root, *The Food of Italy* (Vintage Books, New York, 1992)

William Rubel, *Bread: A Global History* (Reaktion Books, London, 2011)

Michael Ruhlman and Brian Polcyn, *Salumi: The Craft of Italian Dry Curing* (W.W. Norton & Co, New York, 2012)

Silvano Serventi and Françoise Sabban, *Pasta: The Story of a Universal Food* (Columbia University Press, New York, 2002)

Stefano Somogyi, 'L'alimentazione nell'Italia unita' in *Storia d'Italia*, vol. 5, bk. 1 (Einaudi, Turin, 1973)

Ann and Franco Taruschio, *Leaves from the Walnut Tree: Memories of a Lifetime* (Pavilion, London, 1993)

Ulrike Thoms, *From Migrant Food to Lifestyle Cooking: The Career of Italian Cuisine in Europe* (Institute of European History, Mainz, Germany, 2011)

Touring Club Italia, *Guida Gastronomica d'Italia* (1931)

Various Contributors, *Il Cucchiaio d'Argento* (Domus, Rome, 1950); published in English as *The Silver Spoon* (Phaidon, London, 2011)

Oretta Zanini de Vita, *The Encyclopedia of Pasta*, trans. Maureen B. Fant (Columbia University Press, New York, 2009)

Acknowledgements

First, I need to thank my late father Aleco, a great gastronome who taught me to both enjoy food and wine but also inspired me at a tender age to source the best ingredients and cook them. My Italian mother, Anna exposed me to the delights of regional Italian food from a tender age.

My wife Sarah and two sons Alexander and Edward have been great supporters of this project, as well as sounding boards for some of my ideas and guinea pigs for my recipes. Sarah grows superb fruit and vegetables in our allotment in Putney Vale in London, and also bakes beautifully, whilst the boys (currently aged 11 and 14) are already good cooks and epicureans. It should be noted that they can all cook the recipes in this book.

I need to thank Simon Majumdar, as without his original encouragement I would not have seriously considered taking on the task of writing this book. Furthermore, Simon also engineered an encounter with Trevor Dolby, who eventually became my publisher at Random House, as he instinctively knew we would get on and be able to work together. It has been a real pleasure to work with such a consummate professional, as well as other team members, including Katherine Murphy and Neal Townsend. Anna

Koska who I met on social media has produced really wonderful illustrations whilst Trish Burgess has been the perfect editor for someone like me who tends not to use recipes and English is not their mother tongue. Kris Kirkham who was a top chef before turning his hand to photography has produced wonderful pictures that illustrate his empathy for the subject matter.

In a way Oliver Thring is partly responsible for this book as my failure to explain to him my views on Italian Food in 140 characters (on Twitter) encouraged me to write more extensively.

It would be impossible to list all the people I have broken bread with and/or had lengthy discussions with about ingredients, recipes or aspects of Italian cooking, and who directly or indirectly helped or inspired me. However, I would like to mention Mikael Jonsson, Signe Johansen, Fulvio Pierangelini, Giuseppe Mascoli, Sami Wasif, Franco and Ann Taruschio, Francesco Mazzei, Daniel and Viv Young, Andy Needham, Robin and Simona Houldsworth, Eleonora Borgonovi, John and Paola Whelan, Roberto Pisano, Giuseppe di Martino, John Moruzzi, Helen Roe, Bruno and Anna Tanzi, Daniele Camera, Giancarlo Principalli, Alberico Penata, Luca Terraneo, Lello Favuzzi, Chris and Lorna Hayes, Steve Carmo, Hisham Amili, David Bolomini, Robin Majumdar, Maria Elia, Anissa Helou, Andy Hayler, Perm Paitayawat, Silvija

Davidson, Russell Norman, Roberto Della Pietra, Ilaria Padovani, Franco and Alex Fubini, Katie Parla, Mauro Segatta, Marco Canora, Paolo De Marchi, Maria Nava Rondolino, Dario Cecchini, Francesco Cucurullo, Andrea Bezzecchi, Marco Torri, Professor Andrew Cox, Angela Cox, Professor Martin Bull, David Wright, John Harrison, Darragh and Fiona O'Shea, Gennaro Esposito, Claudio Solari, Stefania Cuoco, Mark Britten, Niamh Shields, Chris Golding, Rex Goldsmith, Mat Couchman, Andrea Georghiou, Roger and Julie Ward, Simon and Cathy Berti, Dom Chapman, Diego Jacquet, Pablo Rossi, Alexis Gauthier, Meera Cortesi, Nicola Bertinelli, Bob Granleese, Enzo Cassini, Beatrice Contini Bonacossi, Eleonora Borgonovi, Tony Kypreos, Michael Browne, Alan Bird, Henry and Valeria Blofeld, Elliott John, Alison Elliott, Henry Harris, Leonid Shutov and the Peng family, Niccolo Bittante and Simon Johnson. Needless to say, they bear no responsibility for any errors of fact or interpretation in these pages — those must be laid at my door.

Contributors

Photography

KRIS KIRKHAM was born in
Watford, England and moved to
Canada with his parents when
he was 3 years old. Food and
cooking have been a integral
part of his life from an early age
and he trained for 15 years with
some of the most prominent
chefs in British Columbia and
Quebec. A reverse trip across
the Atlantic to London allowed
him to pursue his passion for
photography. He now lives
there and is a food and drink
photographer.

Illustrations

ANNA KOSKA's passion in
portraying life on paper and
canvas is firmly rooted in
her upbringing on the coast
of Cornwall. As a result, her
sphere of expertise encompasses
all things marine, coastal and
earthbound. Anna is entirely
self taught and, to date, has
worked on over 100 books. She
lives in Sussex with her husband
and three children, and can
usually be found either in the
kitchen, the studio or in the
vegetable garden.

Design

NEAL TOWNSEND is a graphic designer with over 30 years' experience in graphic design and print. He started out as a designer on the *Melody Maker* and then went on to work on various BBC magazines — *Gardeners' World* and *Vegetarian Good Food* — before moving into book publishing where he has designed books for Random House, including *Comptoir Libanais* and *Comptoir Libanais Express*.

Recipes Index

Page numbers in *italics* indicate photographs.

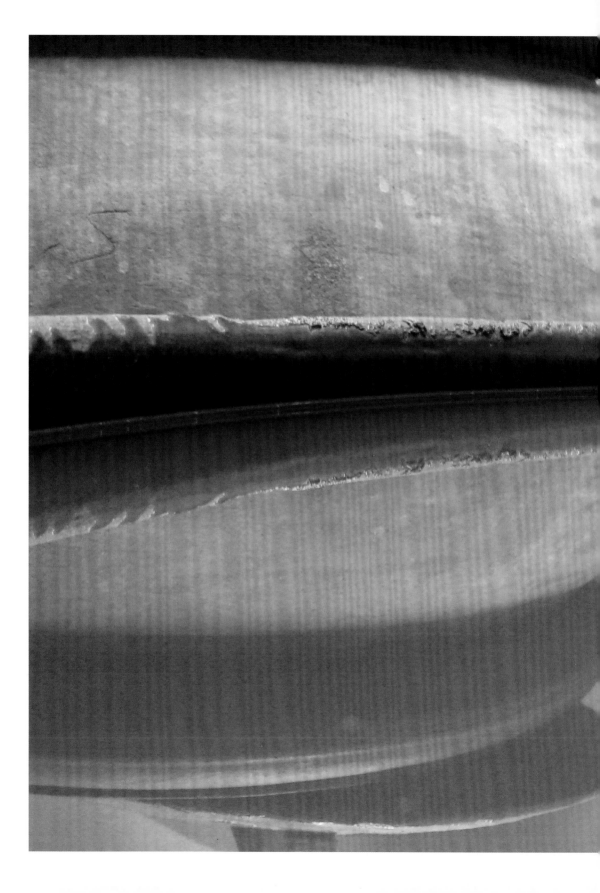

Index

Page numbers in *italics* indicate photographs.

Published by Preface 2014

10 9 8 7 6 5 4 3 2 1

First published in Great Britain in 2014 by
Preface Publishing
20 Vauxhall Bridge Road
London, SW1V 2SA

An imprint of The Random House Group Limited

www.randomhouse.co.uk

Addresses for companies within The Random House Group Limited
can be found at www.randomhouse.co.uk

The Random House Group Limited Reg. No. 954009

A CIP catalogue record for this book is available from the British Library

ISBN 978 1 848 09420 8

The Random House Group Limited supports the Forest Stewardship
Council® (FSC®), the leading international forest-certification organisation.
Our books carrying the FSC label are printed on FSC®-certified paper.
FSC is the only forest-certification scheme supported by the leading environmental
organisations, including Greenpeace. Our paper procurement policy can be
found at www.randomhouse.co.uk/environment

Designed by Neal Townsend
Photographs © Kris Kirkham
Illustrations © Anna Koska
Photograph on page 209 © Paul Winch-Furness, courtesy O'Shea's Butchers
Photographs on page 17 & 454 courtesy of Giuseppe di Martino

Printed and bound in China by C&C Offset Printing Co., Ltd